Signalling Centres in the North East : No 1

York

from Early Days to Rail Operating Centre

Richard Pulleyn

NORTH EASTERN RAILWAY ASSOCIATION

Contents

Published by the North Eastern Railway Association, 2020. Registered Charity No 1164199.
ISBN 978-1-911360-25-4.
Typeset by John G Teasdale.
Printed in Great Britain by The Amadeus Press, Ezra House, West 26 Business Park, CLECKHEATON, BD19 4TQ.

THE NORTH EASTERN RAILWAY ASSOCIATION

Formed in 1961, the NERA caters for all those interested in the railways of north-east England, with particular focus on the North Eastern Railway, its constituents and successors, from their early history down to the present day. This also extends to the many industrial and smaller railways that operated alongside them. Interests range over all aspects of development, operation and infrastructure of the railway, including such diverse activities as locomotive history, rolling stock, train services, architecture, signalling, shipping, road vehicles and staff matters – both for the general enthusiast and model maker.

Regular meetings are held in York, Darlington, Hull and London. The Association also holds an extensive archive of books, documents, photographs and drawings available for study by members and non-members alike.

Members receive a quarterly illustrated journal, the *North Eastern Express*, and a newsletter, covering membership topics, forthcoming meetings and events in the region together with book reviews and a bibliography of recent articles of interest. Over 200 issues of the *Express* have been published to date. The Association also markets an extensive range of facsimiles of railway company documents, including diagram books, timetables and other booklets, while at the same time it is developing an expanding range of original publications.

For a membership prospectus, please contact:

Membership Secretary, 7 Grenadier Drive, NORTHALLERTON, DL6 1SB. e-mail : membership@ner.org.uk

A list of NERA publications is available. Please e-mail or send a Stamped Addressed 9" x 4" Envelope to:

Sales Officer, 31 Moreton Avenue, Stretford, MANCHESTER, M32 8BP. e-mail : sales@ner.org.uk

NERA Website : www.ner.org.uk

Front Cover Illustrations: *(Top) LNER No 4453, a former Great Northern Railway Atlantic, passes Locomotive Yard signal box at the head of a Edinburgh - King's Cross relief circa 1925. The signal box, with 295 levers, was the largest mechanical lever frame ever built. To the right of the express is ex Lancashire & Yorkshire Hughes 4-6-0 No 10431; locomotives of this class were frequent visitors to York, working trains from Liverpool and Manchester via Normanton. (David J Williamson Collection) (Below) In 2019, an Azuma departs York past the Rail Operating Centre. Built close to the site of Locomotive Yard box, York ROC is expected to become the largest on Network Rail, controlling the whole of the ECML from King's Cross to the Scottish border. (Neil Mackay)*

Map : Railways in and around York

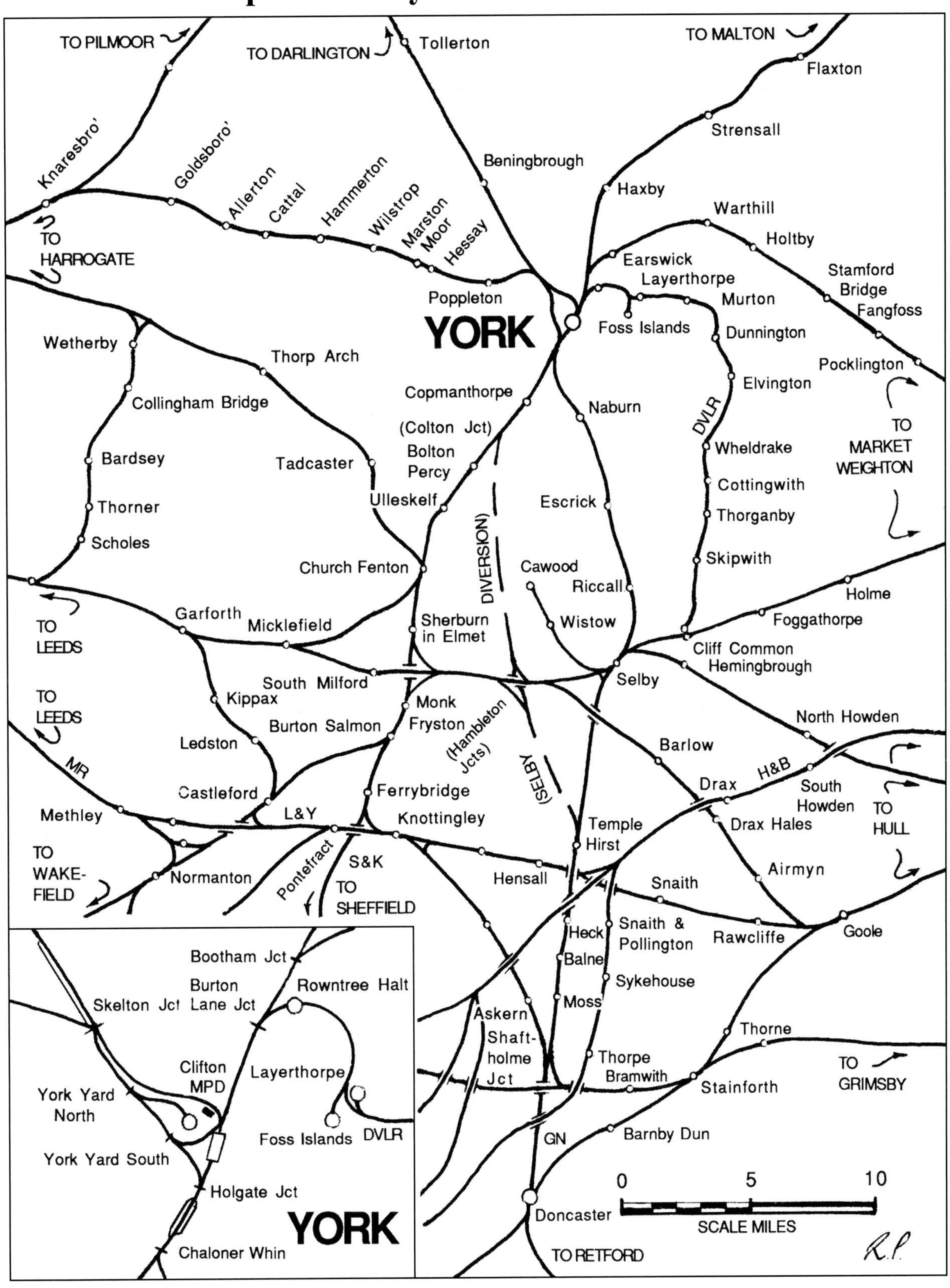

Sketchmap of the railways in and around York at their maximum extent. The Selby Diversion, opened to traffic in 1983 in order to avoid the National Coal Board's Selby Coalfield, is marked as a dashed line. (Richard Pulleyn)

Title Page Illustration: *Class B16/2 No 1327 is seen here in February 1943 at Chaloner Whin at the head of a southbound No 2 Braked Goods. In the left foreground can be seen the fog signalman's levers for placing detonators on the Down Leeds and Down Doncaster lines to be worked in conjunction with the distant signals for South Points signal box; these signals were mounted below the Down Starting signals for Chaloner Whin. It is also interesting to note the mixture of NER lower quadrant and LNER upper quadrant signals on the signal bridge, and one signal even that appears to be a lower quadrant but has been fitted with a metal arm. (P Ransome Wallis, NRM PRW3543)*

Introduction and Acknowledgements

York became a major centre in the early days of the railway – and this remains the case for signalling because it is now the location of a Rail Operating Centre, one of only 12 or so which are planned to eventually control most of the lines across England, Scotland and Wales.

This history concentrates mainly on the area within the City boundary but for completeness it also extends out to a number of places which subsequently became fringe locations to York Power Signal Box (alternatively referred to below as 'York Box'); in most cases these are the first stations on the lines radiating out from York.

For general histories of the development of railways around York, there are many excellent books available such as *Rail Centres: York* by the late Ken Hoole (published by Ian Allan Limited, 1983), and *Britain's Rail Super Centres: York* by the late Ken Appleby (published by Ian Allan Limited, 1993); however, a brief, broad outline is included below as a background introduction. Similarly, the development of NER signalling principles and practices is already covered in detail in *A History of North Eastern Railway Signalling* edited by Neil Mackay (published by the North Eastern Railway Association, 2016).

It will be noted in the text that, until the 1889 issue of the North Eastern Railway (NER) Appendix, the term 'signal cabin' was in general use rather than 'signal box' or the abbreviation SB. After that date either term could be used interchangeably because 'old habits die hard'. The names of locations were also passed down from one generation to the next – and many railwaymen had long memories – so, for example, in the 1960s reference would still be made to South View as a location long after the signal box of that name had closed.

The Signalling Study Group classifications have become a standard method for describing the architectural designs of the cabins and signal boxes so these have been used in the following text where appropriate. These classifications are described in *The Signal Box – a Pictorial History and Guide to Designs* (published by OPC, 1986) and *A History of North Eastern Railway Signalling* mentioned above.

Many of the signal boxes were fitted with lever frames manufactured by McKenzie & Holland, abbreviated in the text as McK&H.

Distances are quoted in the text as shown in the original document, so in some cases these include miles (*m*), chains (*c*) and links (*l*), a method of measurement long superseded.

Where signal cabin dimensions are given they are in the order: Length, Width, and Height of operating floor above rail level. For example 20' 3" x 9' 4" x 8' 0" = 20 feet 3 inches long by 9 feet 4 inches wide by 8 feet from rail level to the operating floor.

Monetary values are also quoted in the text as shown in the original document, generally pre-decimalisation when the units were Pounds (£), Shilling (*s*), and Pence (*d*), shown for example as £45 10*s* 8*d*.

References are included as footnotes where appropriate, with the following abbreviations:

NRM = National Railway Museum
NERA = North Eastern Railway Association
TNA = The National Archives
RM = The Railway Magazine

All of the photographs are by the author or from his collection except where otherwise stated; in particular, I am most grateful to the National Railway Museum (where the author is a regular volunteer) and to the North Eastern Railway Association who have kindly allowed me to include photographs from their collections.

Finally, I would like to record the kind assistance provided by: the staff of the National Railway Museum, especially Ed Bartholomew, Bob Gwynne, John Clarke, Peter Thorpe, Andy Croxton and the team of assistants in the Search Engine; the staff at The National Archive in Kew; the volunteer team at the NERA Archive, core members being Richard Lacey (NERA Archivist), John Askwith, Tom Burnham, Les Cairnes, David Ramsden, Eddie Scarlett and Sam Woods; the staff at the Ken Hoole Study Centre, Darlington, especially Leona White-Hannant and Alison Grange. Also my colleagues including: the late Ken Appleby and his son Geoff Appleby, the late John Bennett, the late John Boyes, John Foreman, Phil Graham, the late Peter Hawes, Neil Mackay, John Midcalf, Mick Nicholson, Andrew Overton, Michael Rising, the late John Talbot, Charles Weightman, the late John Whitaker, David and Claire Williamson, the late Chris Woolstenholmes and John Young. If I have inadvertently omitted anyone I extend my sincere apologies.

Finally sincere thanks to John Teasdale for his skill and patience when typesetting, and to my wife Maggie for supporting me during many years of research and more recently whilst writing this book.

Richard Pulleyn, 2020

Chapter 1 : Historical Outline

South of York, the Leeds & Selby Railway had opened in 1834 and, in the following year, the survey began of the proposed North Midland Railway intended to connect Derby to Leeds. It was to connect with this line (at Altofts Junction, near Normanton) that York's first railway – the York & North Midland Railway (Y&NMR) – was formed, to provide a link in a railway route from York to London (Euston Square) via Derby. The Y&NMR then progressed in stages: on 29 May 1839 the line opened from a temporary station just outside the City Walls at York to a connection near Milford with the Leeds & Selby Railway. On 11 May 1840 the line extended south to Burton Salmon, and finally it reached Altofts on 1 July 1840 – the same day that the North Midland line opened into Leeds (Hunslet Lane). A curve from the Y&NMR at Castleford (Whitwood Junction) to the North Midland at Methley also enabled trains from York to travel to Leeds.

In the meantime, the Great North of England Railway (GNofER) planned a railway from Gateshead to the south via Darlington, and they were persuaded to link up with the Y&NMR at York where a joint station was to be built. Although George Stephenson had recommended that York station should be sited outside the City Walls where there was adequate space, the Y&NMR Act of 1836 provided that it could be built just inside the City Walls – and that is what the company decided to do, even though this site was extremely restricted. That station opened for Y&NMR passengers on 4 January 1841 and for GNofER passengers on 30 March 1841.

Illustration 1. York Old Station fronted on to Toft Green. Originally designed by GT Andrews, principally on behalf of the Y&NMR but also accommodating the GNofER, it opened to traffic in 1841 and was subsequently extended by Andrews and again by Thomas Prosser. (NRM Collection)

The second Y&NMR line, to the east coast at Scarborough, opened on 7 July 1845, with a branch from Rillington just north of Malton to Pickering where it made a junction with the Whitby & Pickering Railway (opened in 1836). This was followed by another branch off the Scarborough line, from Bootham Junction to Market Weighton, which opened on 4 October 1847 and was extended to Beverley on 1 May 1865, thereby providing a line through to the port at Hull via the former Hull & Selby Railway's Hull - Bridlington branch.

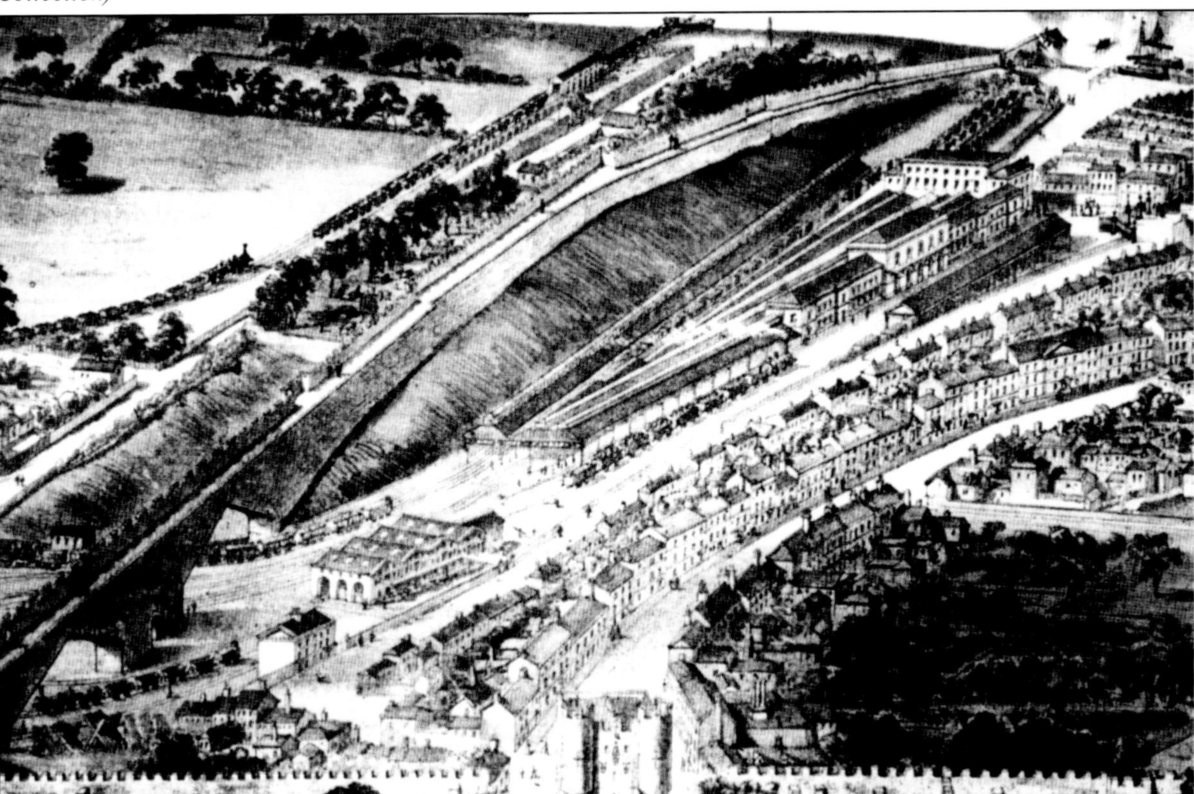

Illustration 2. York Old Station is prominent in this extract from Nathaniel Whittock's 'Bird's Eye View of the City of York', published in 1858. The passenger station is entirely within the City walls, and a coal train can be seen on the GNofER depôt line beyond. (NRM Collection)

To the west, the East & West Yorkshire Junction Railway built a line from Poppleton Junction to Knaresborough, opening to just outside that town on 30 October 1848, then extended to Starbeck on 1 October 1851 and to Harrogate on 1 August 1862.

In 1854, the Y&NMR amalgamated with the YN&BR (York, Newcastle & Berwick Railway, formerly the GNofER), the Leeds Northern Railway, and the Malton & Driffield Railway to form the mighty North Eastern Railway (NER), and further developments will be described in the text as they occurred relative to other events.

Chapter 2 : Signalling in the Early Days (up to 1877)

With few exceptions, the earliest known references to signalling in the York area come from Board of Trade (BoT) Accident Reports so many of these reports provide a useful introduction to signalling in the early days.

After extensive research, the earliest report found for this area was prepared by Captain JLA Simmons and related to an accident just south of York on the Y&NMR. In the early hours of 31 July 1848, about 2 miles outside the city close to Dringhouses level crossing, a goods train from Leeds bound for York came to a standstill due to a burst tube in the engine's boiler. One of the guards went back about half a mile to a previous level crossing on the Askham Bryan road where there was a 'board' signal which he was able to turn to 'Stop'. However, after an assisting engine arrived to take the train forward, he turned the signal back to 'All Right' and returned to the coal train; unfortunately, a mail train then overtook and collided with the rear of the goods train as it moved slowly forward.

To the north of York, the YN&BR undertook a survey of the infrastructure on the line in 1851; they created a volume headed 'Length of Lines' (1) which provides a record of features at that time, as shown in the following table, working from a Zero Point at the buffer stops in York station:

Miles	Chains	Links	Feature as Recorded
	00	00	Buffer Stops at York Station
	03	50	End of York Station
	07	30	York Walls
	09	20	Level Crossing – Thief Lane
	34	78	Scarborough Junction – opposite new Cabin
1	15	03	Bridge over railway – Township Road
1	56	23	East & West Yorkshire Railway Junction [later known as Poppleton Junction]
3	24	00	River Ouse Bridge
4	61	50	Level Crossing – Public Road
5	37	50	Level Crossing – Public Road
5	52	00	Shipton Station

This provides the earliest reference to a cabin at Scarborough Junction.

An accident next occurred on the YN&BR north of York at Poppleton Junction in 1854. This was investigated by Lieutenant H Tyler who reported that distant signals were provided at the junction from both the Thirsk and Knaresborough directions, worked during the day by a pointsman; however, at night train crews were expected to work the point and signal levers themselves. On this occasion, at about 3:5 am, an overnight express from York to Newcastle collided with an empty coal train crossing from the Knaresborough line on to the main line. The express train was eighteen minutes late so it was likely that the driver and guard of the coal train thought that it had already passed. Furthermore, the lamp of the distant signal for trains approaching from York was flickering so dimly as to be invisible through the lamp glass.

The early railway companies were nervous about facing points and, it was not until 1863 that facing points were installed at Poppleton Junction for trains to run straight on to the Knaresborough branch; prior to that date, trains towards Knaresborough had to reverse through a crossover on to the Up Main before proceeding towards Knaresborough.

In 1857, Lieutenant-Colonel G Wynne reported on a collision that occurred on 21 August between a passenger train and a goods train which had been shunting on the curve between North Junction and Holgate Junction. The signalmen at each of the junctions could not see the other because of the curve of the line so 'when a train enters the station by one junction, the signalman rings a bell at the other junction to warn the signalman to expect a train and to act accordingly'. Wynne continued 'this is the only signalling between the two junctions' so he concluded that 'some more efficient arrangements need to be made'.

The cramped station layout within the City walls was also creating operating difficulties. An extract from minutes of the Company Officers' meeting on 29 August 1859, recommended that 'the signal on the arrival platform at York near the turntable be removed and a semaphore signal erected at the West End of the arrival platform, to be worked by a wire from the place where the present signal is erected'.(2) Then, following an accident at York station on 23 May 1860, a further extract from minutes of the Company Officers' meeting on 4 June 1860 recommended that 'a semaphore with a single arm be put up so as to enable the signalman to block the main line against anything coming out of the curve; the semaphore to be worked by a handle in the signal cabin'.(3) So by this time we know that there was a signal cabin at the station.

(1) TNA: RAIL 772/63.
(2) TNA: RAIL 527/1117.
(3) TNA: RAIL 527/1117.

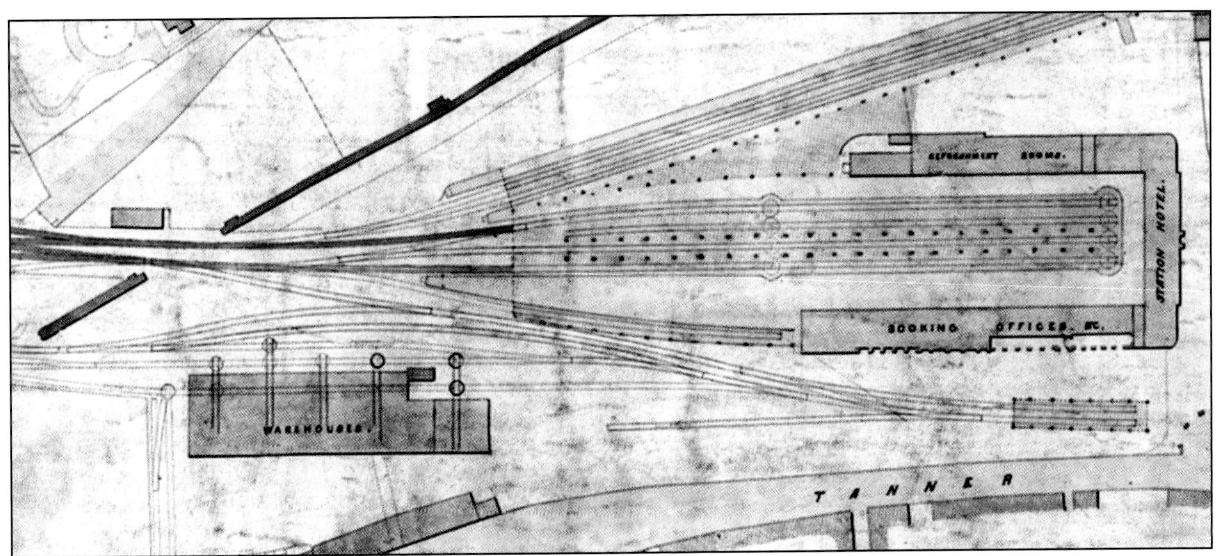

Illustration 3. *York station layout in 1856 (part of a larger plan). The main 'Arrival' platform is alongside the Refreshment Rooms, with the 'Departure' platform alongside the Booking Offices. Note the two sets of four turnplates, used to work an engine and its tender (separately) round its train. Outside the train-shed on the north side are what were referred to as the Scarborough Bays. The station lines converge to pass through the City walls and a building can be seen on the plan which may have been 'Archway' signal cabin, conveniently close to Thief Lane level crossing. (Courtesy of Network Rail Archivist)*

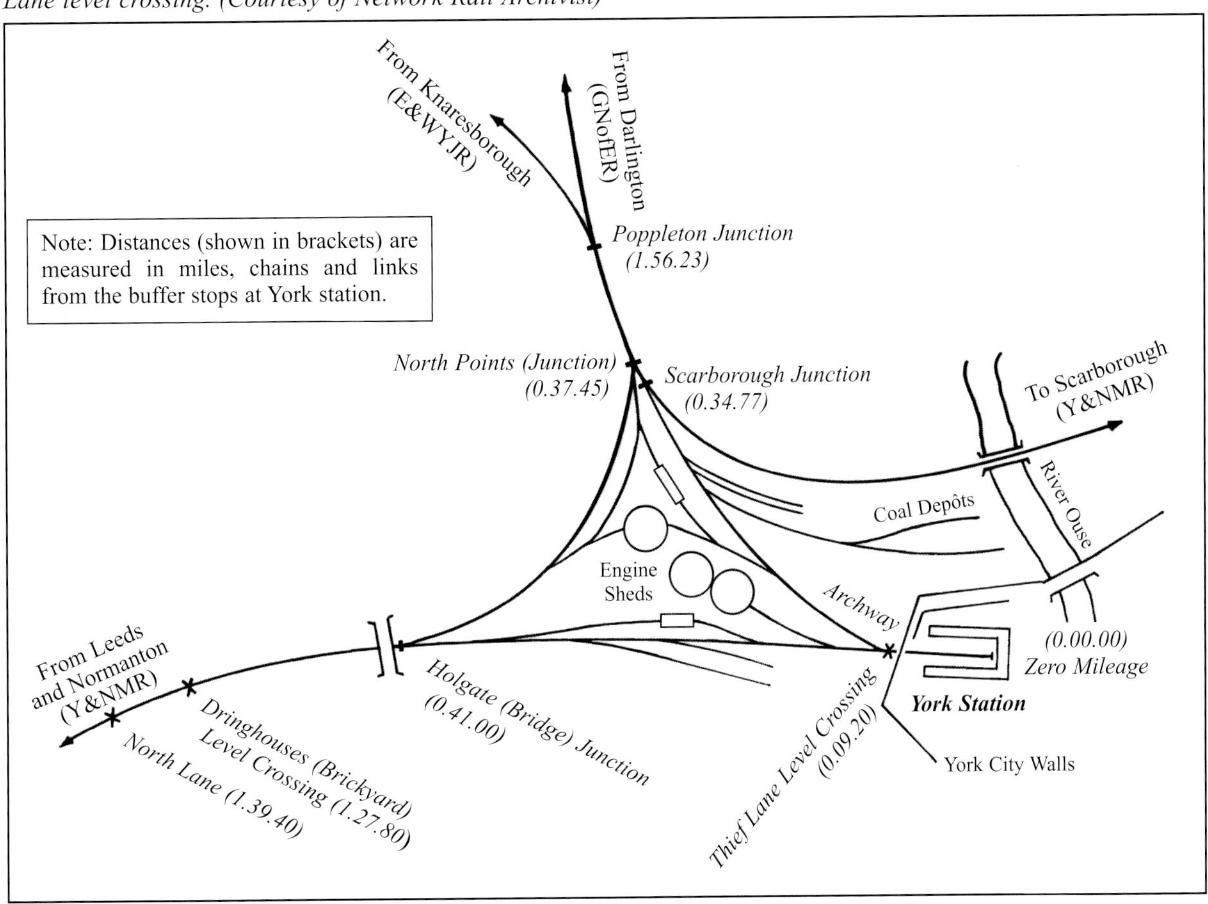

Illustration 4. *Sketchmap showing the railways of York circa 1861. (Richard Pulleyn)*

By the early 1860s, some attempts were being made at a few locations to concentrate together the levers controlling points and signals. For example, on 24 October 1861, Captain William O'Brien, General Manager of the NER, wrote to the Locomotive Committee (made up of NER directors) recommending that the signals at Holgate Junction, York should be raised so that they could be seen at a greater distance. He also recommended that the signalmen at Holgate Junction and North Points (York) should be provided with a platform sufficiently high up to enable them to see trains approaching from a considerable distance.(1)

(1) TNA: RAIL 527/1117.

In 1862, the NER (Southern Division) Line Diagrams (1) provided a record of principal features on the lines south of York – including an extensive number and variety of level crossings:

Miles	Chains	Links	Feature
			End of York station
			Bar Walls
			Level crossing – Thief Lane
	41	00	Holdgate [sic] Bridge (over the line)
1	07	80	Hobb Moor Bridge (under the line)
1	27	80	Level crossing to Brick Yards, Dringhouses
1	39	40	North Lane Gate House
1	53	70	Occupation Gates – level crossing
1	62	70	Occupation Gates – level crossing
2	00	70	Chandley Whins Gate House – level crossing
2	63	50	Bondill's Bridge (over the line) London Road
3	12	95	York Field Lane – level crossing
3	30	10	Wormald's Lane – level crossing
3	54	90	Occupation Road – level crossing
3	68	00	Copmanthorpe station
3	68	40	Copmanthorpe Lane – level crossing
4	22	40	Moor Lane Gate House – level crossing

However, by the mid-1860s, as traffic levels increased, the NER Board recognised that the original station at York was no longer suitable – it was a terminus trying to cope with through traffic; trains had to enter the station then retrace their steps before proceeding. The cramped site of the original station meant that adequate enlargement was not possible so additional platforms were authorised south of Holgate Bridge in 1860. Finally, in 1865 the Board decided to build an entirely new station, outside the constraints of the City walls, which would be able to handle through traffic more readily; work was authorised by an Act of Parliament in 1866 but construction was delayed by financial difficulties being experienced by the NER.(2)

In April 1867, yet another accident occurred on the line between North Junction and Holgate Junction. The Board of Trade Report by Major CS Hutchinson explained that:

> 'York Station is situated such that trains from the north running into it then set off south with the rear of the train now to front. To avoid this with mail trains, a "junction line" has been constructed from North Junction to Holgate Junction, by making use of which the mail trains can be backed into the station, ready to depart in proper order.' He further states that 'Near Holgate Junction, a siding called the "Independent", used for making up goods trains &c., joins the Up Junction Line.'

On this occasion an Up Goods was being shunted on the Up Junction Line but left some wagons which were run into by an Up Mail train, the driver of which stated 'The junction signal and signal at the centre of the Junction Line were all right for him when, a few yards past the latter signal, he ran into the goods wagons loaded with timber'.

Shortly afterwards, O'Brien submitted a report dated 26 November 1867 to the Locomotive Committee regarding the significant 'detentions to trains entering York'. He had arranged for a survey to be undertaken and concluded that the approach from the north was 'so much occupied by trains' that, for example, the 2:20 pm Up train from Newcastle had to be brought in on the Down line on no less than 10 occasions of the 12 monitored, so 'an expedient of somewhat doubtful propriety and only adopted in cases of emergency' had become 'the customary mode of working'.(3)

By 1869, the Board of Trade was pressing hard for the introduction of the 'Block Telegraph System'. O'Brien suggested testing that system on short stretches of line, amongst which the York - Normanton mainline was included and this work was finally authorised by the Board in 1870, installation taking place the following year.

York to Doncaster via Selby

In the meantime, a direct line from York to Doncaster via Selby had been constructed; the BoT sent Colonel W Yolland to inspect it prior to opening, and he prepared his report on 12 December 1870. In addition to various road bridges, there was a swing bridge at Naburn with a fixed span of 103 feet and two openings of 88 feet over the River Ouse.

Naburn station was situated immediately south of the swing bridge and Colonel Yolland's comments were the opposite of what might have been expected; he stated that:

> '...it is over-signalled and two men are proposed to be employed to do what may be better done by one. There are two Distant signals with two repeating signals to the south, both worked from the same box – one intended to cover the Station and the other the Bridge. In the same way, there are two Down signals one for the Station and one for the Bridge, which Bridge works a third Down signal. One signalman is intended for the Bridge signals and a Porter for the Station signals. One Down Distant and repeating signal and one Down Station signal placed at the north end of the Down Platform, and locked at Danger by the Bridge when it is open, will provide for the safety of Down trains – and the Up Station signal should be placed at the south end of the Up Platform. One man can attend to all the signals at this station. In a similar manner, at the Box at the north of the Bridge, the Bridge when open can be made to prevent the signalman at that Box from taking off the Home Up Signal and even the Distant if required – and thus two Home Up Signals, one above the other, at the Box are unnecessary.'

(1) TNA: RAIL 527/958.
(2) NER Board Minutes, 3 November 1865.
(3) TNA: RAIL 527/1254.

The relative distances were as follows:

North Lane (York) to Naburn North	2 miles 465 yards
Naburn North to Ouse Swing Bridge	0 miles 400 yards
Ouse Swing Bridge to Naburn South	0 miles 630 yards
Naburn South to Escrick station	2 miles 1499 yards

Colonel Yolland also inspected the lines into York Station because they did not join the old lines in accordance with the deposited plans, instead the four tracks ran parallel as far as the entrance to the station. He stated that:

'At Selby and at York the signalling is done in a way that is contrary to the usual practice throughout the Kingdom…In approaching a junction from many lines the signal for the left line was shown on the left post, that for the middle line on the middle post, and that for the right line on the right post, and similarly with respect to various lines departing from a junction.'

From what little evidence can be found it would seem likely that signals had been 'stacked' one above another – a practice which subsequently became quite common. Since Parliament had been asked to sanction the trains of other companies to run over these lines, a universal system of signalling should be adopted, so he recommended that the signals should be re-arranged in accordance with usual practice. Robert Hodgson, the engineer of the new lines, undertook to attend to these requirements, so Yolland sanctioned opening of the line via Selby when these alterations had been made.(1)

A New Station is Planned

A plan of the proposed new station at York dated 1871 shows that four running lines were intended through the station with a main platform on the east side and an excursion platform on the west side; bay platforms were planned at the north and south ends. Signal cabins were shown at the south end of the station on the east side, in the centre of the main platform, and between the running lines at the north end near the NER's waterworks.(2)

However, it would not be until 1877 that the new station was ready to be brought into use, and in the meantime another series of accidents had occurred in the vicinity of York station; again, the relevant reports provide further insight into the signalling and train working before that date.

On 1 July 1871 an excursion train from Scarborough collided with an engine and brakevan proceeding from Holgate Junction towards North Junction. Captain Tyler's report to the Board of Trade paints a vivid picture in words. He described the arrangements outside York station as:

'…very complicated, comprising four junctions for the lines from Newcastle, from London, from Scarborough, and from York station, and numerous sidings in connection with the main lines in every direction. There is also a triangle, each side of which is nearly half a mile long, and which is used partly as a means of sending through traffic past the station without entering it, partly as a means of turning the trains end for end by backing them into the station,

(1) TNA: MT 6/69/11.
(2) TNA RAIL 527/498.

Illustration 5. *Naburn Swing Bridge with the cabin mounted above, seen in an engraving dated 1871. The Board of Trade Inspector Captain Henry Tyler, RE, was critical of the over-signalled and over-staffed arrangements. Note the semaphore 'River Signals'. (Engineering, 27 October 1871)*

and partly as a means of running the engines round the trains and turning them at the same time without either taking the engines to the turntable or bringing them into the station.'

In North Junction signal cabin there were:

'Six telegraph bells – from Shipton, Haxby, Stockton (Warthill), York Station, Holgate Junction and Gas Works; a Block Telegraph instrument from Gas Works cabin, and a double needle speaking instrument from Malton on the Scarborough line. There are no levers for working the points and signals inside the cabin, but under the cabin roof and scattered outside the platform round the cabin there are levers for working seven pairs of points and handles for working five signals.'

Amongst the signals described was:

'...a square board which applies to trains running from the south along the south-west side of the triangle...and two signals at the signalmen's cabin which are used as Home signals for the Up & Down Main lines. There is no locking apparatus in the cabin in connection with any of the points or signals.'

Signalling on the line towards Scarborough was also described:

'180 yards on the south of the North Junction cabin is Scarborough Junction cabin...there are two Home signals, one applying to the main line from Scarborough and the other applying to a coal depot line which joins at this point; and there is a Distant signal towards Scarborough about 650 yards south of the cabin. There is also an Auxiliary Distant signal 800 yards further from the cabin, with a handle near the Distant signal, which is intended to be applied by the guards of trains detained at or near the Distant signal, on occasions of obstruction at the junction.'

(At that time, drivers were required to bring their train to a stand if a Distant signal was placed at 'Danger'. Then, if the line ahead was clear, to proceed at a speed not exceeding 5 miles per hour until the whole of the train was at least 300 yards within the signal, so that their train was protected by the Distant signal from any other trains following.)

Tyler continued:

'There are no means of communication between Scarborough Junction cabin and North Junction cabin other than by hand signals, including flags by day and hand-lamps by night. The signalman at Scarborough Junction makes signs with his hand-signals on each occasion to ask leave of the signalman in North junction when a train approaches from the direction of Scarborough before he lowers his signals, and he depends for replies made by the latter signalman by means of hand-signals also. The signalman in North Junction cabin, who is really the principal signalman for this portion of line, has thus no signal except the Home signal above his cabin which he can work either in the direction of Scarborough, or of the siding connected with that line, or of the station or sidings connected therewith; and he is obliged to depend entirely upon hand-signals for affording indications either to the signalman in Scarborough Junction cabin or to the engine-drivers of trains approaching from any of those directions.'

Tyler concluded that:

'The lines outside York have grown to their present condition in the course of several years and are in a most unsatisfactory condition; modern appliances have not yet been made use of for working the very complicated and constant traffic...'

In this instance, the driver of a train approaching York 'found the Distant signal at 'Danger' but upon the whistle being sounded, the signal was lowered, and the engine ran forward ... towards Scarborough Junction cabin.'

On nearing that cabin, the signal was again lowered so the train carried on towards North Junction, but as it approached the driver noticed the signalman calling out and making signs to an engine propelling a brake van, approaching from Holgate Junction, to get a move on, but the inevitable occurred – the two trains collided at the convergence of the lines.

The signalmen at each cabin were experienced: remarkably, the Scarborough Junction man had served for 20 years, and the other for 9 years, in their respective posts. They were working for 12 hours by day and 12 hours by night on alternate weeks and 'they were further relieved such that they take 11 shifts in each fortnight'.

Both signalmen were aware of the approach of the train from Scarborough by:

'...the bells in their cabins ringing on the instruments from Haxby. The Signalman at Scarborough Junction kept his signals at Danger until he heard the whistle of the expected train approaching. He then blew a whistle which he kept in his pocket for that purpose and held up his hand to ask permission from the signalman at North Junction to lower his signals. The signalman at North Junction waved his arms as the usual form of reply, so the signalman at Scarborough Junction lowered his signals... When the bells are rung correctly, there is usually an interval of from 7 to 10 minutes between the ringing of the bell from Haxby and the arrival of the train at Scarborough Junction.'

The signalman at North Junction thought that there was adequate time, therefore, to allow the engine and brake to pass before the Scarborough train; when he saw that was not the case he tried to change the points for the latter to run on to the Up Independent, but, before the collision occurred 'the lever, although near him, was blocked in its position by a wooden key, such as is used to key the rails in the chairs; and he was unable to get this key out, and to push the lever over…'

It was not recorded whether this wooden key was an official device or something introduced by the signalmen to wedge facing points.

Although the North Junction signalman was clearly to blame, Tyler emphasised that:

'…it could not have occurred if he had been provided with those modern improvements and better appliances which are indispensable to safety in working junctions, crossings, and complicated systems for through traffic and shunting traffic, such as are to be found in the neighbourhood of this cabin… It is to the want of such improvements and such appliances that this accident is really to be attributed. There has for some time been a project for a new station at York, and the alterations will no doubt make a great difference in the working of traffic.'

But, as there was no certainty about when these works would be carried out, he recommended that, in the meantime 'the cabin should be raised, the signalman should be provided with levers, conveniently arranged, and interlocking with one another…and with the means of inter-communication with signalmen near him. Without these improvements a reasonable degree of safety cannot be expected to be secured.'

Some four months later, in November 1871, another accident occurred, inspected by Colonel Yolland for the Board of Trade. He noted that:

'There are two modes of entering York station by trains arriving from the north. One, which is unobjectionable, is by running directly in by the north curve, with the engine in front; and the other, which is very objectionable, by running south through Holgate Bridge, and thence backing by a cross-over road and reaching the Down Normanton line, thence shunting back along it in to York station, a distance of 1200 yards in length.'

On this occasion a train from the north reached Holgate Bridge but there was already a train on the Down Normanton line, so the signalman at Holgate Junction decided to back the train along the Independent line normally used for engines proceeding from the shed. He realised that there were hand points along that line so he 'sent one of the boys employed in the signal cabin to hold up the points which lead to the coke shed siding'.

The boy did as he was bid – but both the signalman and the lad forgot that there were other hand points which were not held over, so the train from the north collided with an engine. Yolland commented:

'The accident was due to an objectionable system of shunting trains for more than half a mile into York station, and to the fact of the points not being worked from the signal box and properly interlocked with the signals and with each other...The company have powers to construct a new station at York, and I trust when it is constructed these objectionable arrangements will be done away with.'

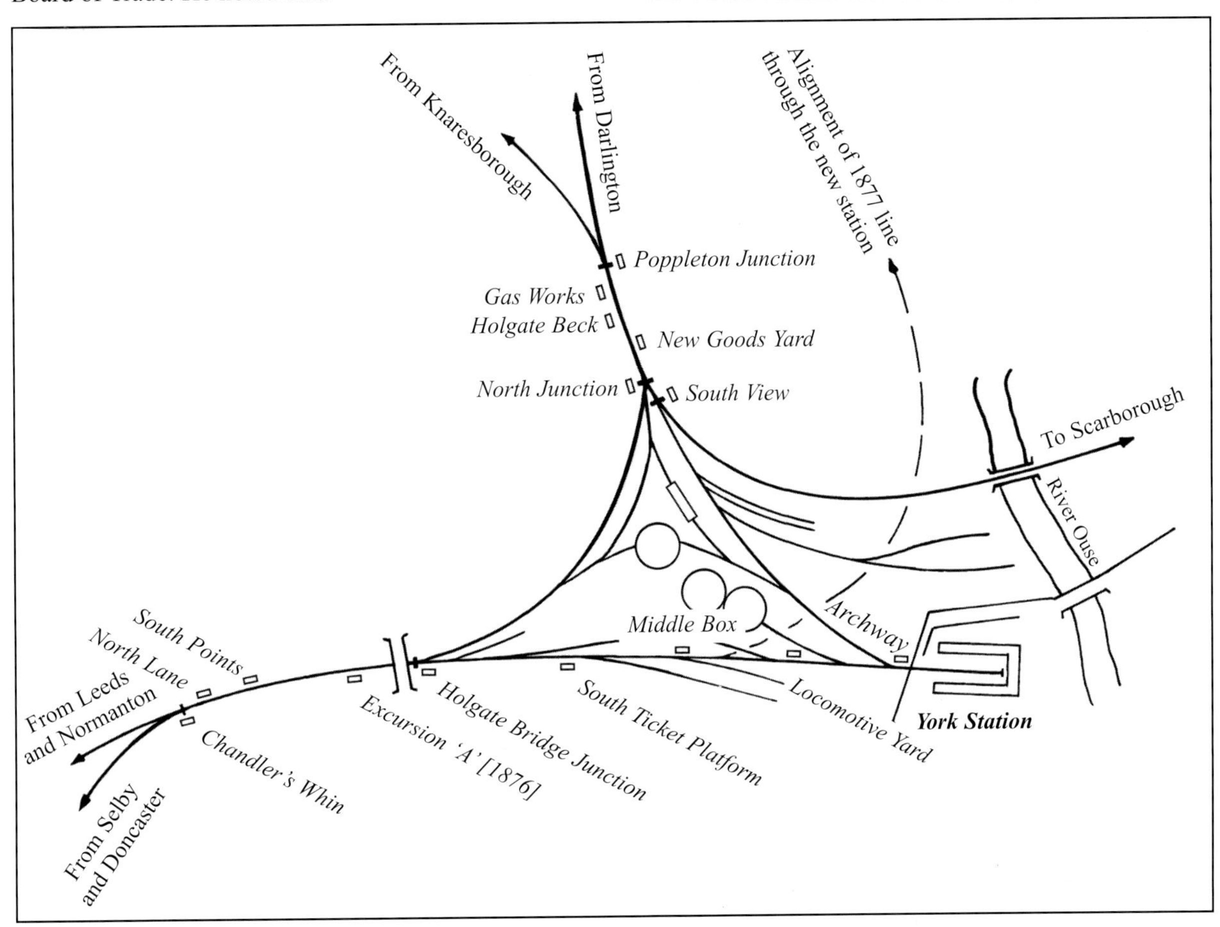

Illustration 6. *Sketchmap showing the signal cabins in and around York circa 1872. (Richard Pulleyn)*

However, the following year, in August 1872, there was a similar accident when a train from the north was backing in to York station and collided with a train already in the platform. Tyler was again called to investigate, and he provides another detailed description of the working:

> 'There are two platforms, one on the north and another on the south side of the station, and there are lines on both sides of these platforms….. The total length of these platforms is 195 yards, and there is a carriage turntable at 95 yards from the west end.'

The approach was obstructed by an archway 35 yards from the end of the platform, and the line curved such that a driver approaching could not see whether the destination platform was clear.

> 'There is a signal cabin close to the archway, and the signalman there stationed controls the approaches to the various lines in the station; and he uses his fixed signals and hand-signals according to circumstances; but he is frequently obliged to let a train into the station when the line on which the train is about to run is partially occupied, and in which case he gives the driver a hand-signal or calls to him as he is backing in to warn him of the obstruction.'

The train standing in the platform had come from the south 'with an excess of passengers going northwards for the opening of the grouse shooting season.' Its departure was delayed whilst passengers were taking their refreshment. The signalman had lowered his signal to permit the train from the north to back in, and shouted as it passed; the guard heard and applied his brake, but neither the driver nor the fireman had heard. The signalman could not give a hand-signal because he was already making hand-signals to an engine crossing from the goods yard to the shed. Once again, Tyler commented that:

> 'The condition of York station has already been subject of remark in a sufficient number of reports. Nothing can be more inconvenient than the mode in which the traffic is worked into and out of the station… I cannot blame any of the men concerned in this case. The only wonder is that they are able to work the traffic as they do without accidents constantly occurring.'

The cabin referred to by Tyler was known as Archway; even today, there is a small brick building adjacent to an arch in the City walls, and a plaque is mounted on the footpath above that arch pointing to 'Old Signal Cabin'. Illustration 7 is a photograph of the building seen in 2013 from above the archway in the City walls; although there are no familiar signs to confirm that this building was indeed a signal cabin, it cannot be disproved since, at that time, points and signals were worked outside or hand signals sufficed.

As may be expected, the NER Directors were keen to progress building of the new station, and work was indeed underway, when in December 1872 a further accident took place at North Junction, described as being about 700 yards from York station. A GNR engine left the station for the shed and proceeded tender-first towards the junction where the signal was at danger so the engine was brought to a stand. The driver whistled three or four times and eventually the signal was lowered briefly before being replaced to danger, so the engine started to move then came to a stand again; no sooner had that occurred than a passenger train leaving the station ran into the engine. Lieutenant-Colonel Hutchinson noted that the line curved sharply between the station and the junction and, running alongside were numerous sidings occupied by wagons *etc.* By this date, there was telegraphic communication between the station and the junction cabins but only for announcing the arrival and departure of trains; Hutchinson recommended that Block Working should be adopted whereby no passenger train should be allowed to leave the station until the line was clear up to the junction. He added 'Should such a mode of working be incompatible with the exigencies of the traffic with the

Illustration 7. *This building, adjacent to York City walls, is reputed to be Archway signal cabin. However, positive evidence of this has yet to be found. During the 1930s the building was used as a store by the LNER locking fitters based at York. (John Whitaker)*

present arrangement of the station (which arrangements will, of course, be entirely altered when the new station is completed), it would be some improvement to provide the junction with a Distant signal placed 200-300 yards on the station side of the junction.'

Adoption of Block Working

The NER Board had at last accepted the need for action in this regard, and Block Working had already been introduced on the line between York and Altofts (Normanton). Furthermore, surveys were being undertaken by Alexander Christison, the NER Passenger Superintendent, to determine what was required on those lines not currently equipped with Block Working and interlocked signal cabins. The following is extracted from his *Memorandum of the Proposed Block Signal Stations between Holgate Bridge Junction (York) and Shaftholme Junction* dated 14 December 1872 with the information shown from south to north to describe signalling on the lines approaching York at that time:(1)

At Chandler's Whin a cabin opened in 1870 to control a temporary junction during construction of the direct line via Selby to Doncaster. Traffic commenced running by that route on 2 January 1871. However, the cabin was not in use at the time of Colonel Yolland's inspection of the new line, nor was it included by Christison in his 1872 report, so for a period the Doncaster lines simply ran parallel with the Normanton lines as far as Holgate Bridge Junction where they joined together to run into the station. Incidentally, derivation of the unusual name 'Chaloner Whin' goes back to the Court Rolls of 1625 when tenants of the Manor of Dringhouses were accused of stealing Chandlers Whin – Chandler being a surname and 'whin' being a local name for gorse. Local mispronunciation is believed to have corrupted the name to Chaloner Whin. It became Chaloner's Whin in 1900, then reverted to Chaloner Whin, and the LNER changed it to Chaloners Whin; thereafter, it was not unusual to see any of those spellings used.(2)

NABURN STATION CABIN and NABURN NORTH CABIN
Distance 0m 41c
The Block instruments may be placed in the temporary Cabin which stands at the north end of the Up Platform, but a permanent and elevated Cabin should be erected at the south end of the same platform, so that the Station Points may be connected with, and worked from it. This change of Cabins would in no way interfere with the proper arrangements for securing the safety of trains passing over the Bridge**. The Bridge Signal which stands at the north end of the platform would be continued in its present position and worked by wire from the permanent Cabin, being controlled as at present mechanically by the Bridge itself. An advance semaphore should be provided for the Up line.
[** *i.e.* the swing bridge over the River Ouse]

NABURN NORTH CABIN and NORTH LANE CROSSING
Distance 2m 21c
The advance Cabin for the Bridge is of wood, on the level of and at the east side of the Main Lines. It will be suitable as a temporary Cabin for Block working, and only requires the Instruments for the line to and from the north.
There is at present a special system of Block working between this Cabin, the Cabin on the Bridge, and the Station Cabin, which has worked well, and I think it is desirable not to disturb it; so that the Block section will end at the North Cabin in the direction of York, and at the South Cabin in the direction of Doncaster. An advance semaphore will be required for the Down line.
There are a Foreman and 8 men employed at the Bridge, and houses for only 4 men are provided. It is desirable that at least 4 additional houses should be built here.

NORTH LANE CROSSING and HOLGATE SOUTH POINTS
Distance 0m 46c
At the North Lane Crossing, a private siding connected with the York and Doncaster line, is being put in for the use of Mr. Nelson, the Contractor. An interlocking frame is now in position on the west side of the lines. A ground Cabin will be placed over it, and it will be suitable for Block working. The points and signals will be connected and interlocked. An advance semaphore will be required for the Up line.
On account of the Level Crossing, day and night attendance will be required.

HOLGATE SOUTH POINTS and HOLGATE BRIDGE JUNCTION
Distance 0m 30c
These Cabins are now fitted up for Block working on the York and Normanton lines, and only require the instruments and their fittings for the line from York to Doncaster.

(1) TNA: RAIL 527/1117.
(2) *24 Hours at York*, OS Nock, RM September / October 1949.

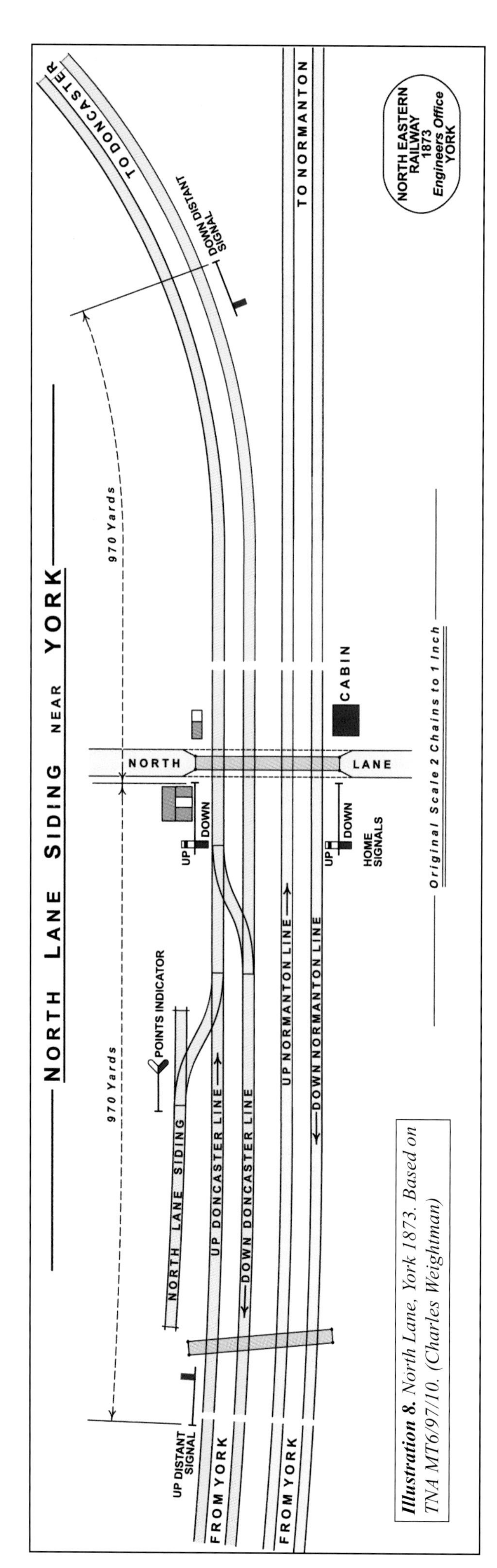

Illustration 8. North Lane, York 1873. Based on TNA MT6/97/10. (Charles Weightman)

Progress with Interlocking

Under pressure from the Board of Trade not only to introduce Block Working as described above, but also to extend interlocking of lever frames, a report was submitted to the NER Committee on 29 November 1872. This included that, on the line from York to Darlington, Poppleton Junction and Gas Works Junction were already provided with locking frames, although they had not yet been ordered for the cabins at the station, North Junction or Shipton. On the Normanton line, Holgate Bridge and Copmanthorpe cabins were so fitted, but locking apparatus had still not been ordered for Loco Sidings, South Sidings, Middle Junction or South Points. Finally, on the Scarborough line, Bootham Junction cabin had an interlocked lever frame, but nothing had been ordered for South View Junction. Given the Board of Trade reports into accidents in and around York at that time, it is inevitable that the Inspectors became increasingly frustrated.(1)

Places supplied with Locking Apparatus

Darlington to York

Poppleton Junction
York Gas Works Junction

York to Normanton

York Holgate Bridge Junction
Copmanthorpe Station

York & Scarborough

Bootham Junction

Places for which Locking Apparatus are not ordered

Darlington to York

Shipton Station
York North Junction
York Station

York to Normanton

York Loco Sidings
York South Sidings
York Middle Junction
York South Points Junction

York & Scarborough

York South View Junction

North Lane

The private siding at North Lane referred to by Christison above was inspected by Lieutenant-Colonel Hutchinson on 24 February 1873 who also noted a new crossover road at that place; the points and signals were properly interlocked and he gave his approval subject to a signal being repositioned.(2) See Illustration 8.

(1) TNA: RAIL 527/1117.
(2) TNA: MT 6/97/10.

North from York

On the line north from York, Christison's *Memorandum of the Proposed Block Signal Stations between North Junction (York) and Dalton Junction* dated 1 January 1873 included the following useful descriptions.(1)

	Distance Apart	Gradients
1. NORTH JUNCTION CABIN and HOLGATE GOODS SIDING CABIN.	0m 33c	1 in 1123 Falling
2. HOLGATE GOODS SIDING CABIN and SEVERUS JUNCTION CABIN. The line between the above places is now worked on the Block system. The junction for the new station will commence at a point about 70 yards north of the present Cabin at Severus Junction, and it may be necessary to build a new Cabin at the facing points further north, on the west side of the main lines. There is a siding north of this junction, connecting with the Up Main line, for the use of the Water Works Company. It is necessary that this siding should be extended to the Severus Junction, and catch points be placed upon it, to be worked from the Cabin.	0m 27c	1 in 1178 Rising
3. SEVERUS JUNCTION CABIN and POPPLETON JUNCTION CABIN. The Block system is in operation at present between these two points but not beyond, and Poppleton Junction will therefore be the starting point for commencement of the extension of Block working northwards to Darlington. A permanent Cabin is built at Poppleton Junction on the east side of the lines. It is rather small, but with a little alteration will do for the extended Block working. An advance Semaphore will be required for the Down line. At present there is a Bell communication to the Shipton station, which will be available for Block Working.	0m 48c	1 in 1178 Rising
4. POPPLETON JUNCTION CABIN and SKELTON BRIDGE CABIN. A permanent Cabin should be erected at Skelton Bridge, on the west side of the lines, at a point about 10 chains less than mid-way between Poppleton Junction and Shipton station. An advance Semaphore should be provided in each direction. Two houses should be provided for Signalmen. Being so close to York, there will necessarily have to be day and night attendance.	1m 43 c	1 in 3882 Rising
5. SKELTON BRIDGE CABIN and SHIPTON STATION CABIN. A Cabin should be erected at the Shipton station, on the east of the lines, at the north end of the Up platform, to admit of which the shed should be removed.	2m 26c	1 in 3882 Rising

With the line so divided into sections, and the Signalmen in Telegraphic Communication with each other, and aware of the position of Passenger and fast Goods trains, a great amount of the delay which now unavoidably occurs at York, Thirsk , and Darlington will be saved, and the working of the traffic, as a result, much facilitated.

A. CHRISTISON

H. TENNANT, Esq.

1st January 1873

(1) TNA: RAIL 527/1117.

It will be noted that Christison anticipated a junction for the new station at a point about 70 yards north of the existing cabin at Severus Junction. However, as constructed, the new lines ran parallel to the existing lines until they joined at Poppleton Junction.

Shortly after Christison's reports, the first NER *Appendix to the Working Timetable*, issued in May 1873, shows a number of additional signal cabins suggesting that the Block system was indeed being extended.(1) See the table below.

Strangely, although Severus Junction and Skelton Bridge cabins are both referred to by Christison neither is included in the 1873 Appendix; evidence in the 1874 Return to the Board of Trade suggests that 'Gas Works Junction' (the NER had opened their own gas works nearby in 1869) was close to the later site of Severus Junction so it may have been one and the same. It will be noted that the next cabin north from Poppleton Junction was not until Bishophouse at Pilmoor.

The 1874 NER Appendix (see below) lists the same cabins as a year earlier but includes that 'Speaking Instruments' were available at these locations: Copmanthorpe, South Points, North Junction, Gas Works Junction and Shipton station.

During the same year, in May 1874, Colonel Hutchinson was back at York to investigate the derailment of a passenger train from Scarborough which was backing through a pair of points at North Junction towards a ticket platform on the line to the station when one of the carriages left the rails and was tilted up. The circumstances provide a further insight into signalling and train working at the station when Hutchinson reported:

> 'According to the present arrangements of the York station yard (which is now in course of alteration), all trains from Scarboro' to York run up to North Junction, and then set back through two pairs of points (one of which is worked by the North Junction signalman) and along a short piece of single line common to both incoming and outgoing Scarboro' trains, and then through a pair of points at which these lines diverge, and which are weighted to lie right for the line leading to the ticket platform, from which they are distant about 100 yards. A signalman who is stationed at a ground cabin (called South View), not very far from these points, works the signals for incoming and outgoing Scarboro' trains, the North Junction signalman having control over the former, but not over the latter of these signals.'

Station	Cabin	Weekday Hours	Sunday Hours
COPMANTHORPE	Copmanthorpe	Always	Always
	Chandler's Whin	Always	Closed from passing of 2-10 Up and 2-49 a.m. Down Mails on Sunday, to 1-0 a.m. on Monday
YORK	South Points	Always	Ditto
	Holgate Bridge	Always	Always
	Middle Box	Always	Closed from 4-0 a.m. on Sunday to 5-0 a.m. on Monday
	South Ticket Platform	Closed from 8-0 p.m. to 8-0 a.m. Daily	No Sunday duty
	Locomotive Yard	Always	Closed after passing of 3-41 a.m Down Mail to 8-30 p.m. on Sundays
	Archway	Always	Always
	North Junction	Always	Always
	Holgate Beck	Always	Closed from about 2-0 p.m. to 11 00 p.m. on Sunday
	New Goods Yard	Always	Ditto
	Gas Works Junction	Always	Always
	Poppleton Junction	Always	Closed from 6-00 a.m. to 6-00 p.m. on Sunday
PILMOOR	Bishophouse	Closed from 6-0 p.m. to 9-0 a.m. Daily	No Sunday duty
	Sessay Wood	Closed from 9-0 p.m. to 7-0 a.m. Daily	No Sunday duty
	Station Junction	Closed from 8-35 p.m. to 6-30 a.m. Daily	Open on Sundays for passenger trains only

(1) KH.1992.

As the train reversed towards the station, the guard noticed that the set of points was standing partly open, so he put on his hand-brake as hard as he could despite which part of the train went one way, and part the other. The driver stated that it was not customary for anyone to hold over these points. The South View signalman was holding another pair of points over whilst the train had set back, but he could not see the points where the derailment took place; however, he stated that a number of trailing moves had taken through those points, and the upper part of the point lever (on which was fastened a weight which kept the points in the required position) was subsequently found to have broken off. It was concluded that this was the cause. Hutchinson also emphasised that:

'This accident points to the danger of unlocked facing points, especially if unattended by any Pointsman when trains are passing over them...The existing state of points and signals at York station will happily soon (as new arrangements are fast progressing) be a thing of the past. It is to be regretted that the necessary improvements should have been so long delayed.'

The next accident was only five months later, in October 1874, once again at North Junction. Colonel FH Rich described the signals as follows:

'The junction is protected by Home signals, and...Distant signals from both Newcastle and Leeds, but not from York station. The points and signals are not interlocked...There is a bell communication between the signal cabin at the north end of York station platform, which is called Archway cabin, and the North Junction cabin.'

It would seem that the bell announcing the departure of a train from the station to Newcastle was rung after the signals had been lowered at North Junction for a mineral train to pass from the north towards Leeds. The signalmen at North Junction and South View saw that the Newcastle train was travelling at speed and unlikely to stop before North Junction so they tried to attract the attention of the driver who looked out and saw the junction home signal at danger and tried to stop, but there was a minor collision. Rich concluded that the driver of the Newcastle train was responsible because he had not kept a good look out for the junction signal which could be seen for about 400 yards. He stated that:

'It would be very desirable that the signals and points at North Junction should be re-arranged and interlocked; but as the NER are at present changing their station at York, and the approaches to it, they have allowed the old arrangements to remain... The new arrangements are to be on the locking principle.'

Sadly, there were to be two more accidents in this vicinity before the replacement York station was brought into use. However, some progress was being made: in the 1874 Return to the Board of Trade, the NER report included that Absolute Block working was in place in the York area as follows:(1)

York to Altofts Junction (Normanton)	23m 12c
Holgate Junction to Shaftholme Junction	27m 45c
Poppleton Junction to Gas Works Junction (York)	0m 46c
South View Junction to Scarborough	42m 15c
Worked by Electric Telegraph (but not on Absolute Block)	
Poppleton Junction to Otterington	24m 66c
Poppleton Junction to Knaresborough Goods	14m 47c
Gasworks Junction to York station	1m 10c
Bootham Junction to Beverley Junction	31m 43c

In the 1875 Return, two further routes were upgraded to be worked by Telegraph on the Absolute Block system:

Darlington South Junction to North Junction (York)	43m 30c
Bootham Junction to Earswick	0m 63c

Still worked by Electric Telegraph (but not on Absolute Block):

North Junction to York station	0m 40c
Poppleton Junction to Knaresborough Goods	14m 47c

In March 1875, five months again after the previous reported accident, yet another collision occurred at North Junction and Colonel Hutchinson was appointed to investigate. An Up Mail train collided with a goods train which had been propelled along the Up Line from Gas Works to North Junction where it was waiting for a signal to allow it to enter the station. The report provides a description of the telegraphic bell communication between Gas Works cabin and North Junction cabin, about three quarters of a mile apart:

'Instruments were provided for block telegraph working in case of either main line being occupied or of crossing moves taking place. The telegraphic bell signals were: one ring for goods, mineral, cattle trains or light engines; two rings for ordinary passenger trains; three rings for mail, special, or express trains; the acknowledgements being the same as the announcements.'

On this occasion, the Gas Works signalman sent one ring to North Junction and received a reply 'with unusual promptitude'; he was then notified that the Up Mail was approaching so he sent three rings on the bell – but received only two back; he persisted by repeating three bells but each time received only one or two back, so the telegraph boy at Gas Works was instructed to keep sending three bells until it was correctly acknowledged which it was eventually. At North Junction neither the signalman nor the assistant signalman were aware of the goods train being propelled towards them, but Gas Works cleared the signals for the mail train which then collided with the

(1) TNA: RAIL 1053/189.

goods train. The malfunction of the bell had been reported and attended to on a number of occasions and, after the accident, the telegraph inspector concluded there was some fault in the coils so fresh ones were substituted; he suggested that the immediate response to 'one bell' may have been due to a short circuit. Therefore, the cause of the accident was unclear – it was possible that the Gas Works signalman had failed to bell on the goods train, but equally the North Junction may have forgotten that he had received the signal, or that the faulty bell had misled the Gas Works signalman. Hutchinson concluded that:

'Had the Absolute Block system been in constant and not merely occasional use between the two cabins, the collision would very probably have been prevented. It is now in force from Berwick to Thirsk, and I understand that in a month's time it will be extended from Thirsk to York.'

In February 1876, an accident occurred at Holgate Junction when a passenger train from Normanton split in two, the front portion continuing on the correct line, but the rear portion being diverted to the Down Independent line the train then became derailed. This time Colonel Rich reported on behalf of the Board of Trade. The junction home signal worked to 'Danger', 'Caution' and 'All Right'; on this occasion it was lowered to Caution for the train to pass. The points and signals were interlocked with each other, and were worked from a raised cabin about 62 yards from the points where the accident happened. The points were well made and secured by:

'Mr Harrison's wedge apparatus. This wedge apparatus does not prevent the lever and points from being moved by the Pointsman while a train is passing but it, together with the tie-bar between the stock rail, as fitted by the NER, presses the points against the stock rail, and holds them close and firm while a train is passing, if the lever is not moved by the Pointsman.'

Therefore, Rich concluded, the points must have been moved by one of the men in the cabin.(1)

Holgate Excursion Platforms

A short distance south of Holgate Junction, outside the six running lines, were two 'Excursion Platforms', one on each side of the line. These platforms were especially useful for passengers attending the horse racing held on York's Knavesmire course which was a short walk away. For the race meeting in May 1876, HJ Winspear of the NER Southern Division Engineer's Office wrote to A Almgill requiring two temporary connections and a temporary cabin, 'Excursion Platform A', to be installed in accordance with the plan reproduced as Illustration 9.

The Board of Trade appointed Colonel Hutchinson to inspect the altered arrangements for these platforms adjacent to Up and Down Independent Lines. He noted that the platforms were used about three times a year for excursion traffic to 'York Feaste' (sic); a new frame 'Platform A' had been installed at the south end of the Up Platform to work a connection from Up Independent to Up Normanton or Up Doncaster, with a slot on the Down Doncaster Home and Up Doncaster Home signals for South Points. His only requirement was that the arms of the distant signals were to be notched.(2)

Out at Poppleton Junction an additional siding had been connected with the Up Branch from Harrogate. Since there were no spare levers in the cabin, which was soon to be replaced in connection with the new station at York, interlocking was simply achieved by a wire attached to the protecting home signal. This was not acceptable to Colonel Hutchinson but he agreed to the temporary arrangement provided that a newly installed Up Distant signal was also brought into use together with Block Working on the affected line.(3)

Finally, in September 1876, with the new station almost ready, Colonel Hutchinson was called upon to investigate yet another accident between North Junction and Archway just outside the 'old' station, providing a final description of the signalling and working to and from the 'Old' station. Trains from North Junction proceeding into the station could use either the Main Line or the Scarborough Line, at the discretion of the signalman; these lines ran either side of a ticket platform, at the station end of which was a double-armed signal post worked from the station (Archway) cabin, the upper arm applying to incoming trains on the Main Line, and the lower arm applying to the Scarborough Line. Close to that signal were facing points on the incoming line leading to the outgoing Scarborough Line, normally set for the latter. At South View cabin, some 200 yards from North Junction, the signalman controlled incoming and outgoing Scarborough trains in order to prevent them from coming into conflict at points near North Junction. Telegraphic bell communication was available between North Junction cabin and South View, and between North Junction and Archway, but there was no code by which the North Junction signalman could inform Archway on which line (Main or Scarborough) a train was approaching; North Junction had no telegraph with Locomotive Cabin, and South View had no telegraph with Station / Archway cabin.

On this occasion a train was backing in to the station from North Junction along the incoming Scarborough Line; the driver thought he was on the Main Line (also known as the Station Line) and mistook the signal lowered at the end of the ticket platform so his train met a mail train coming out on the same line. Hutchinson noted that the alterations at York were fast approaching completion so he did not recommend any significant changes, although he did mention that it would be simple and desirable to immediately establish a code of telegraph signals so that the North Junction signalman could advise the Station signalman on which line a train was to approach.

(1) A description of the Harrison's wedge apparatus can be found in *A History of North Eastern Railway Signalling* page 132.
(2) TNA: MT 6/166/3. (3) TNA: MT 6/162/24.

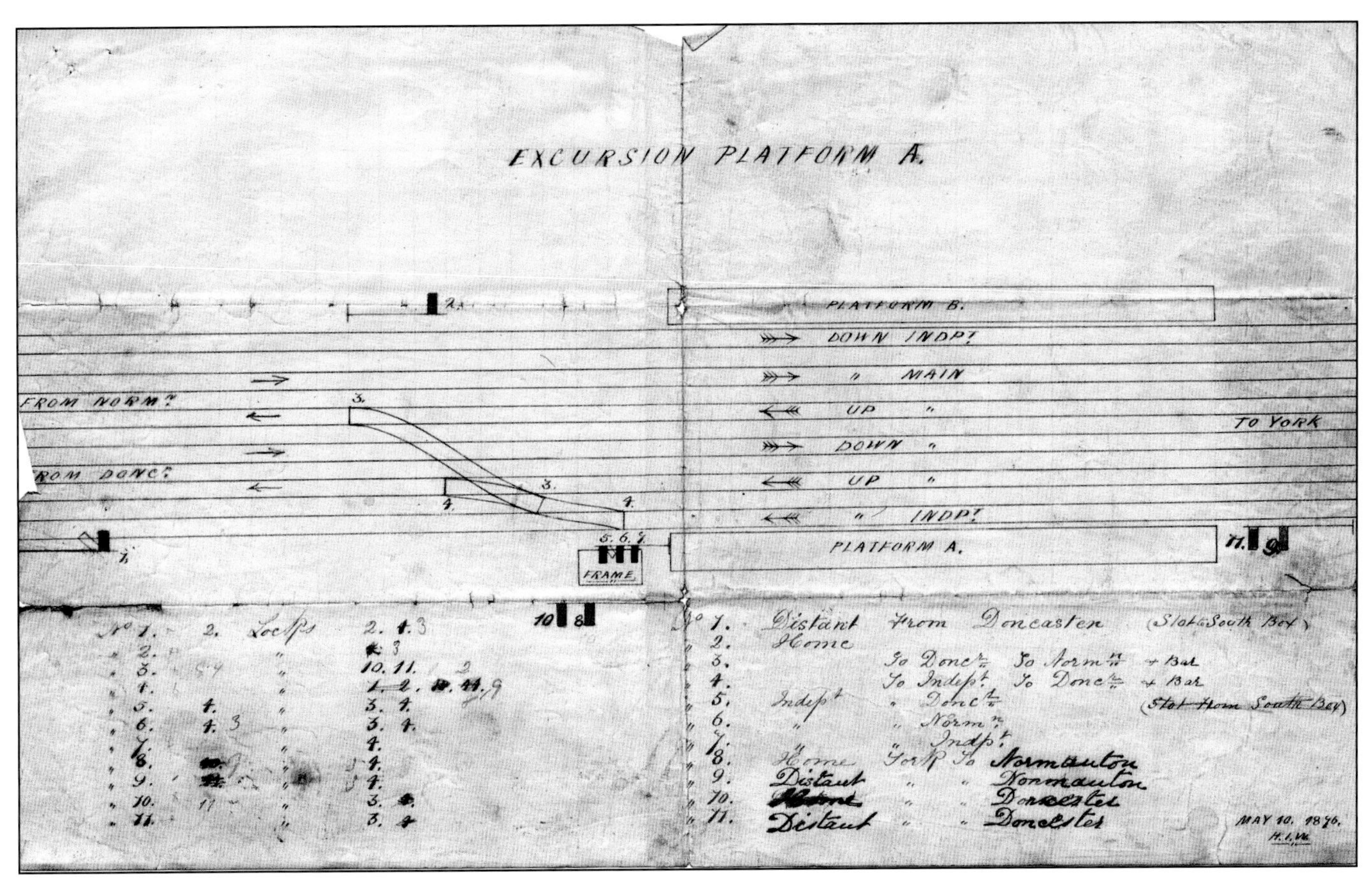

Illustration 9. *This diagram accompanied Henry John Winspear's memorandum dated May 1876 concerning the installation of temporary connections and a temporary cabin, 'Excursion Platform A', at Holgate Excursion platforms (note his initials in the bottom right corner of the diagram). By 1876, Winspear had been serving as an NER signal inspector for several years. The 1891 census records Winspear as being a railway signal engineer, and it is believed that he was in charge of York signal workshop at that time. (David J Williamson Collection)*

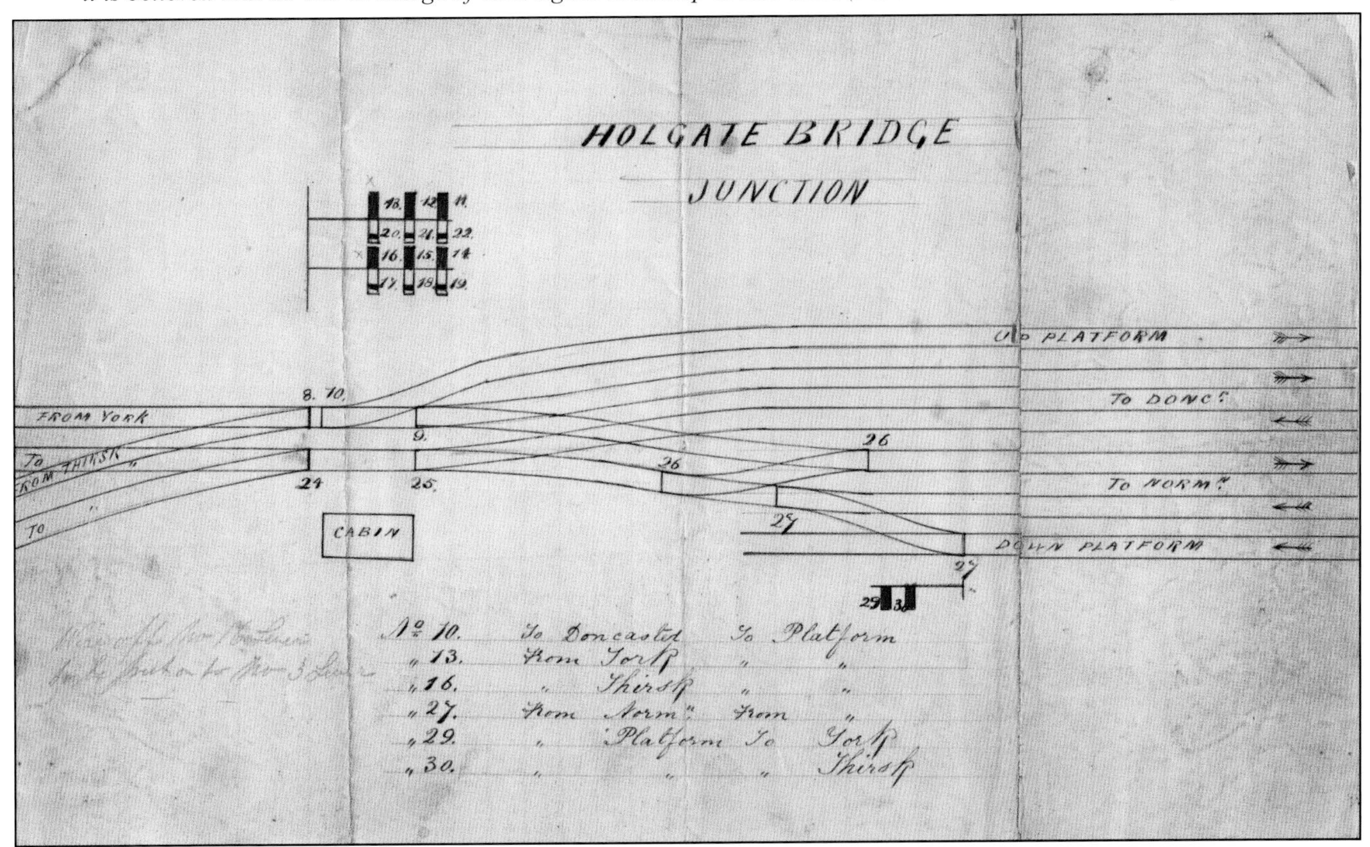

Illustration 10. *In preparation for opening the new station at York, various temporary signalling arrangements were made on the approaches. Illustrations 10 and 11 show the arrangements at Holgate Bridge Junction and Locomotive Yard signal cabin respectively. (David J Williamson Collection)*

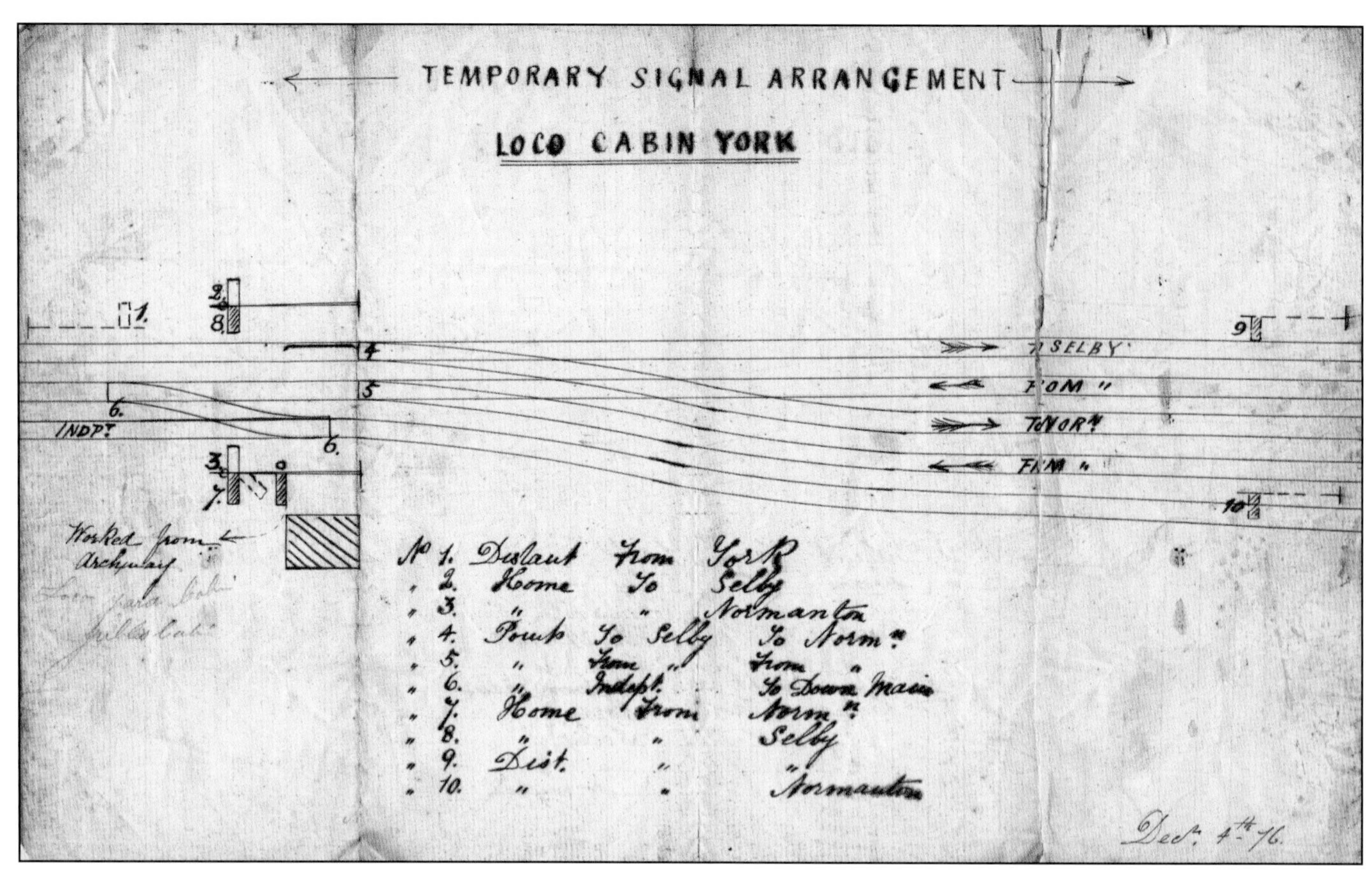

Illustration 11. *'Loco Cabin York' as described in the caption for Illustration 10. (David J Williamson Collection)*

In preparation for opening the new station at York, various temporary signalling arrangements were made on the approaches, as exemplified by the diagrams of signalling for Holgate Bridge Junction and Locomotive Cabin, dated 4 December 1876 (Illustrations 10 and 11). The diagrams were accompanied by a brief note from HJ Winspear to A Almgill requiring these arrangements to be put in place as soon as possible since they would be required for Christmas Day.

South Points

On 6 December 1876, Colonel Hutchinson inspected the new cabin and junction at South Points where the lines to and from Normanton and Selby were joined by new Up and Down Independent lines which proceeded to and from the station as Excursion lines, being placed outside the existing Up and Down Doncaster and Up and Down Normanton lines; this made a total of six running lines between South Points and the station. The arrangements were considered satisfactory, but the points and signals had not been connected up. The lever frame had a total of 25 levers, six of which were spare, and the cabin was brought into operation early in 1877.(1) See Illustration 12.

When all of the above works were completed, early in 1877, the original Y&NMR road overbridge at Holgate Junction dating from 1839, and which had spanned only two tracks, was also reconstructed to span up to six lines.

(1) TNA: MT 6/173/7.

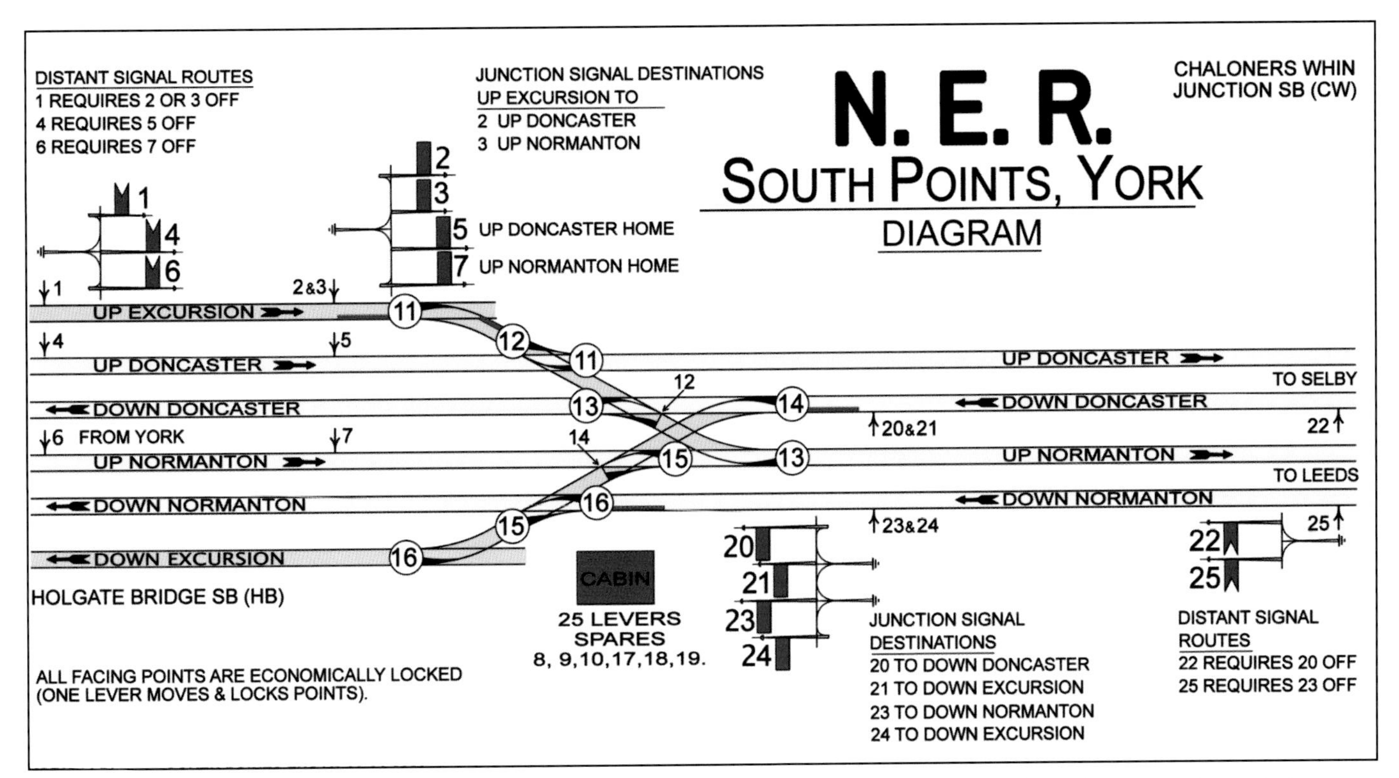

Illustration 12. *South Points, York, 1876. Colonel Yolland's comments made in 1870 about the siting of signals is amply illustrated in this diagram on which small arrows have been inserted to clarify which lines the signals refer to; of course, for drivers the positioning of these signals must have caused difficulties. (Diagram based on TNA MT6/173/7 and drawn by Charles Weightman)*

Illustration 13. *This is a view of the 1841 York station, taken from the city wall long after its closure and replacement by a new station outside the wall. After closure, the station sidings were used for carriage storage as seen here. The station buildings and the Royal Station Hotel (built across the end of the station and opened in 1853) were used as offices. Looming over the station in the background is the North Eastern Railway's headquarters building, completed in 1906. (DS Barrie / Locomotive & General Railway Photographs / John Alsop Collection)*

Chapter 3 : 1877 – the New Station

The NER wrote to the Board of Trade on 9 March 1877 regarding alterations at Holgate Bridge and Poppleton Junctions which were in preparation for opening the new station.(1)

Holgate Bridge

At Holgate Bridge Junction a new cabin had been provided on the Up side to control the following lines:
* From South Points: a Down Independent, Up and Down Normanton, Up and Down Selby, Up Independent.
* From North Junction: Down Independent, Down and Up Goods, Second Down and Up Goods, Up Independent.
* From the station: Back Road (Siding), lines to and from station, Centre Back Line (Siding), from station, Up Independent.

The cabin was fitted with a 44-lever frame, of which eight levers were spare; however, by August 1877 an additional connection had been made from the Down Independent to the Down Main, so only three levers remained spare. See Illustration 16.

(1) TNA: MT6/267/7.

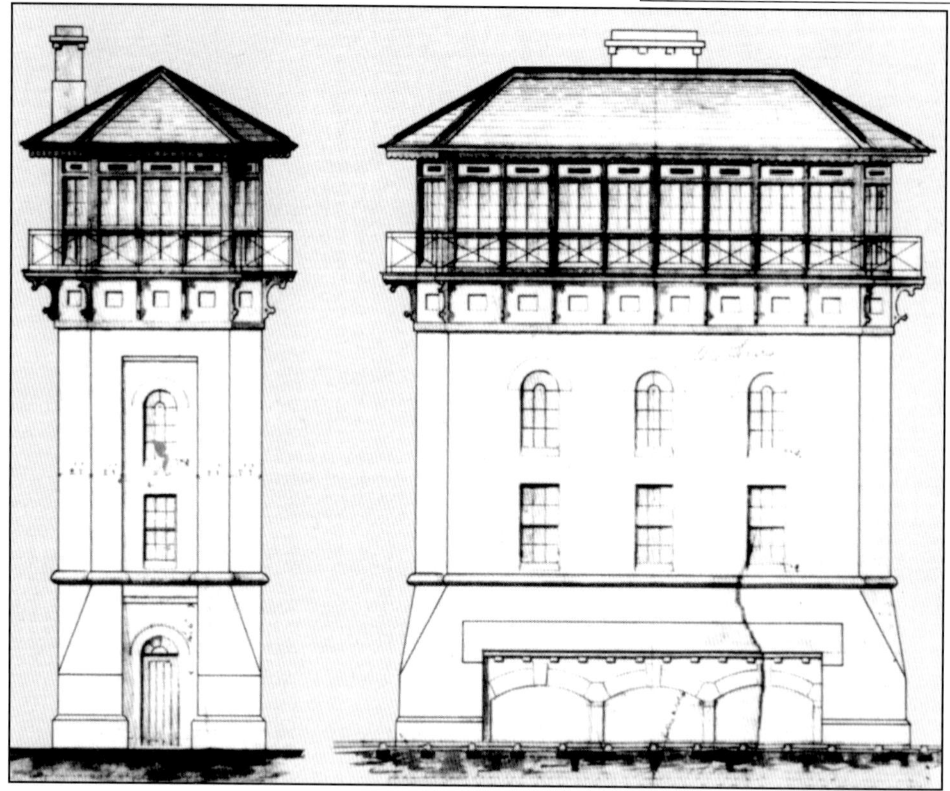

Illustration 14. *Holgate Junction Cabin, York, from an NER drawing dated June 1876. This was a special design for a prestige location; built of brick with a wooden top 27' 8" x 11' 0", the operating floor was 30' above rail level to allow signalmen to see over Holgate Bridge.*

Illustration 15. *Holgate Junction. On the right, a corner of the signal cabin can be seen. On the Up Doncaster line a passenger train approaches the convergence of lines from York Yards. (Arthur & Company / John Alsop Collection)*

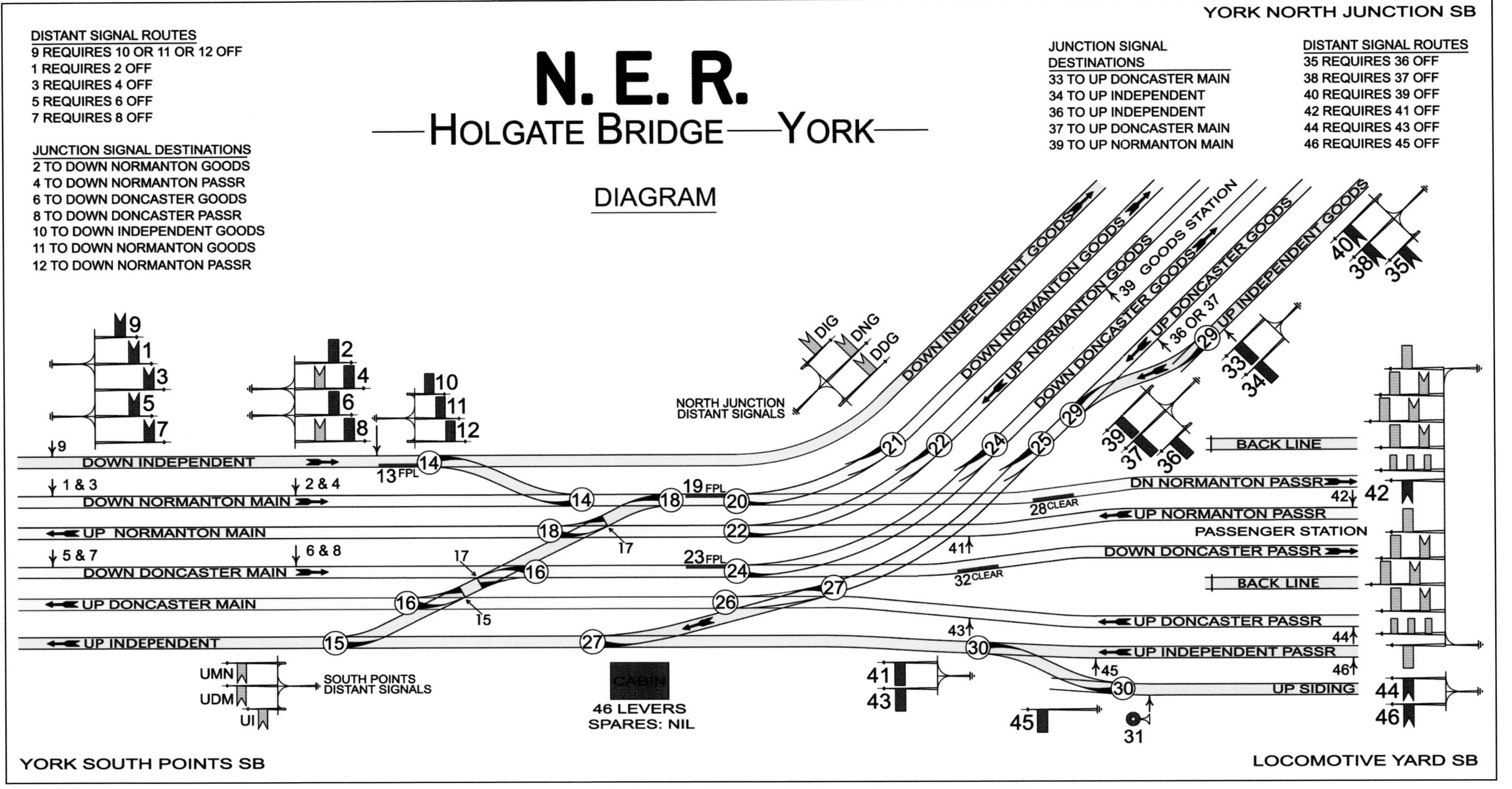

Illustration 16. *Holgate Bridge Junction: this diagram is based on a sketch made by Colonel Thomas Preston circa 1910. However, despite some minor alterations and subsequent re-locking of the frame, the layout was largely unchanged and usefully illustrates arrangements similar to those in 1877. The colours used on this diagram (and others like it elsewhere in the book) follow NER practice. Principal running lines were normally coloured yellow, and secondary lines, sidings and connections either blue or grey. Facing point lock bars and clearance bars were shown as short red lines. (Charles Weightman)*

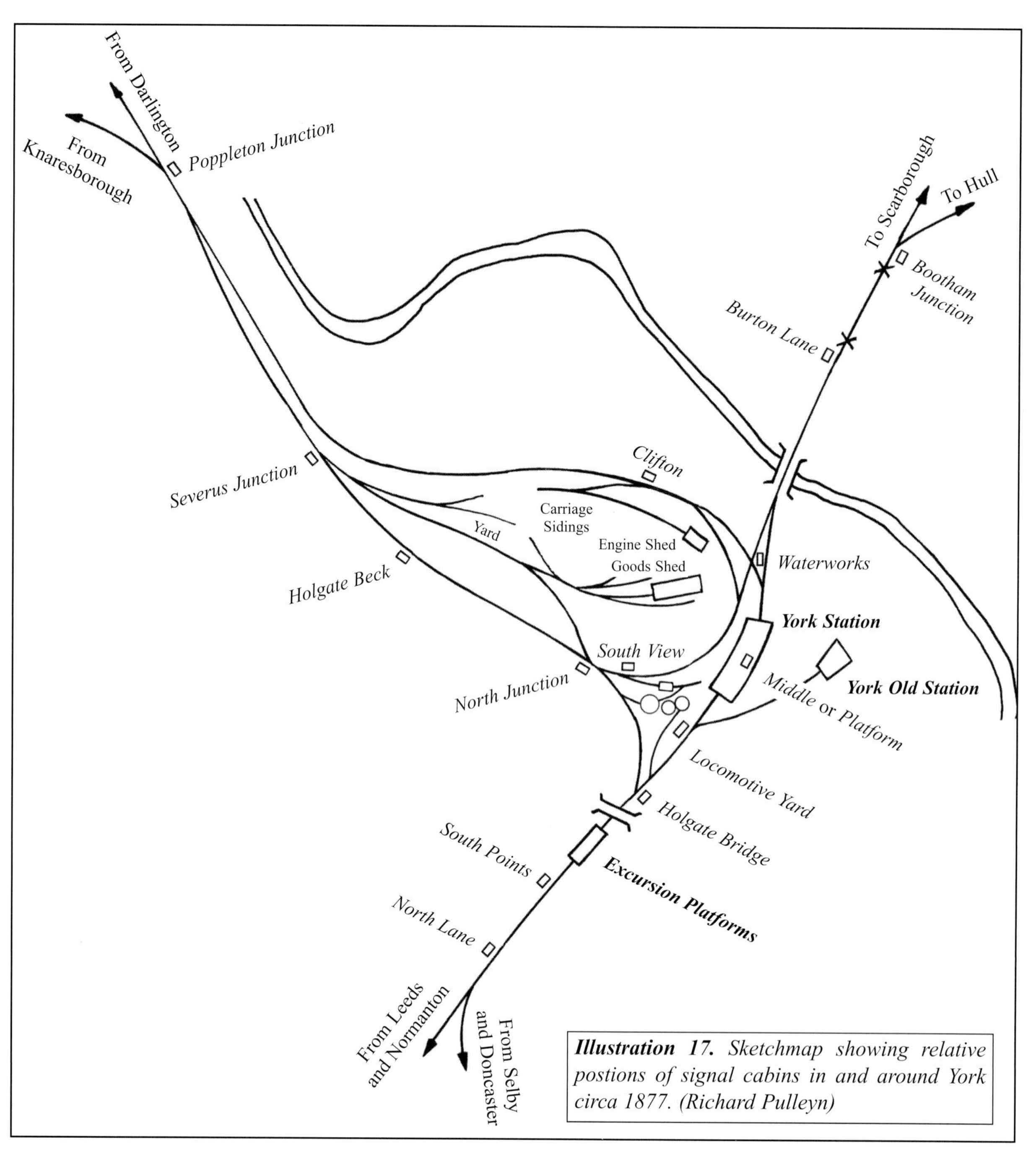

Illustration 17. *Sketchmap showing relative postions of signal cabins in and around York circa 1877. (Richard Pulleyn)*

Poppleton Junction

At Poppleton Junction, a new cabin was provided at the junction with the Harrogate lines to control the additional junction where the Up and Down Passenger lines from the new station ran parallel with then joined what became the Up and Down Goods from Severus Junction. This cabin had a 32-lever frame, of which five levers were spare.(1) See Illustration 18.

Following this inspection, the NER were advised by letter dated 5 April 1877 that the Board of Trade had no objection to the above arrangements subject to two provisos: at Holgate Bridge 'the ends of the catch sidings should be provided with some description of wheel or buffer stops'; at Poppleton Junction 'a set of facing points has not been provided with wedges or locking bolts'.

Regarding the proposals for the new station there was no objection in principle, subject to inspection and various requirements being addressed; importantly, this included whether the level crossing of the goods and passenger lines at the Waterworks cabin and at the north end of the station had received Parliamentary sanction. Thomas Harrison, the NER Chief Engineer, wrote back to the Board of Trade on 21 April 1877 stating his opinion that no special Parliamentary sanction was necessary, furthermore 'these places will be entirely interlocked and with catch point sidings so collisions will be impossible'. However, the Board of Trade was not satisfied so Major-General Hutchinson and Captain Tyler agreed to meet Harrison on 3 May in London, following which they agreed that any other arrangement would 'introduce greater disadvantages'. That matter resolved, Harrison then had to arrange another meeting with the Board of Trade, this time with the President, because it was 'very undesirable to work through traffic by passing Down trains through the Up platform'; nevertheless, no formal objection was made by the Board.

(1) TNA: MT 6/267/7.

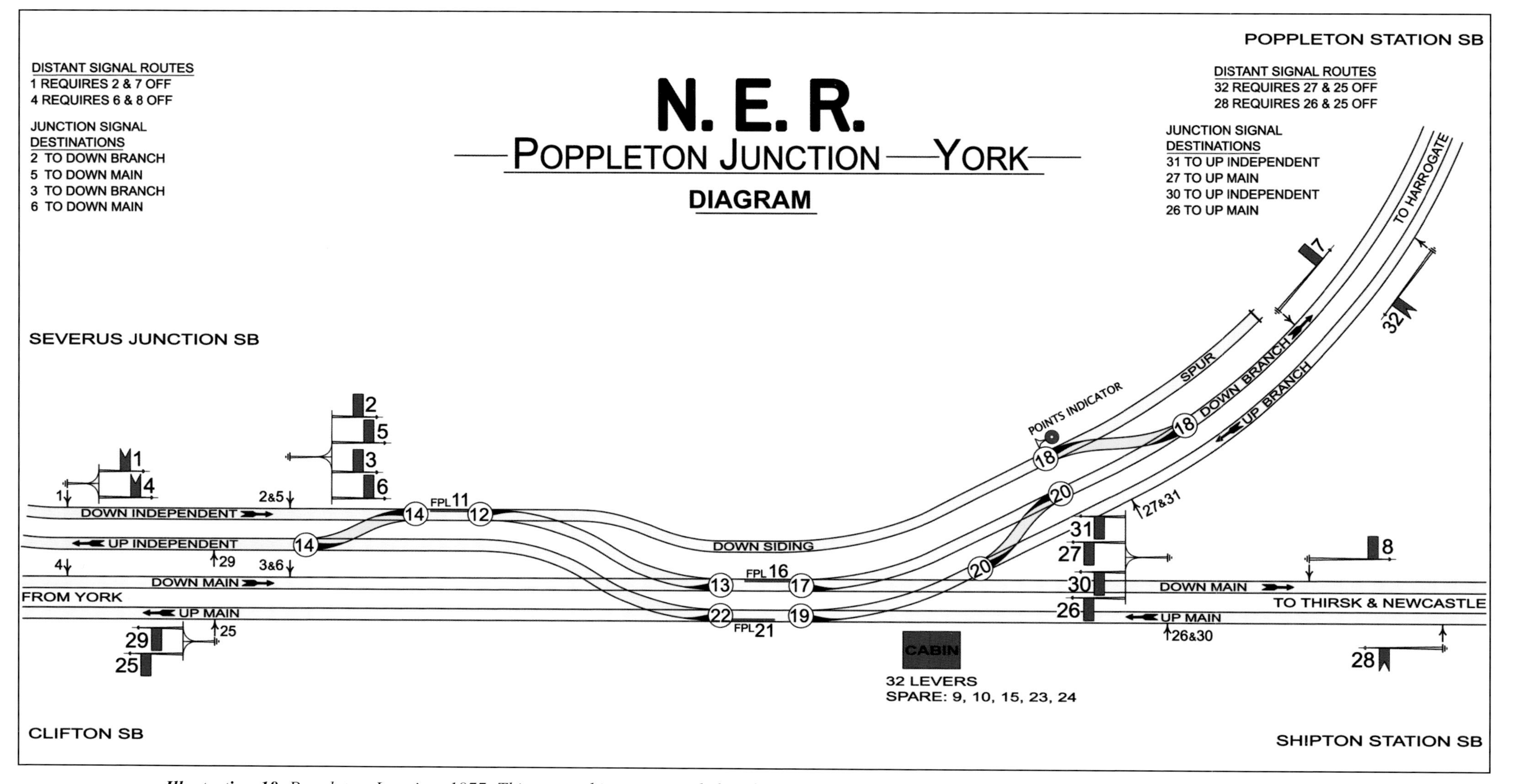

Illustration 18. *Poppleton Junction, 1877. This new cabin was provided at the junction with the Harrogate lines to control the additional junction where the Up and Down Passenger lines from the new station ran parallel with then joined, the Independent lines that became the Up and Down Goods from Severus Junction. Based on TNA MT6.267.7. (Charles Weightman)*

Having already agreed arrangements at Holgate Junction and Poppleton Junction, the remaining four new cabins were inspected on 26 May 1877; from south to north, these were:

Locomotive Yard – fitted with 89 working and five spare levers. (Note: this was the second cabin to carry that name.) The previous cabin was 56' 3" x 12' 0", with the operating floor 8' 0" above rail level, containing 46 working and one spare lever.

Central – fitted with 64 working and six spare levers. The cabin was situated on the main Up platform and was of an attractive, non-standard design with an octagonal footprint. Although referred to as Central at this time, it became Platform at an early date following.

Waterworks – fitted with 75 working and three spare levers in two back-to back McK&H No.12 frames of 39 levers each. Like Holgate Junction, the cabin had an attractive, non-standard design with an octagonal footprint, 28' 0" x 14' 6" in brick, with the operating floor 10' 0" above rail level.

Clifton – fitted with 23 working and six spare levers, built in wood (because it was at the top of a steep bank), 22' 0" x 11' 3" with the operating floor 8' 0" above rail level. The cabin controlled connections to the new York North engine shed: this consisted of three adjoining roundhouses in the shape of an 'L', on the west side of the line. The earlier roundhouses south of the station (behind Locomotive Yard Cabin) and the straight shed at Queen Street (the former York Locomotive Works opposite Locomotive Yard Cabin) remained in use as York South engine shed.

Although he was satisfied in all other respects, Hutchinson was concerned at the large number of facing points, but accepted that they were necessary for working the traffic at the station. However, the matter of working Down trains through the Up platform (so that passengers could readily access the Refreshment Rooms) as mentioned earlier was raised again because he considered that passengers were put at unnecessary risk.

Illustration 19. *A view looking north towards the new York station. The 1877 Locomotive Yard signal cabin is in the left foreground. (NERA V Rippon Collection VRP15_0271)*

Illustration 20. *On the right, partially hidden behind the columns, is Central (soon to be re-named Platform) signal cabin. This photograph was evidently taken before construction of the pedestrian bridge, and is believed to have been taken shortly after the opening of the new station. (NRM Collection)*

Illustration 21. *This view north from the new station pre-dates the installation, in 1900, of an additional connection across the main lines towards Scarborough on the station side of Waterworks signal cabin; the cabin is left of centre. Lines to the north bear left and lines to Scarborough bear right. (NRM Collection)*

On 6 June 1877, Hutchinson completed his inspection; he had no objections except, once again, the working of certain Down trains through the Up platform, so he concluded that 'the new station at York cannot be sanctioned without danger to the public'. According to a note dated 16 June on the file, however, the matter 'had already been disposed of by the Board's letter of 7 June so the Board of Trade will sanction the use of the new station and lines'.(1)

Indeed, the new station was brought into use on Monday, 25 June 1877, the first train to depart being the 5:30 am to Scarborough, and the first train to arrive the 8:30 am from Leeds..

Contrary to some sources, when first opened the station had 10 platforms (although two were incomplete). In the centre of the station were two long, through platforms: Nos 4 (on the east side) and 5 (on the west side), with two through lines (the Down and Up Main lines) between them. An additional through 'Excursion Line' (Platform No 6) was provided behind Platform No 5. Bays at the south end, behind Platform No 4, were numbered 3, 2, and 1 (incomplete); at the north end, again behind No 4, the bays were numbered 7, 8, 9, and 10 (incomplete).

For clarity, the list of signal cabins through the station in order was as follows:(2)

Chandler's Whin
South Points
Holgate Bridge
Locomotive Yard
Platform
Waterworks
Clifton
Poppleton Junction
Skelton Bridge

The original route from Holgate Bridge to Poppleton Junction became York Main Goods lines (or simply York Yards), and henceforward the former station was referred to as York Old station. Again for clarity, the list of signal cabins through the Yard in order at that time was as follows:(3)

Holgate Bridge
North Junction
Holgate Beck
Severus Junction
Poppleton Junction

In the York area, the Block Telegraph Regulations applied on the following lines:

Holgate Bridge Junction to Shaftholme Junction
Holgate Bridge Junction to Milford North Junction
Poppleton Junction to Poppleton station
Bootham Junction to Earswick station
South View cabin to Washbeck cabin (Scarborough)
North Junction (York) to Thirsk South Junction

In the station area, yet more facing connections were brought into use in August 1877 and again these were inspected by Hutchinson: he was unhappy that in this case the points, bars and wedges were all worked from one lever and the NER were instructed to use two separate levers. This is a further reference to Harrison's wedges which, nevertheless became quite widespread throughout the NER.

Of greater impact, by October 1880, Hutchinson had again become increasingly concerned at what he perceived as that regular practice of Down trains using the Up platform, so the NER Directors were asked to comment. According to the correspondence, it was their view that no conditions relating to the number of trains making this move had been agreed with the President of the Board of Trade; however, it would also seem that the Directors had given the impression this practice would only apply to three or four express trains each day. Since the practice had increased significantly, the Board of Trade supported Hutchinson regarding the risks and firmly placed responsibility on the NER Directors. Henry Tennant, the General Manager, wrote back that the Directors fully accepted those responsibilities, although commenting that he could see no difference between their responsibilities at York and those at other stations.

Hutchinson had also raised the question whether anything could be done to make the working safer, such as 'the Sykes system for preventing mistakes being made by the signalmen' and evidence suggests that a version of 'Lock & Block' was subsequently installed on a number of lines at least.

(1) TNA: MT 6/267/7. (2) NER, *Appendix to Working Timetable*, in effect from 1 November 1877.
(3) NER, *Appendix to Working Timetable*, in effect from 1 November 1877.

Chapter 4 : Through York Yards 1873 to 1909

On the original line between North Junction and Poppleton Junction, before the new station opened, the following signal boxes were listed by the NER in their *Appendix to the Working Timetable* (WTT) issued on 1 May 1873:

North Junction
Holgate Beck
New Goods Yard
Gas Works Junction
Poppleton Junction

However, when the 1877 passenger station was brought into use these former GNofER lines from the north became goods lines between Holgate Junction and Poppleton Junction. The new passenger lines curved round through Clifton before running parallel to and alongside (but not joining) those goods lines at the north end between Severus Junction and Poppleton Junction. Consequently a large area of land effectively became rail locked, and this is where the main York Marshalling Yards (known simply as York Yards) were established from the early 1880s onwards.

The main requirement for through traffic was for staging sidings where, for example, locomotive or crew changes could take place, leading to the establishment of the following: Nos 1 and 2 Up Yards, No 1 Down Yard (which included an early hump), and No 2 Down Yard (known locally as 'Klondyke' – a name thought to derive from the Klondike Gold Rush of 1896 to 1898 in Canada, suggesting perhaps that the yard was built at that time). Also branching off at Severus Junction were lines to York Warehouse and Leeman Road Goods Depot.

When the next NER Appendix was issued on 1 November 1877, between North Junction and Poppleton Junction, only Holgate Beck and Severus Junction were listed. It would seem that Severus Junction had replaced both New Goods Yard and Gas Works Junction cabins; certainly, the NER Coal Gas Works were originally situated close to what became known as Severus Junction. ('Severus' is an unusual name in modern times – it was the name of a famous Roman Emperor who died in York in AD 211 and his body was said to have been consumed to ashes on Severus Hills in this vicinity.) Between Severus Junction and Poppleton Junction additional Down Departure lines and Up Arrivals lines were also constructed. On the former Scarborough lines, South View cabin was still in place between North Junction and Waterworks.

When the next NER Appendix was issued, dated 1 April 1889, on the York Main Goods Lines between North Junction and Severus Junction, the cabins were now No.1 Down Goods, No.2 Down Goods, No.1 Up Goods, and No.2 Up Goods. However, by the early 1890s, yet further space was required for marshalling local traffic so Branches Yard was formed to the west of the station, together with Leeman Road coal depots which ran parallel with the former Scarborough lines between North Junction and the north end of the passenger station. An additional No.3 Up Goods cabin was included in the 1892 NER Appendix.

The cabins and distances listed below from the NER *Appendix to the WTT* dated 1898 also accord with the map opposite (Illustration 22):

Down Direction from Holgate Bridge:
Holgate Bridge 516 yards to North Junction
North Junction 1183 yards to Severus Junction
Severus Junction 986 yards to Poppleton Junction
North Junction 428 yards to No.1 Down Goods
No.1 Down Goods 212 yards to No.2 Down Goods
No.2 Down Goods 551 yards to Severus Junction
Up Direction from Severus Junction:
Severus Junction 452 yards to No.3 Up Goods
No.3 Up Goods 113 yards to No.1 Up Goods
No.3 Up Goods 715 yards to North Junction
No.2 Up Goods 363 yards to North Junction
No.1 Up Goods 245 yards to No.2 Up Goods

The following details for each of the Yard Boxes were recorded by the NER in 1893:(1)

Up Goods No.1
22' 8" x 11' 0" x 8' 0"
2 x 'NE Old Pattern' frames, each with 11 working and one spare levers.
Up Goods No.2
24' 0" x 10' 0" x 9' 6"
14-lever 'NE Old Pattern' frame with no spare levers.
Up Goods No.3
17' 3" x 9' 9" x 8' 6"
17-lever Stevens frame including one spare lever.
Down Goods No.1
10-lever 'NE Old Pattern' frame including two spare levers.
Down Goods No.2
32' 0" x 10' 0" x 8' 6"
37-lever Saxby frame including five spare levers.

Numbered cabins were not unusual on other companies' lines but on the NER were quite rare; as far as is known, there were only four locations, all on or close to the ECML: York Yards, Ferryhill, Baxter Wood (Durham) and Newcastle Central.

The Board of Trade was not required to inspect any of the cabins in York Yards because their Inspectors were only concerned with passenger lines, so it is difficult to find out some of the history. However, it would seem that both No.1 and No.2 Down Goods cabins were closed on 26 January 1901, when a new No.1 Down Goods cabin was opened, combining the functions of both predecessors; the new cabin had a frame of 40 levers.

In 1903 York Marshalling Yards were extended and remodelled yet again. Consequently, a new cabin with a 125-lever frame was installed at North Junction.

(1) NERA.1539.

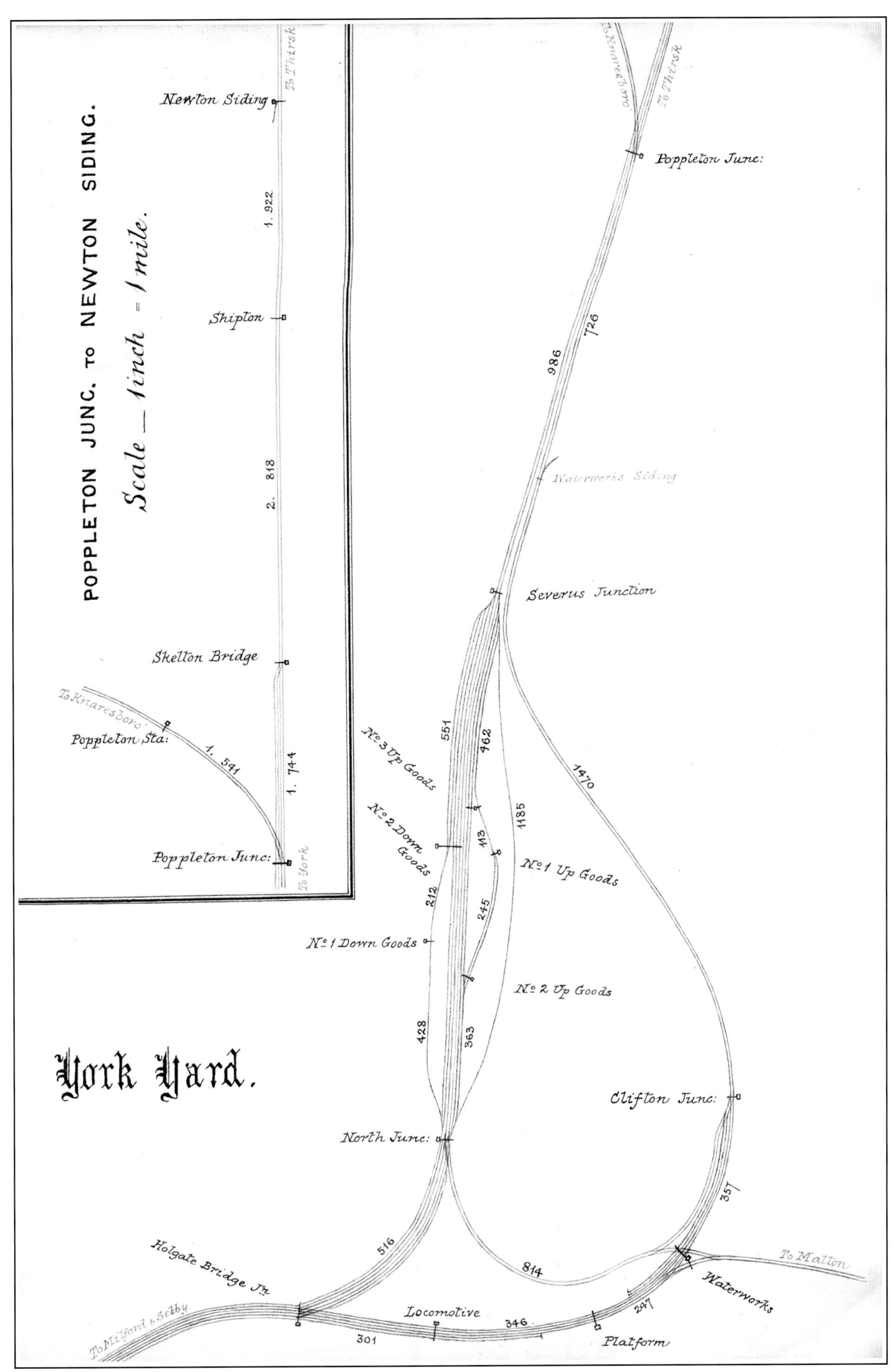

Illustration 22. *York Yards, 1898, from Appendix B to the General Rules, Regulations & Working Time Table. (NER / NERA Collection 0809-1)*

Severus Junction

At the north end of the yards, however, a more radical approach was adopted when the old cabin at Severus was demolished on 19 August 1903 and on 21 September 1903 a new box was opened.(1)

The NER had already installed Westinghouse power-operated miniature lever frames around Tyne Dock in 1902 but at Severus Junction they experimented with the 'Crewe' system of power signalling which had been invented by the LNWR then manufactured and supplied by the Railway Signal Company. With 101 working and 32 spare levers, the frame occupied a space of just over 21' 10" in a cabin with an interior length of 28' 4"; it was estimated that a 5 inch mechanical frame would have occupied 55' 10" so the cabin would have been twice the size of the Crewe frame cabin.

The 133-lever frame was set up in two tiers with levers placed alternately: odd numbers in upper tier and even numbers in the lower tier, although levers in both tiers could work either points or signals. All point levers and most signal levers had to be moved to the mid position to send power to the outside equipment; a check-lock then prevented the lever from completing its full stroke until a 'Return Indication' was received. Mechanical tappet locking was provided in six locking boxes, with contacts and switches fixed below.

Illustration 23. *Severus Junction cabin was opened in September 1903. It is the fairly standard NER Type 3 cabin design with two-pane deep upper lights above three-pane deep main windows, although it retains arched locking room windows. (RM, 1908)*

Illustration 24. *Here we have a closer view of the Severus Junction signal bridge in a photograph taken in 1904. The view looks north towards Poppleton Junction, with Landing Lane bridge immediately behind the signal bridge. Manufactured by McKenzie & Holland, the signal bridge includes signals in the Up direction along the Goods Lines, into the Reception Lines and Yards. In the Down direction the signals read towards the Main and Shunting Lines. (Railway Engineer, 1904)*

The system was 'all electric': point motors were fixed below rail level so that there was no obstruction to staff walking on the line. Signals were worked by electro-magnets: when the coils were energised a rod was lifted which in turn raised the signal rod and a small residual current held the arm in the 'off' position. Rotating ground discs were also operated by an electro-magnet which moved a rod to create a quarter revolution.(2)

Unfortunately, the system proved unreliable with the following repair and renewal costs being recorded: 1905 Nil; 1906, £151; 1907 £672; 1908 £1515; 1909 £1118.(3)

(1) NER Programme 0.8638.
(2) *The Railway Engineer*, May 1904, pages 152-157.
(3) TNA: 527/411.

Illustration 25. *Severus Junction cabin interior, showing the 'Crewe All-Electric' frame with block instruments on cupboards along the back and side walls; above the frame, the Sykes Release instrument and bell were used in connection with Leeman Road Permanent Way ground frame which was located on the Warehouse Lines. (Ken Hoole Study Centre Collection)*

Furthermore, the equipment was prone to significant over-heating: instructions were issued dated 25 November 1903 and revised on 12 March 1910. These included 'When a signal has been pulled off, the signalman must, as soon as the train has passed, return the signal to the danger position. Should he not do so there is a great danger of the coils becoming unnecessarily heated.' Perhaps rather more alarmingly, the instruction continued: 'In the event of fire breaking out, the signalman should first switch off the electrical current .... and then put out the fire by smothering it with a damp sponge cloth ...' Consequently, the system was replaced, after a life of less than 20 years, by a conventional mechanical frame and signalling in April 1922.(1) See also the photograph inside the front cover.

In addition, there were ground frames as follows: Severus Junction GF; York Warehouse Yard GF; Permanent Way Stone Yard Siding GF.(2)

No.2 Down Goods cabin was no longer listed by the time that the 1904 NER Appendix was issued and, following re-arrangement of various lines, No.3 Up Goods closed on 30 September 1909; the estimated cost of this latter work was £60, but the value of work recovered was £32, together with an annual saving of £143.(3) However, No.1 Down Goods and No.1 Up Goods and No.2 Up Goods remained operational cabins within the yard at this time.

(1) NRM 2011-7074: *NER Instructions to Signalmen working the Electric Signalling Apparatus at Severus Junction, York*, O.258, 1910.
(2) NER (Southern Division) *List of Branches, Signal Boxes, Ground Frames, and Level Crossings*, 1909.
(3) TNA: RAIL 527/411.

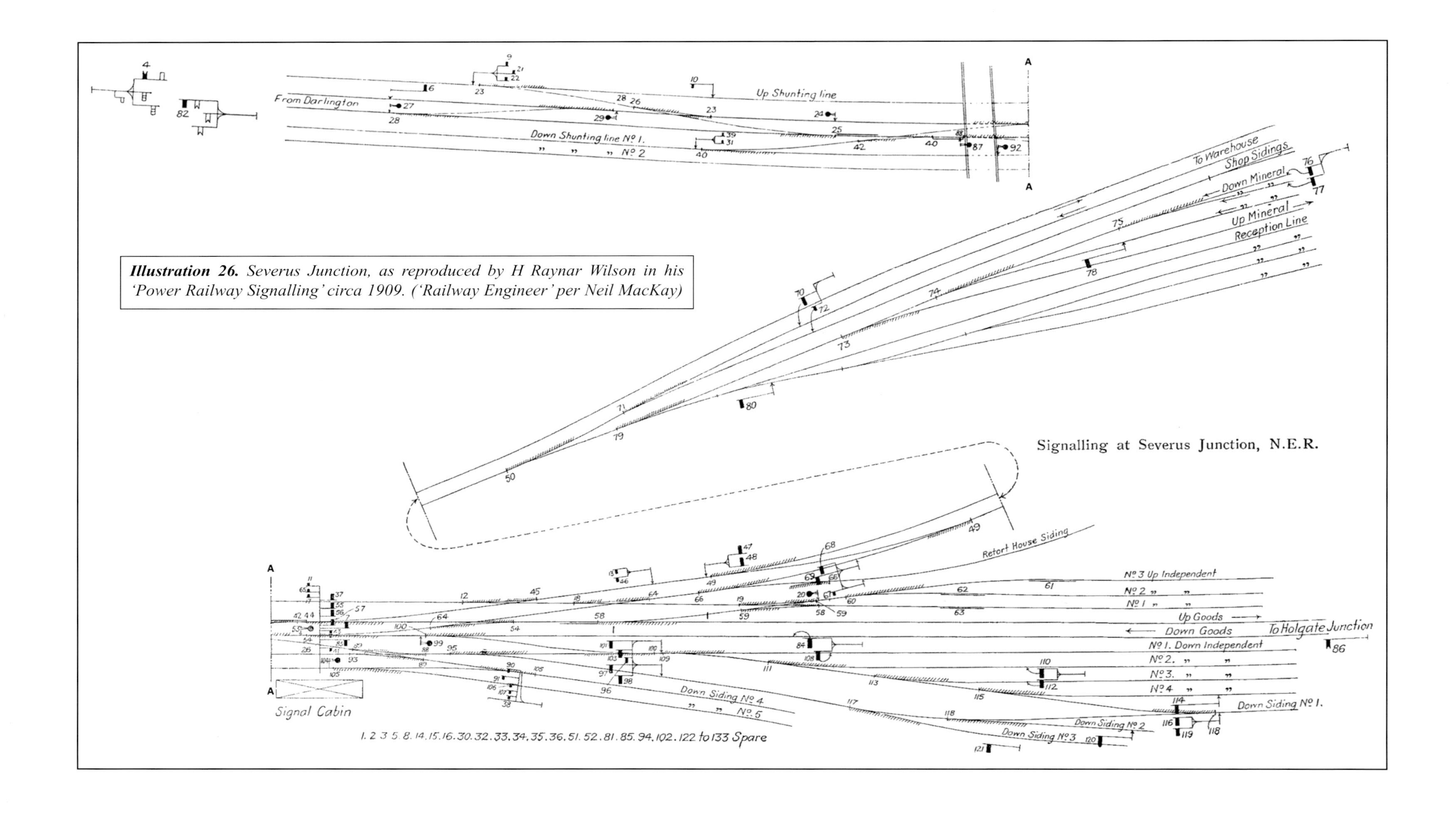

Illustration 26. *Severus Junction, as reproduced by H Raynar Wilson in his 'Power Railway Signalling' circa 1909. ('Railway Engineer' per Neil MacKay)*

Chapter 5
Towards Scarborough and Harrogate 1874 to 1908

Proceeding out of York along the Scarborough line in early days, the first level crossing of many along the Scarborough line was encountered just beyond the 2 mile post at Burton Lane gate house, followed by Bootham Stray gate house at 2*m* 41*c* 20*l*, with the Market Weighton line junction just 4*c* 30*l* beyond.(1)

On the Scarborough line, prior to the new station opening at York, South View cabin worked to Bootham Junction cabin. Below is an extract from the first known NER Appendix dated May 1873.

Station	Cabin	Weekday Hours	Sunday Hours
YORK	North Junction	Always	Always
	South View	Always	Closed from 6-00 a.m. to 8-30 p.m. on Sunday
HUNTINGTON	Bootham Junction	Always	Always
CASTLE HOWARD	Crambeck Lane	Closed from 8-00 p.m. to 6-00 a.m. Daily	No Sunday duty

Christison's *Memorandum of the Proposed Block Signal Stations between North Junction and Scarborough* dated 1 January 1873 included the following useful descriptions.(2)

NORTH JUNCTION and BOOTHAM (1 Mile 70 Chains apart)
The line between these two junctions is at present worked on the Block system, but an intermediate Block Cabin will shortly be required at the west end of the Ouse Bridge, when connections with the New Station lines are made; the position of the junction will determine the site of the Cabin.
At Bootham Junction an elevated and permanent Cabin is erected south of the lines and immediately on the east of the Turnpike Level Crossing, having the Junction lines brought up to it by parallel lines for a distance of about 115 yards from the converging point. The signals and points are connected and interlocked, but the gates are not yet connected; it is desirable that they should be.
An advance Semaphore is required for the Down line. There is day and night attendance, and houses are provided for the men.

Scarborough Bridge

As suggested by Christison at this time, alterations were needed to the bridge over the River Ouse, a short distance outside the station: temporary Scarborough East Junction and West Junction Cabins were erected south and north of River Ouse Bridge for Single Line Working over the Up Scarborough line. The signals protecting entrance to the single line were slotted by each cabin.(3) Lieutenant-Colonel Hutchinson later reported on 25 September 1875 that, in connection with continuing alterations to the bridge over River Ouse, Single Line Working had been switched over to the Down Scarborough line. He also noted that a new connection had been installed at Scarborough West Junction for construction of the connecting line north of the new station. The cabin had a 10-lever frame of which one lever was spare; East Junction cabin had a 6-lever frame, all in use.(4) See Illustration 28.

Burton Lane

Although Burton Lane had already existed as a gate house a cabin was opened at that location in 1878; the gates were now interlocked and a double to single junction had been constructed in readiness for the Foss Islands branch. The cabin had a 23-lever frame, of which five were spare.(5) See Illustration 29.

By 1896 Burton Lane still had a 23-lever frame but with only three spare levers.(6) According to NER records, the brick-built cabin dimensions were 20' 3" x 9' 4" x 8' 0". See Illustration 31.

In 1906 Burton Lane was chosen as the location for an experimental arrangement whereby emergency detonators could be placed on the line by operation of a 'Stirrup' handle placed in a segment of the lever frame; after tests, this equipment was subsequently installed at many other NER cabins.

In 1908 a new 32-lever frame (including Gate Wheel No.1) was installed and inspected.(7)

Bootham Junction

At Bootham Junction, the line to Beverley and Hull diverged from the Scarborough line to the east; this was opened as far as Market Weighton on 4 October 1847 and on to Beverley on 1 May 1865. Initially, it was operated as a double-line but by the time of the extension to Beverley the line had been divided into four single-line sections worked by Pilot Staffs and Pass Tickets as follows: Bootham Junction to Stamford Bridge; Stamford Bridge to Pocklington; Pocklington to Market Weighton; Market Weighton to Beverley.

By 1877 the whole of the lines from South View to Scarborough, and the Market Weighton line from Bootham Junction to Earswick Station were being worked by Block Telegraph.(8)

Illustration 27. *Bootham Junction: the heavy brass Train Staff for the section to Stamford Bridge when the single line to Market Weighton opened in 1865; this was taken out of use when the line was doubled in 1890. (NRM 2003-7461)*

(1) TNA: RAIL 527/958: NER (Southern Division) Line Diagrams 1862.
(2) TNA: RAIL 527/1117. (3) NA: MT 6/116/11. (4) TNA: MT 6/144/1. (5) TNA: MT6 /214/14.
(6) TNA: MT 6/222/0. (7) TNA: MT 6/1727/4. (8) NER Appendix 1877.

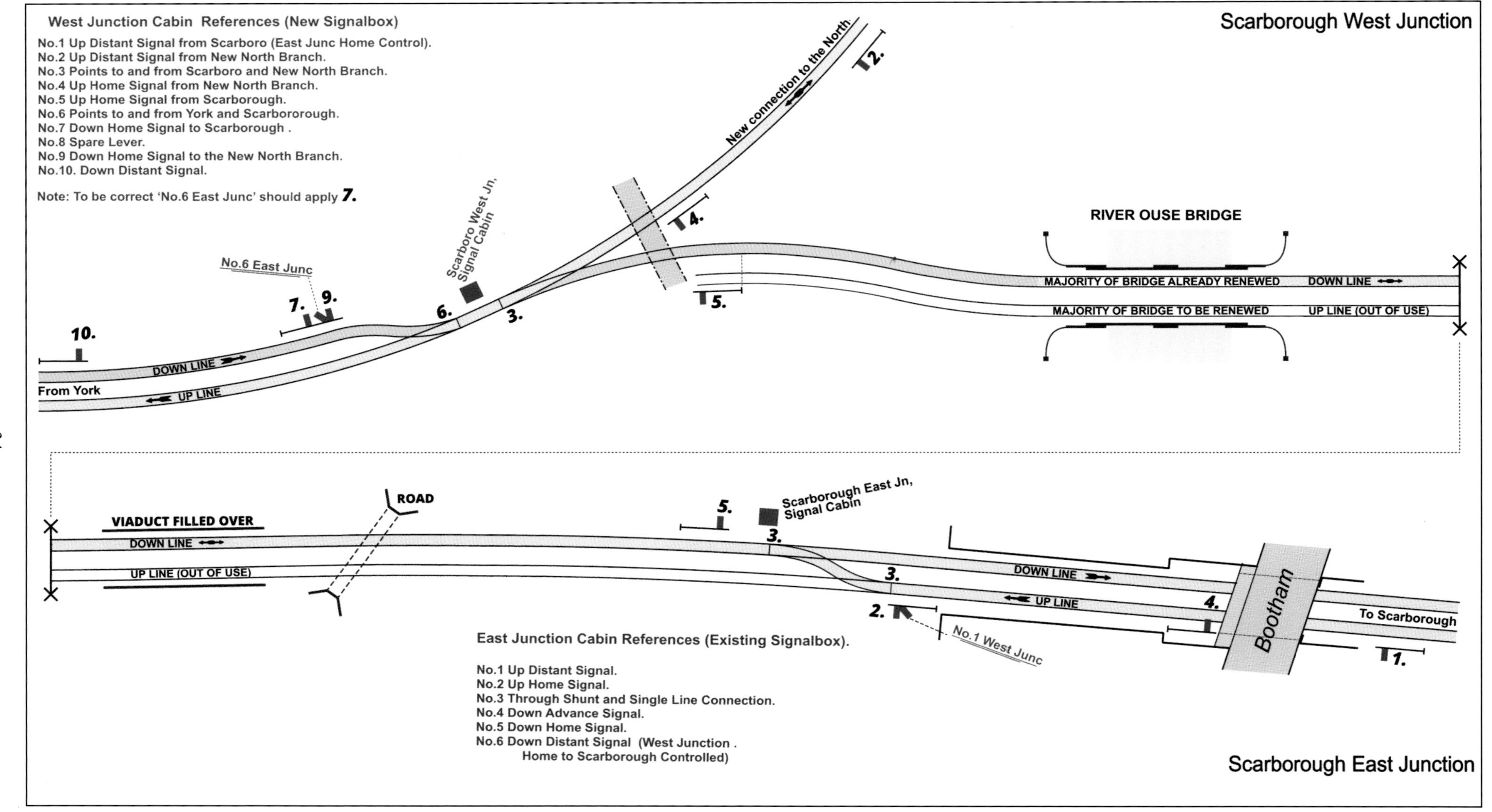

Illustration 28. *In preparation for the new station, alterations had to be made to the bridge over the river Ouse in 1874 and 1875. Temporary cabins were erected at Scarborough East Junction and West Junction with signals slotted at either end to enable Single Line Working initially over the Up Scarborough line but subsequently switching over to the Down Scarborough line as illustrated here (based on TNA MT6.144.1).(Charles Weightman)*

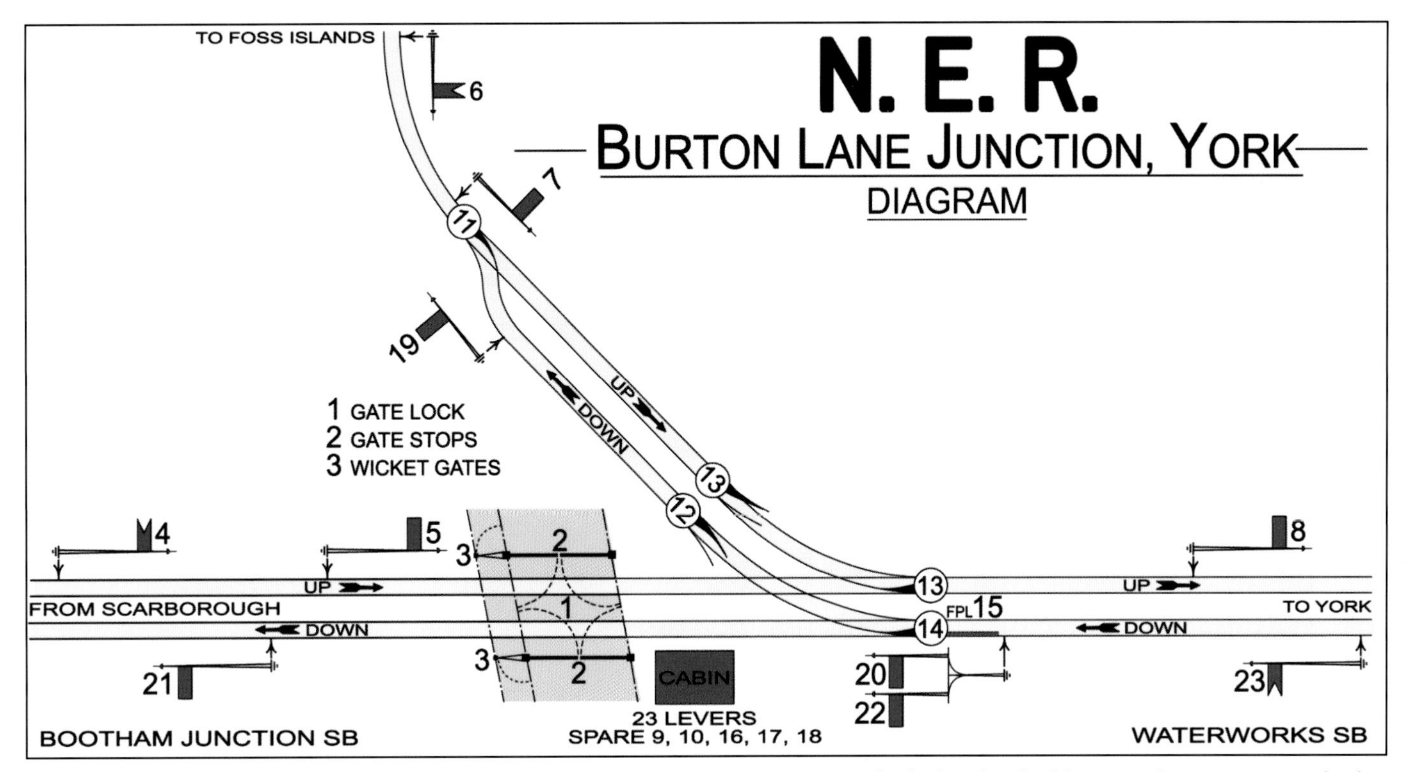

Illustration 29. *Burton Lane: the cabin opened in 1878 when the gates were interlocked and a double to single junction was laid in readiness for the Foss Islands Islands Branch. Based on TNA MT6.214.14. (Charles Weightman)*

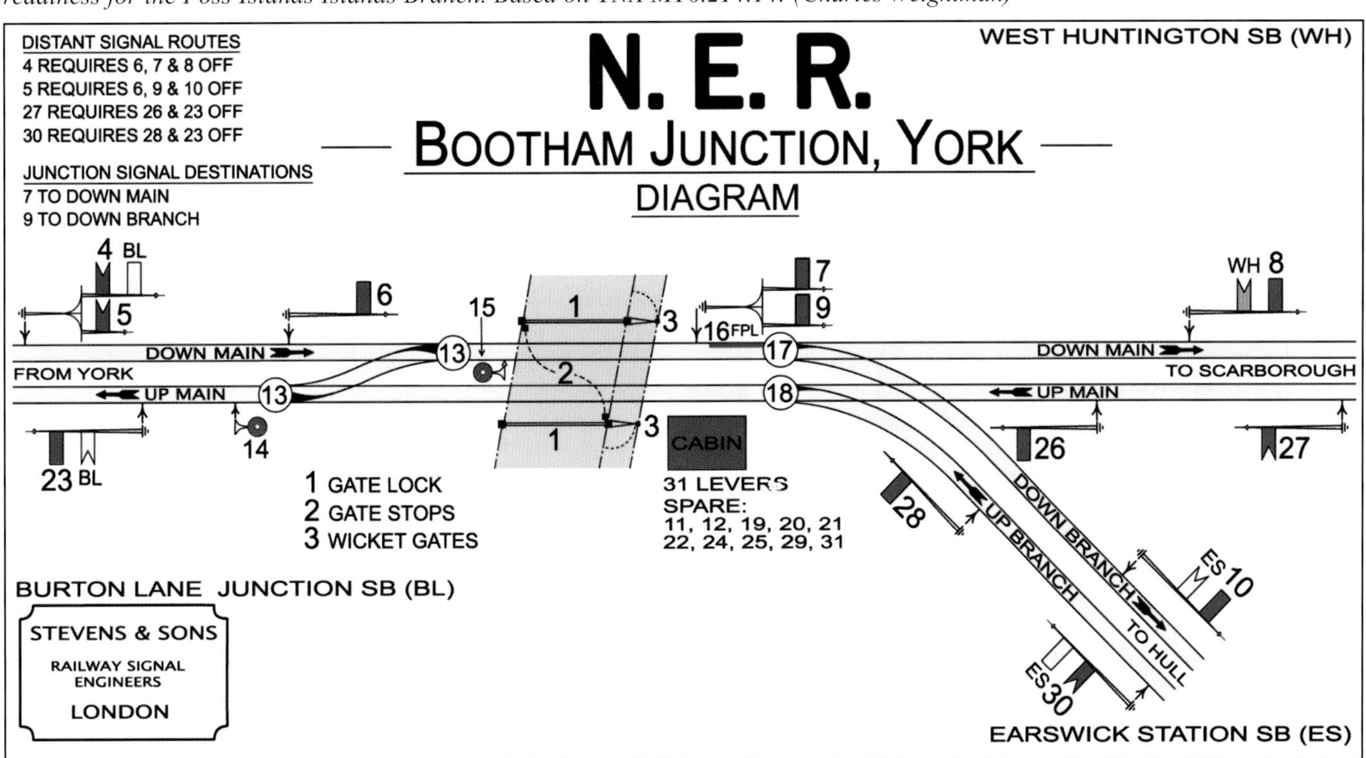

Illustration 30. *Bootham Junction circa 1910. Based on a sketch by Colonel Preston and TNA MT6.594.5. (Charles Weightman)*

In 1892, a replacement cabin was brought into use at Bootham Junction a few yards south of the existing cabin, closer to and immediately alongside the level crossing where the road crossed the railway at an acute angle; see Illustration 30. Built of brick, the cabin was 21' 0" x 10' 0" x 8' 0". A crossover road south of the level crossing was also provided. The gates were worked by a McK&H wheel (No.1) and a 30-lever Stevens frame Nos.2 to 31 (including 10 spare levers) was provided; it was inspected by Major HA Yorke on 14 September 1892.(1)

North from Bootham Junction, the next regular Block Post was Haxby Road cabin but during summer months when traffic was heavier a temporary cabin was opened each year at West Huntington; for example, in 1903 the cabin was open from 1 July to 30 September.(2) However, in the half year to June 1906, an outer home signal was erected at Bootham

(1) TNA: MT6/594/5.
(2) NER Appendix, *Supplement No.3*, 1903.

Junction which enabled trains from the Malton direction to be accepted at the same time as a train was passing to or from the Market Weighton line. This enabled West Huntington cabin to be dispensed with at a cost of £45 10*s* 8*d*, but the value of work recovered was £21 8*s* 0*d*, and an annual saving of £35 was achieved.(1)

(1) TNA: RAIL 527/411.

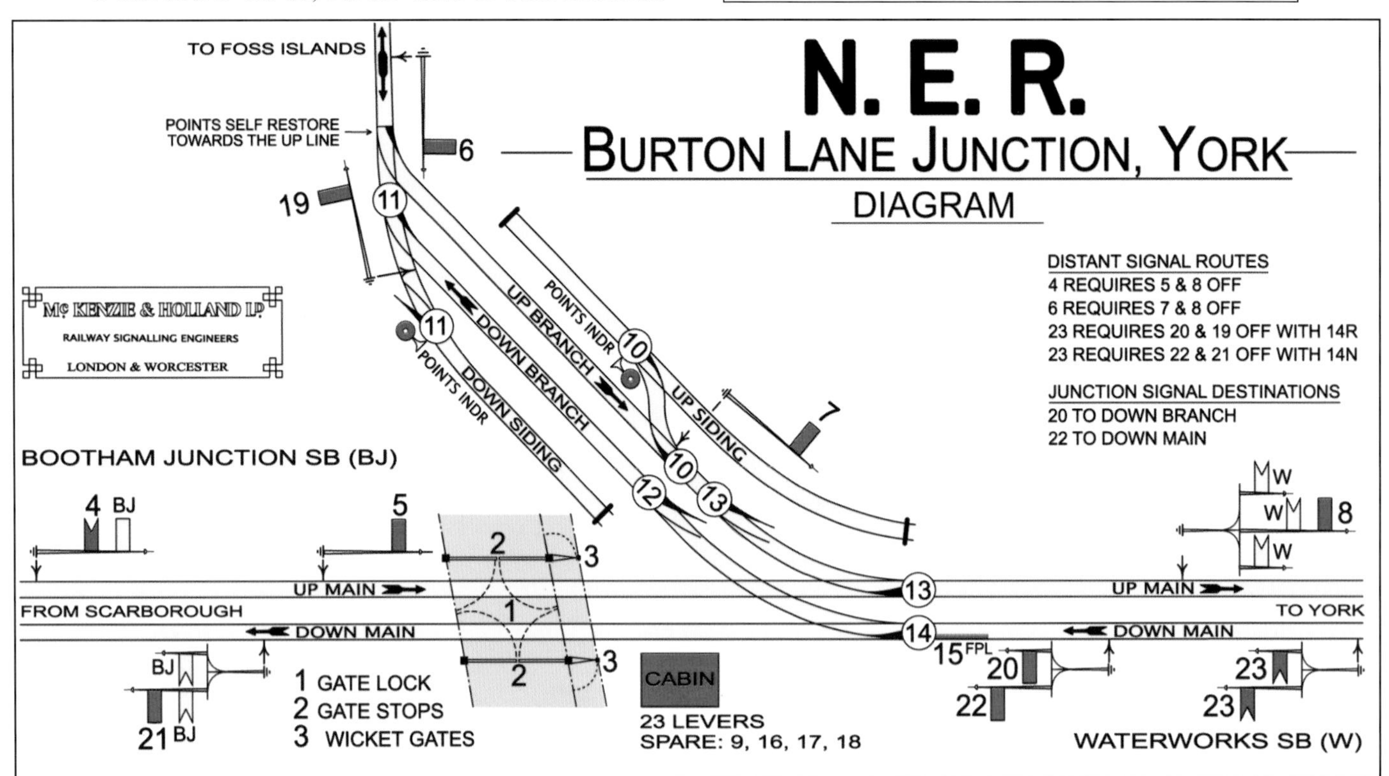

Illustration 31. *Burton Lane cica 1890. This diagram appears to pre-date the connection to Rowntree's sidings. Unusually, the Down splitting distant signals were both worked by lever No.23 and were selected by No.14 points. (Charles Weightman)*

Illustration 32. *Burton Lane. The red Staff & Ticket box was fixed to the booking desk table. When not in use, the staff could be inserted into the side of the box to unlock the lid, thereby allowing access to the metal tickets. Mounted above the telephones on the board behind the desk is the tannoy announcer which repeated calls between York box and shunting staff. (Richard Pulleyn)*

Illustration 33. *Burton Lane. The staff and tickets have been removed so that they can be photographed. The staff is No.1 and the tickets were numbered 2 to 6. The Annett's Key, attached to the staff by a chain unlocked the ground frame which gave access to the Derwent Valley Light Railway from the Foss Islands Branch. (Christopher J Woolstenholmes, CJW178 19)*

Foss Islands Goods Branch

The Foss Islands goods branch was opened officially on 1 January 1880: it terminated in a yard situated just outside the City walls near to Walmgate Bar and, importantly for traffic, close to the cattle market on Barbican Road. Connections were also made to the York City Gas Works, the Electricity Generating Station and to the NER laundry close to Malton Road; subsequently, they were also made to the Derwent Valley Light Railway and to Rowntree & Company Cocoa Works. Rowntree's, the famous confectionery manufacturer, had moved to a site on Haxby Road by 1891 and a steeply-graded private siding connection was made at the end of a short double track section from Burton Lane Junction. See Illustration 135 on page 111.

From the outset, the Foss Islands branch was worked by Staff & Ticket. As illustrated here, there were five oval metal tickets numbered from 2 to 6, the train staff itself effectively being No.1.

Although there was no signal cabin at Foss Islands, the yard foreman operated from a ground level hut which included a single lever (working a signal on the approach to the goods station); between 8 am and 8 pm he acted as 'Staff Attendant' from that hut, there also being a Staff & Ticket box, and a telephone to Burton Lane cabin which enabled him to control the passage of trains. When a driver of a train was about to enter the single line at either the Burton Lane or Foss Islands end and was given a Ticket, he was shown the Train Staff and informed how long the preceding train had been gone and told to proceed at caution. When there was no one on duty at Foss Islands the driver simply retained the Train Staff for the return journey.

The Gas and Electricity Works were accessed via siding connections from the north end of Foss Islands Yard, but the connection from the single line to Rowntree's sidings was worked by a ground frame released from Burton Lane cabin, and the Derwent Valley Light Railway (DVLR) ground frame (brought into use in 1912 when that railway opened) was released by an Annett's Key attached by chain to the Train Staff.

Towards Harrogate

On 8 October 1861, Captain William O'Brien, General Manager of the NER, wrote to the Locomotive Committee recommending that 'a Distance Signal be erected on the Down line at Poppleton', also 'the signals at all the stations on the East & West Yorkshire branch are single disc signals so that the signalman cannot open or close one of the lines without opening or closing the other also. I recommend that these be removed and replaced by the usual semaphore signals.'(1)

Poppleton Junction was 1*m* 60*c* 10*l* from York station; towards Harrogate this was followed by Nether Poppleton gate house at 2*m* 47*c* 40*l*, and Poppleton station at 3*m* 5*c* 35*l*.(2)

The NER Interlocking Report in 1872 noted that interlocking had been ordered for both Knaresborough Goods and Station cabins, but not for any of the stations between Poppleton Junction and Knaresborough.(3)

Similarly, Christison's *Memorandum of the Proposed Block Signal Stations* in 1873 included proposals for interlocking on the line between Knaresborough Goods and Wortley junction (Leeds) but no mention was made of the Poppleton Junction to Knaresborough line.(4)

The first NER *Appendix to the Working Timetable* issued on 1 May 1873 did not list any signal cabins on the line until Knaresborough was reached, and in the 1874 Return to the Board of Trade, the NER report included that Poppleton Junction to Knaresborough Goods (a distance of 14*m* 47*c*) was worked by Electric Telegraph but not on Absolute Block. However, the cabin at Poppleton station finally appeared in the 1877 Appendix and cabins were listed for other intermediate stations by 1889.

(1) TNA: RAIL 527/1117.
(2) TNA: RAIL 527/958.
(3) TNA: RAIL 527/1117.
(4) TNA: RAIL 527/1117.

Chapter 6 : Around York 1880 - 1908

Although the new station made a huge difference to operations, and to safety in particular, traffic levels continued to rise and further developments became necessary. For example, in 1883 some alterations were made to the connections from the Scarborough bays to the Down Scarborough, worked from Waterworks cabin; these were inspected by Major-General Hutchinson and recommended for approval in his report dated 27 July 1883.(1)

Additional bay platforms were provided on the west side of the station in 1894: Platform No 7 was an additional bay for trains to and from the south; it was worked from Platform cabin (which then had 65 working and five spare levers) with control on the signals from Locomotive Yard cabin. Platform No 8 was an additional bay platform for trains to and from north, worked from Waterworks cabin (where all 78 levers in the frame were then in use). Hutchinson again made inspections in August and November 1894, then recommended the alterations for approval in a report dated 22 November 1894.(2)

In the centre of the station were scissors crossovers linking the platform lines with the through lines; these enabled connecting trains to share the platforms, and one of the station Pilot locomotives to attach or detach vehicles on the rear of trains. For example, trains from the north could run to the south end of Platform No 4, with a Scarborough train arriving at the north end to make a connection. Furthermore, if the Scarborough train was due to depart towards Leeds before the train for the south (as was often the case) it could run through the scissors crossover and get on its way. (See Illustration 40.)

It will be recalled that Chandler's Whin cabin, at the junction of the direct line to Doncaster, had closed in 1877 when the actual junction was made at Locomotive Yard cabin or Holgate; however, by the late 1880s, traffic levels on the adjacent Normanton line resulted in an additional break-section block post being installed at Askham Bog between Copmanthorpe and North Lane.

To summarise, by 1898, cabins on the main line were as follows:

Name of Cabin	Distance from previous Cabin above
Copmanthorpe station	
Askham Bog	1 m 315 yards
North Lane	1 m 337 yards
South Points	0 m 868 yards
Holgate Bridge	0 m 855 yards
Locomotive Yard	0 m 301 yards
Platform	0 m 345 yards
Waterworks	0 m 247 yards
Clifton	0 m 357 yards
Poppleton Junction	1 m 436 yards
Skelton Bridge	1 m 744 yards
Shipton station	2 m 815 yards **

** Shipton station was renamed Beningbrough on 1 December 1898.

The following details are included in NER signal cabin records dated 1893:(3)

South Points
21' 8" x 12' 3" x 8' 0"
25-lever McK&H frame including six spare levers. Brick.

North Lane
20' 4" x 9' 2" x 14' 0"
20-lever Saxby Spindle frame including one spare lever. Brick with wood top that oversailed at the front. Inside brickwork measured 19' 6" x 7' 0".

Askham Bog
10' 0" x 9' 0" x 1' 6"
6-lever NE Love Locking only.

Copmanthorpe
12' 9" x 9' 9" x 8' 0"
10-lever Saxby Spindle frame.

Copmanthorpe Moor Crossing
8' 9" x 8' 6" x 2' 0"
7-lever frame including one spare lever.

In the station area, according to a report dated 1896 sent to the Board of Trade as required under the Regulation of Railways Act, 1889 (regarding the block system, interlocking, continuous brakes, *etc.*) it is evident that the lever frames in a number of the cabins had been extended.(4)

Holgate Bridge
46-lever frame, of which two were spare.

Locomotive Yard
97-lever frame (Numbered A to C, and 1 to 94), of which two were spare.

Platform
70-lever frame, of which two were spare.

Waterworks
82-lever frame (Numbered 1 to 78 and A to D), none spare.

Clifton
34-lever frame (Numbered A to D, and 1 to 30), of which one was spare.

Poppleton Junction to Skelton Bridge

North of the station, the Up and Down Goods lines, which had previously terminated at Poppleton Junction, were extended north in 1896 by $1^1/_2$ miles to Skelton Bridge (just south of the River Ouse). A new McK&H frame of 62 levers (including 13 spare) was installed at Poppleton Junction. The cabin was built of brick and 24' 6" x 10' 0" with the operating floor only 5' 6" above rail level.

(1) TNA: MT6/347/5.
(2) TNA: MT6/676/15.
(3) NERA 1539.
(4) TNA: MT 6/2200.

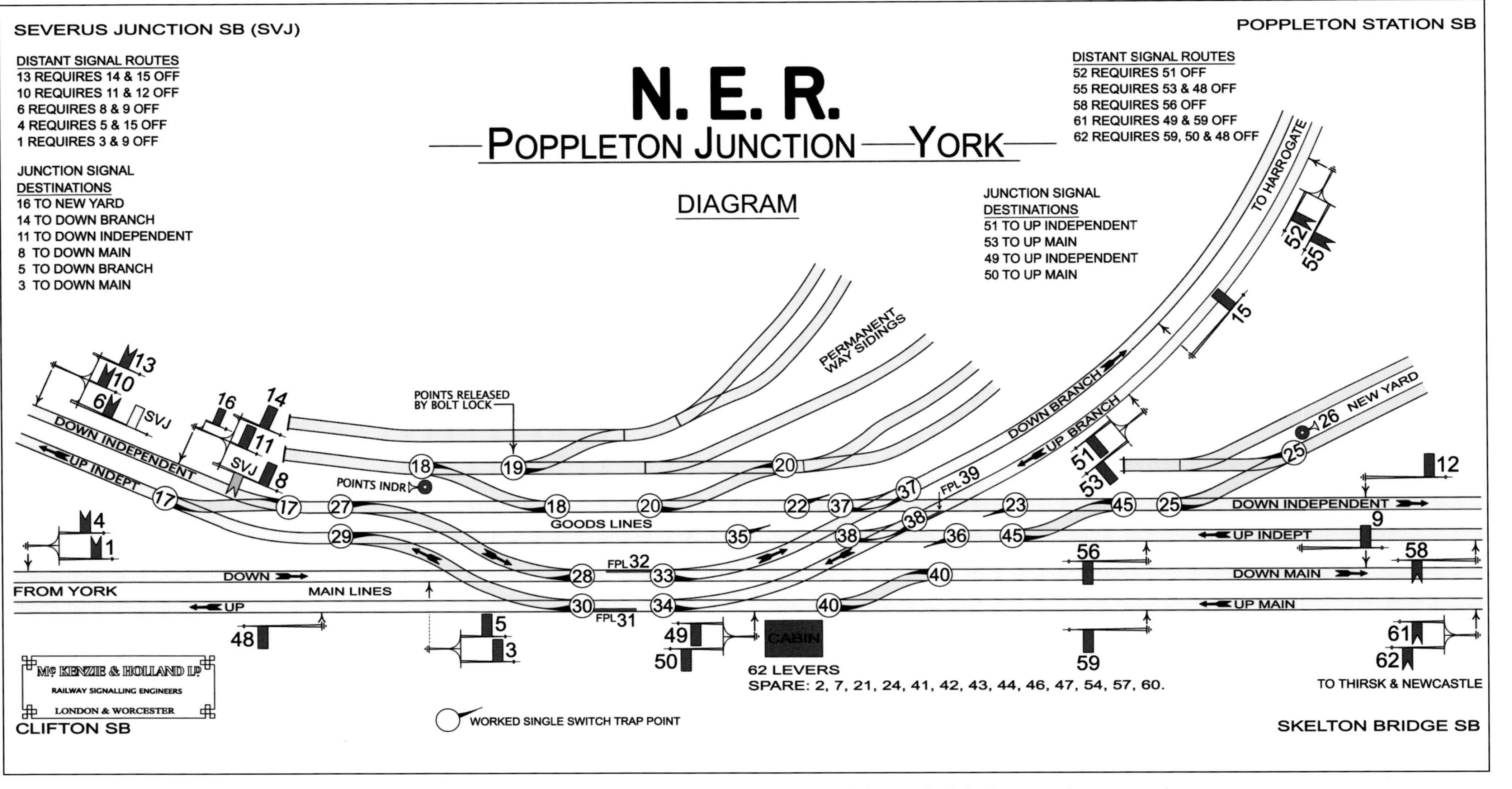

Illustration 34. *Poppleton Junction; in 1896 the Up and Down Goods lines, which had previously terminated at Poppleton Junction, were extended north to Skelton Bridge. Based on TNA: MT6.760.5. (Charles Weightman)*

In connection with the same work, reported on 18 October 1896, the existing cabin at Skelton Bridge (which had a 6-lever NE-pattern frame) was replaced by a new cabin, immediately to the south of the previous cabin; the 22-lever frame in the new cabin was described as 'old style, with T bar locking'. Both the old and the new cabins were built of wood because they were located at the top of embankments.(1) See Illustrations 36 and 37.

Clifton

New Carriage Sidings (which became known as Groups 1 and 2) were opened in 1900 on the Down side of the line at Clifton, and provision was made for additional sidings on Up side (which became Group 3); to accommodate this work, a new cabin was opened at Clifton with a 120-lever frame, including 37 spare levers.(2) See Illustration 69.

Locomotive Yard

In the same year, 1900, to accommodate Royal Show traffic, a temporary, wooden Down platform was added outside the main station building on the south-west side, with a new Platform Line and Up Engine Line alongside. Locomotive Yard cabin had to be lengthened at the north end to accommodate 35 new levers which were added to the frame, making 129 in total, of which only six were spare. Initially the temporary platform was referred to as Platform No 7A, and was worked in the Down direction only. It was inspected and recommended for approval by Colonel PG Von Donop in his report dated 16 June 1900.(3) Surprisingly, traffic between Locomotive Yard cabin and Platform cabin was still worked entirely by telephone – there were no block instruments. See Illustration 39.

Illustration 35. *Poppleton Junction: looking south towards York with the Main Lines to the left and the Goods Lines to the right, intersected by the Branch Lines coming in from Knaresborough. (Kidderminster Railway Museum, 068127)*

Illustration 36. *Skelton Bridge: this is the new cabin, commissioned in 1896. Situated on the Up side of the line, immediately south of the bridge over the River Ouse, the cabin controlled the connections between the Main and Goods Lines. This photograph shows 'Raven's Fog Signal Apparatus' located in the Down Main as described in 'A History of NER Signalling'. (Kidderminster Railway Museum, 068125)*

Leeman Road and Waterworks

Meanwhile, Platform No 7A became Platform No 14, and connections were also being made at the north end of station towards the north and Scarborough. In 1900, this extended layout required an additional cabin named Leeman Road and sited immediately opposite the existing Waterworks cabin. It had a 60-lever frame, of which eight levers were spare. In addition to the new connections, it took over control of some points which previously had been worked from Waterworks cabin.

(1) TNA: MT 6/760/5.
(2) TNA: MT 6/976/5.
(3) TNA: MT 6/970/3.

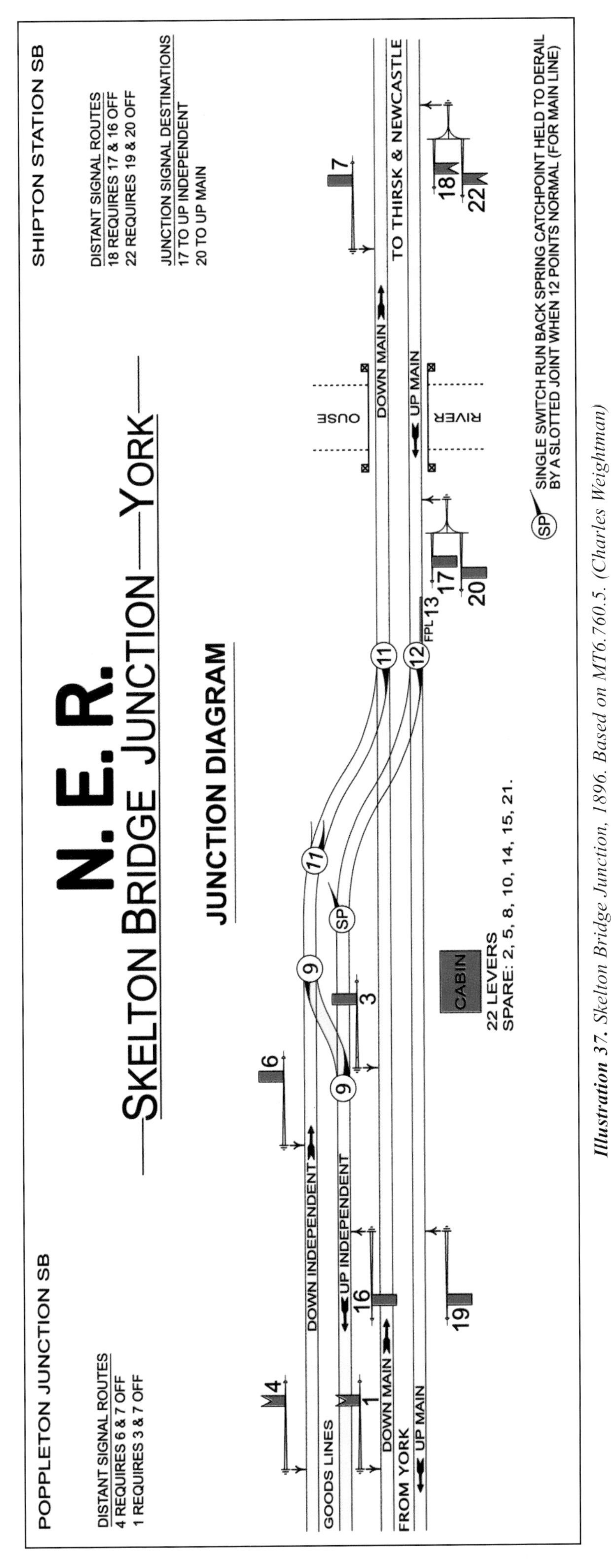

Illustration 37. *Skelton Bridge Junction, 1896. Based on MT6.760.5. (Charles Weightman)*

Working these cabins in such close proximity to each other required a complex assortment of signal slotting, point controls, releases and back-locks. Leeman Road cabin controlled the Down Main from the platform starting signals northwards, the Up and Down Goods to the west of the passenger lines, and connections with Branches Yard west of the station. See Illustration 38.

Waterworks cabin controlled the Up Main where it entered the station, the Scarborough lines, and the connections into and out of bay Platforms Nos 4, 5, 6 and 7. The box was modified internally to accommodate 132 levers, being arranged with 66 levers facing the main lines and 66 levers facing the Scarborough lines. The name was derived not from York Waterworks (which had a ground frame connection off the Up Main south of Poppleton Junction), but from the NER pumping station by which water from the River Ouse was pumped into a huge storage tank at the locomotive running sheds, also serving water columns in the station area.(1)

Chaloners Whin to Copmanthorpe

By 1900, the NER had decided that traffic levels justified quadrupling the lines south from Chaloners Whin to Church Fenton by installing duplicate lines on the east side of the existing Normanton lines. The first stage involved quadrupling from Chaloners Whin to Copmanthorpe in 1901, with new signal boxes at both locations. At Chaloners Whin the new cabin had a 110-lever McK&H No.11 frame to control a whole series of double junctions; plans also show proposed new Up and Down Goods lines from Chaloner's Whin towards York, although no evidence has been seen to confirm that these were actually installed. The cabin was to the S1a design which appears unusual given that most cabins by this date were built to the S3 design; however, it is possible that this was an old cabin extended. See Illustration 47.

At Copmanthorpe, the new cabin (S3 design, 25' 0" x 12' 0" x 8' 6") had a 45-lever McK&H No.16 frame (14 of which were spare) to work a new double junction between the Normanton Main and Duplicate lines.

(1) TNA: MT 6/970/4.

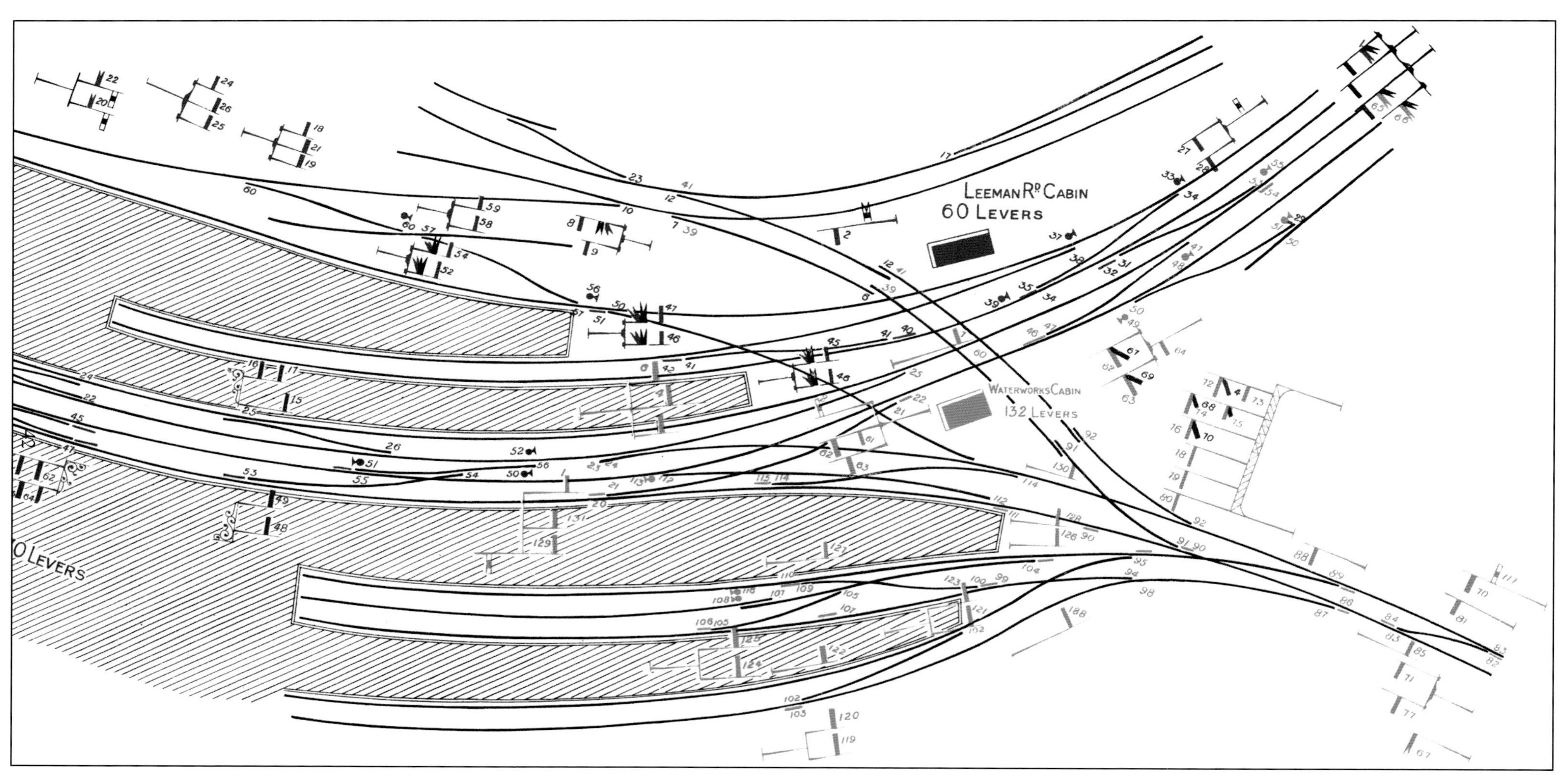

Illustration 38. *York North End: in 1900 new connections and an extended layout at the north end of the station required provision of an additional cabin named Leeman Road, whcih was situated directly opposite the existing Waterworks cabin. It had a 60-lever frame, of which 8 levers were spare. In addition to the new connections, Leeman Road cabin took over control of some points which previously had been worked from Waterworks cabin. Points and signals shown in blue were worked from Platform signal box. (Author's Collection)*

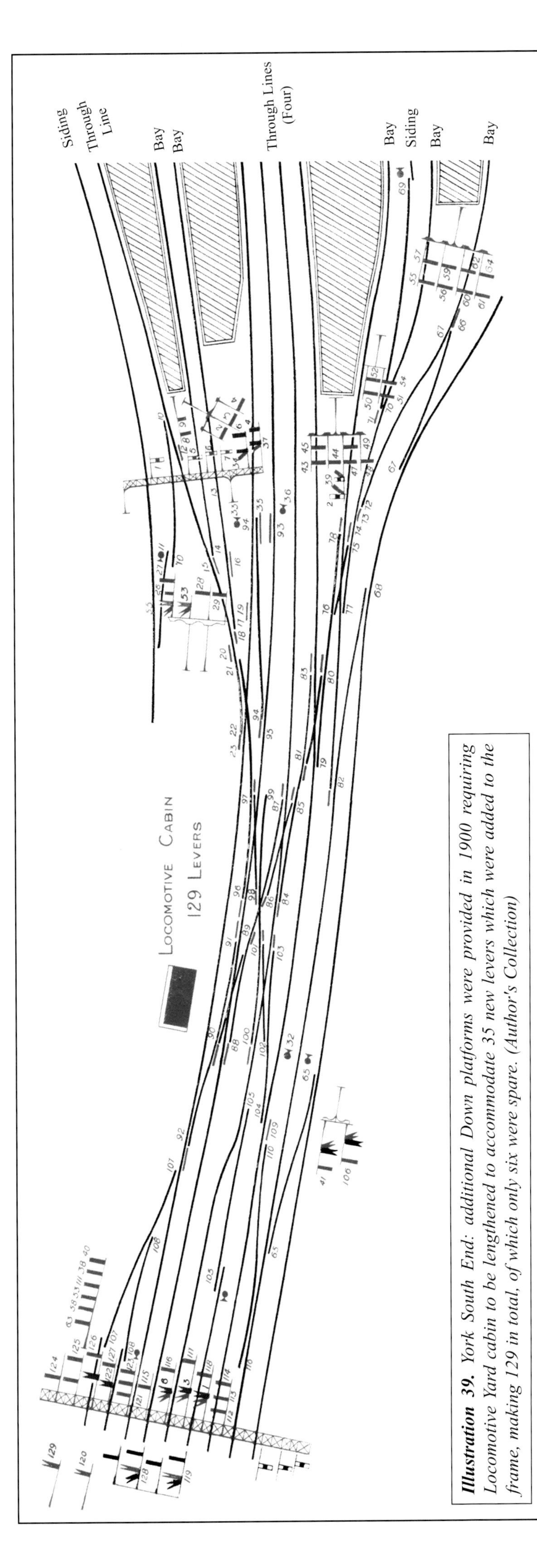

Illustration 39. *York South End: additional Down platforms were provided in 1900 requiring Locomotive Yard cabin to be lengthened to accommodate 35 new levers which were added to the frame, making 129 in total, of which only six were spare. (Author's Collection)*

Between Chaloner's Whin and Copmanthorpe a new cabin was also opened at Askham Bog (the second of that name) on the Down side of the line; this was a block post only, with no connections, and had a 24-lever McK&H No.11 frame (12 of which were spare). The box was 1607 yards from Chaloner's Whin and 1513 yards from Copmanthorpe; on both the Normanton and the Leeds lines, the Up distant signals for Askham Bog were mounted below the Up advance signals for Chaloner's Whin, and the Down distant signals were below the Down starting signals for Copmanthorpe station cabin. It was brick built, 18' 0" x 12' 0" x 8' 6".(1) See Illustration 48.

Minor changes were made at the south end of the station in 1901 when a new crossover road between the Up Main and Platform No.4 replaced slip points worked from Locomotive Yard cabin which still had a frame of 129 levers, but only four of which were now spare.(2)

At Clifton, on the Up side of the line, new Fish Dock Sidings were brought into use in 1903. The 118-lever frame in that cabin now had 23 spares.(3)

Working Naburn Bridge

The NER *Appendix to the Working Timetable* effective from 1 January 1904 provides a useful insight into the method of operating Ouse Swing Bridge at Naburn at that time. In addition to Bridge cabin there were 'outpost cabins' situated at least 400 yards on each side of the bridge:

Naburn Bridge North was a brick cabin 9' 9" x 8' 0" at ground level with a 6-lever NE Lovelock frame (including one spare lever).

Naburn Bridge South was also a brick cabin but 12' 0" x 9' 9" with the operating floor 9' 0" above rail level; it had an 11-lever Stevens frame (including two spare levers).

Both of these cabins were provided with home and distant signals which were kept at danger except when required to be lowered for a train to pass, the home signals also being controlled by the working of the bridge. An indicator semaphore signal was also provided in each direction at the ends of the bridge; these indicators were worked by the bridge machinery and stood at danger except when the bridge was set for the passage of trains.

(1) TNA: MT 6/1006/5 & MT 6/1006/15.
(2) TNA: MT 6/1026/22.
(3) TNA: MT 6/1201/8.

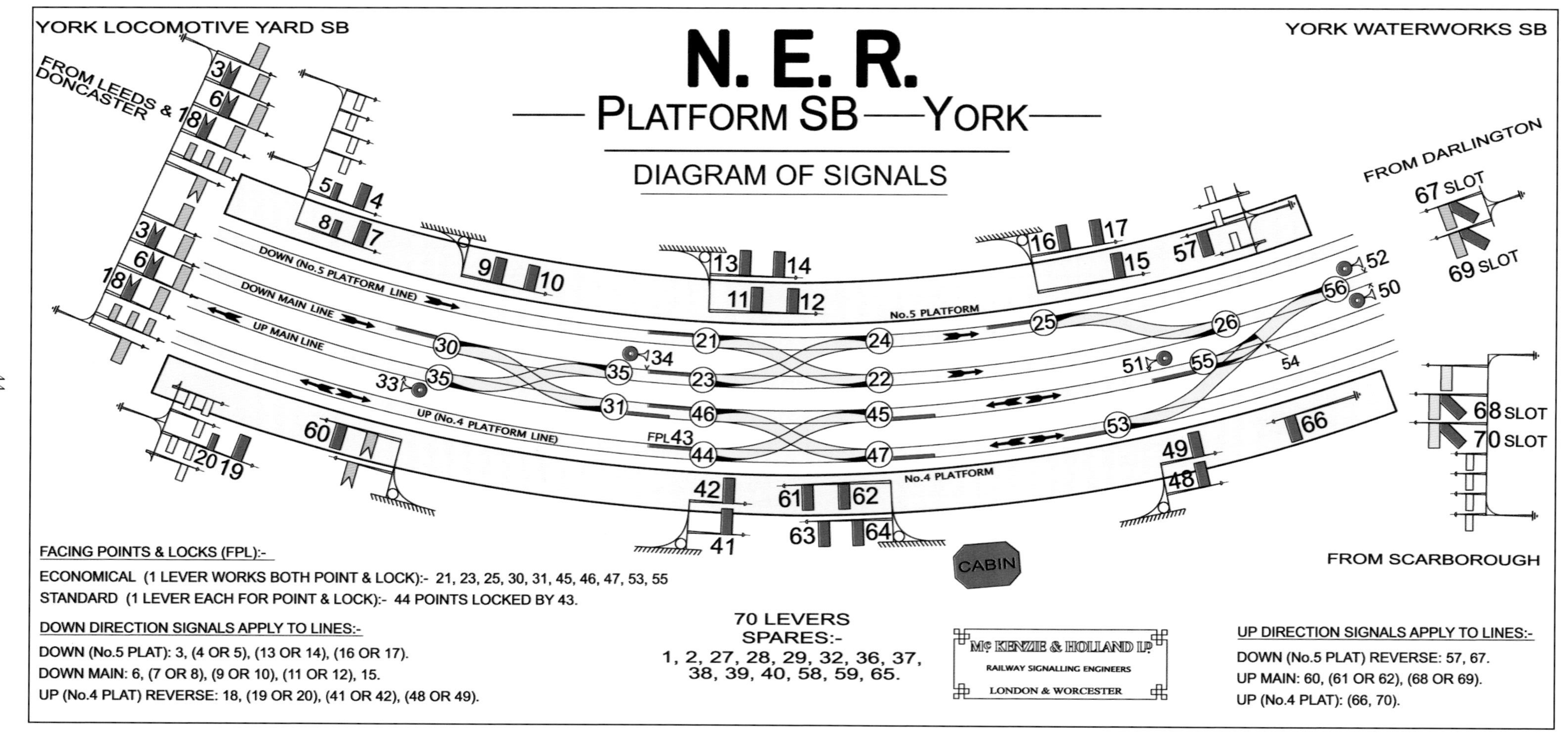

Illustration 40. *York Platform signal box: based on a diagram drawn circa 1910 by Colonel Thomas Preston. Preston was an interesting character. He was born in 1887, grandson of William Thompson, Archbishop of York and was a pupil at Eton College by the age of 14. He worked for the North Eastern Railway from about 1905 until 1911 when he was Personal Clerk to the General Superintendent, taking a particular interest in signalling. (Charles Weightman)*

Telegraphic communication was provided between all three cabins; the needles of the instruments were vertical when the bridge was open for river traffic and when it was not prepared for the passage of rail traffic. The following code of bell signals was used between the outpost cabins and the bridge cabin:

Call Attention	
For an Up non-passenger train approaching	3
For an Up passenger train approaching	4
For a Down non-passenger train approaching	2 - 1
For a Down passenger train approaching	2 - 2
Obstruction Danger	6
Cancelling signal	3 - 5

When dealing with passenger trains, the signalman at an outpost cabin was not permitted to accept the 'Is Line Clear?' signal until the proper signals had been given and acknowledged by Bridge cabin which pegged the needle of the bridge block instrument to 'Bridge right for train'. However, when dealing with engines and non-passenger trains in clear weather, if the proper bell signals were not acknowledged by the Bridge signalman, trains could be accepted at caution by the outpost cabin signalman; in these instances, to prevent trains from being cautioned unnecessarily, the outpost signalman did not accept the train at caution until the 'Is Line Clear?' signal was repeated.

Illustration 41. *Naburn: originally, the swing bridge was provided with 'indicator semaphore signals' in each direction at the ends of the bridge; however, this photograph was taken much later, on 20 September 1937, and the indicators appear to have been replaced by two arms on a single post. This makes an interesting comparison with the engraving dated 1871 seen in Illustration 5. (LNER / NERA Collection CE201*

Illustration 42. *Waterworks and Leeman Road cabins: the 1877 Waterworks cabin is on the left with Leeman Road cabin, dating from 1900, directly opposite. The 1937 view looks south towards the station. (LNER / NERA Collection CE183-03)*

When the Bridge signalman received the signal for a train approaching in either direction he had to first check that the bridge was set ready, that the lock-bolts and rest-bolts were properly 'in', that the bridge ends were lowered on to the bed-plates of the piers, and that the arms of both semaphore indicator signals were down; only then he could peg the appropriate block instrument before acknowledging the bell signal by repetition. After the passage of the train, he called attention and unpegged the block instrument.

Illustration 43. *Waterworks and Leeman Road cabins: another view, dated 20 September 1937, showing how close the two cabins were, requiring close cooperation for a number of moves. (LNER / NERA Collection CE183-12)*

Illustration 44. *Waterworks signal cabin, showing the impressive signal bridge facing engine drivers as they approached the station from the direction of Scarborough Bridge. (LNER / NERA Collection CE183-11)*

Illustration 45. *Chaloner Whin: the cabin was to the NER S1a design which appears unusual given that most cabins by this date were built to the S3 design; however, it is possible that this was an old cabin extended for its new purpose. Date of the photograph is 20 September 1937. (LNER / NERA Collection CE183-07)*

Illustration 46. *Chaloner Whin: the signal cabin dated from 1900, when work commenced on quadrupling the lines to Church Fenton. At this stage it had a 110-lever McK&H No.11 frame to control the junction towards Selby and Doncaster, together with a whole series of double junctions between the running lines. (The Railway Magazine, 1908)*

Bishopthorpe Lane

Between Naburn and Chaloner Whin a minor road known as Bishopthorpe Lane crossed the line; signalling protection was minimal with only an NER rotating board provided. During the Royal Agricultural Show in 1900, however, it acted as a temporary block post.

Widening to Church Fenton

In connection with widening of the lines through to Church Fenton in 1904, the original Normanton lines were renamed Up and Down Leeds, and the Duplicate lines became the new Up and Down Normanton lines. North Lane cabin closed in March 1904 when St Helens Road Bridge replaced the level crossing; the value of work recovered was £70, with a saving of saving £325 per annum. The siding connection was then worked from a ground frame. Also, Copmanthorpe Moor closed as a block post in the half-year ending June 1904 and was converted into a gate box resulting in a saving of £74 15*s* 0*d* per annum. The gate box had a 7-lever frame with two gate wheels and was released from Copmanthorpe station cabin separately for either the Leeds or Normanton lines. See Illustration 49.

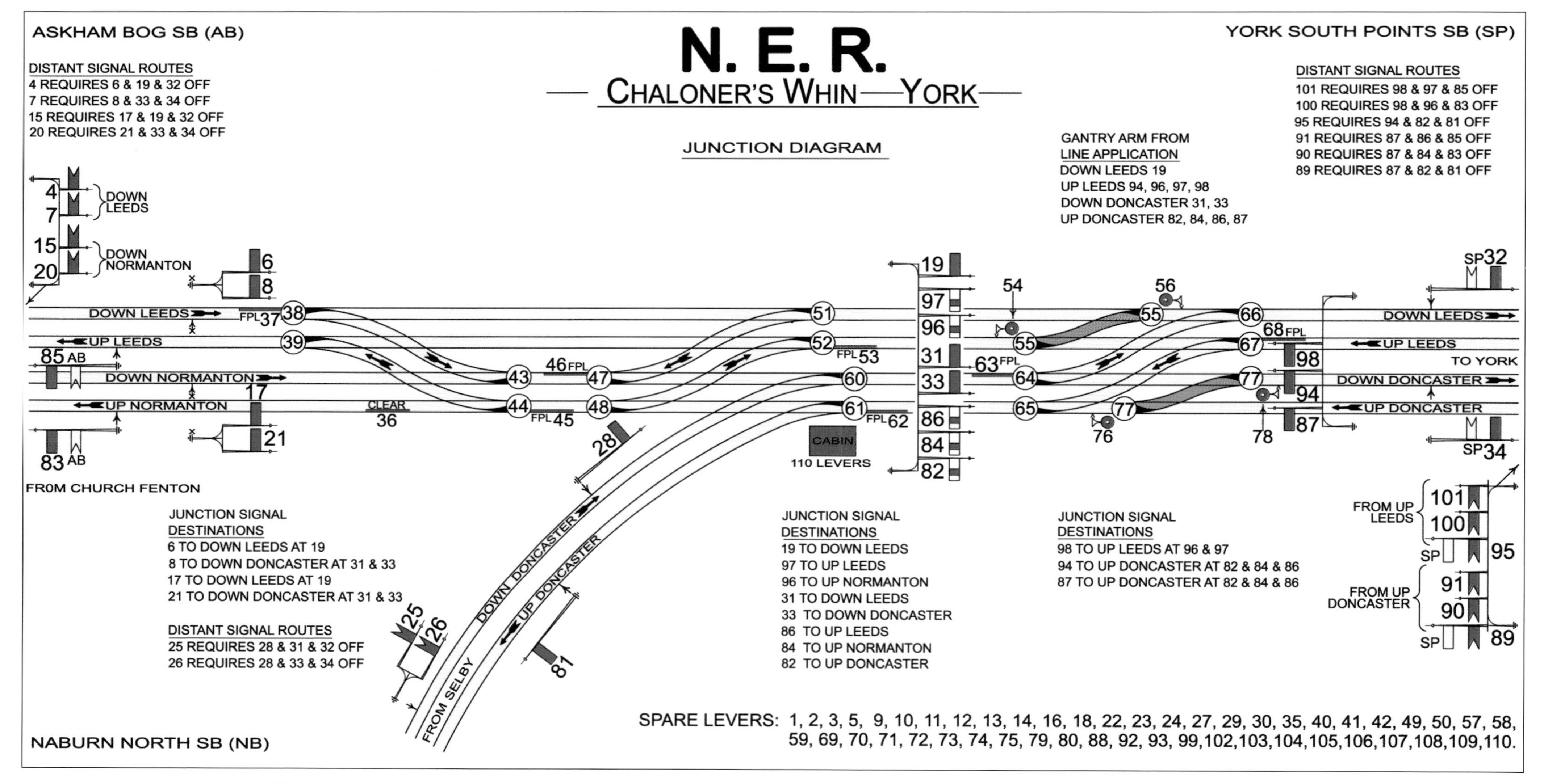

Illustration 47. *Chaloner Whin 1911 showing the quadrupled lines towards Church Fenton. The number of spare levers is accounted for because the NER had planned to install a pair of goods lines north alongside the Leeds lines towards Holgate Junction, but these were never installed. Diagram based on TNA MT6.1957.11 and sketch by Colonel Preston. (Charles Weightman)*

The widening to Church Fenton was completed on 5 June 1904 when the level crossing at Ulleskelf was replaced by an overbridge and a new cabin 471 yards south of its predecessor. In the half-year ended December 1904, Askham Bog closed for 4 hours per day, saving the equivalent of one man (1) and finally, the cabin was closed on 14 August 1909.

(1) TNA: RAIL 527/411.

Illustration 48. *(Left) After closure, Askham Bog signal cabin was adapted for use by Permanent Way staff by removing the operating floor and lowering the roof. The cabin is seen from a passing train on 11 June 1989; it has since been demolished. (Claire E Williamson)*

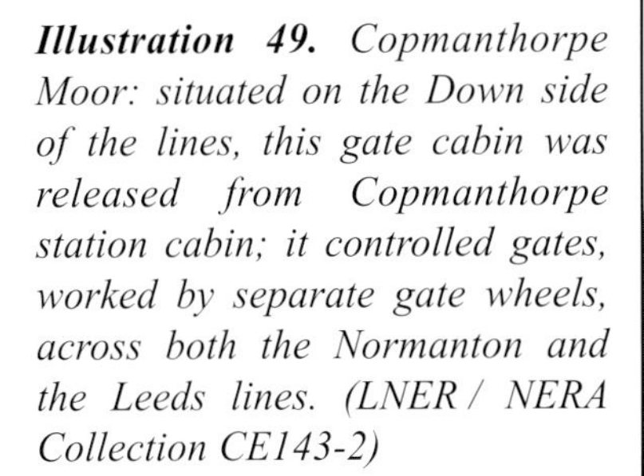

Illustration 49. *Copmanthorpe Moor: situated on the Down side of the lines, this gate cabin was released from Copmanthorpe station cabin; it controlled gates, worked by separate gate wheels, across both the Normanton and the Leeds lines. (LNER / NERA Collection CE143-2)*

Illustration 50. *Copmanthorpe: constructed in 1900 in connection with the widening between Chaloner Whin and Church Fenton, the cabin was to the distinctive NER S3 design, common to many locations between York and Burton Salmon. To the right of the cabin is an NER 'Both-Ways' signal which applied to trains approaching from either direction, so the back of the signal, which would normally be painted white with a black stripe in this case is painted red with a white stripe – exactly the same as the other side of the arm. Evidently this signal replaced signals 14 and 17 shown in Illustration 51. (LNER / NERA Collection NERA CE143-1)*

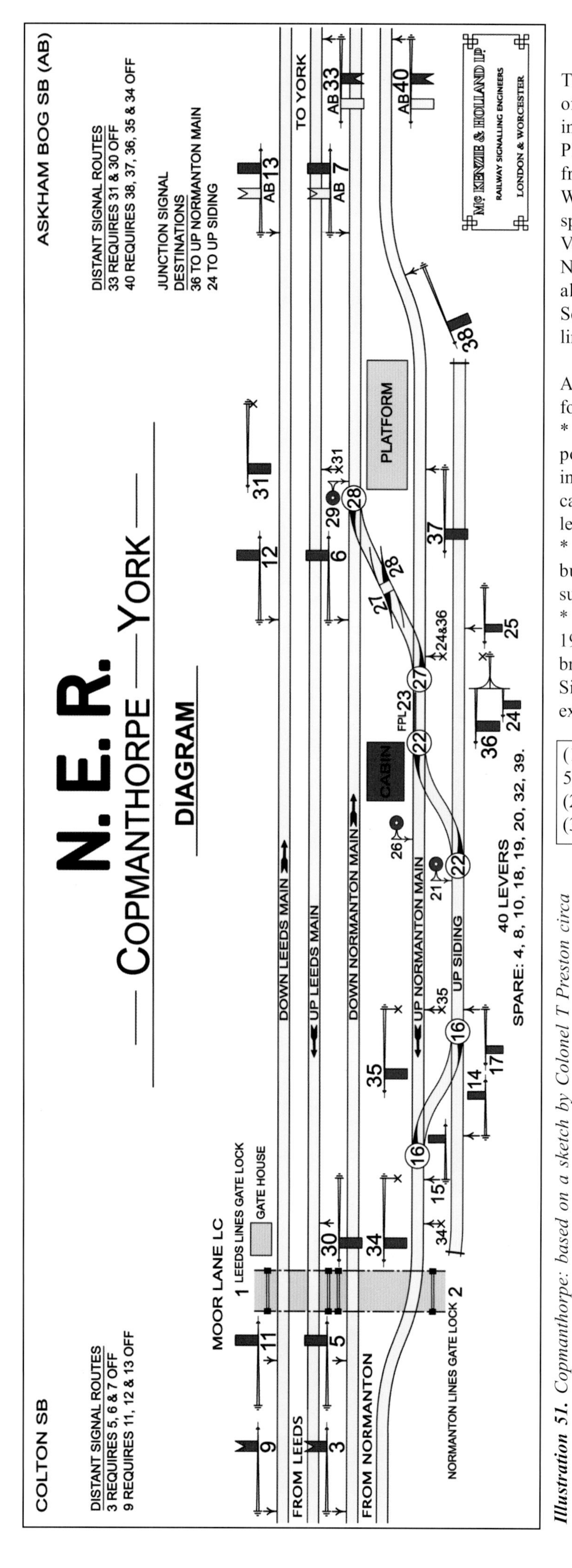

Illustration 51. *Copmanthorpe: based on a sketch by Colonel T Preston circa 1906. When trailing points were installed to the horse dock they were placed just in advance of No.37 signal, and levers 18, 19, 20 were brought into use to work the points and the additional shunting signals. (Charles Weighman)*

Waterworks

The following year, in 1905, at the north end of the station new connections were brought into use from the Up Scarborough line into Platform Nos 10 and 12; these were worked from the existing 132-lever frame at Waterworks cabin, where there were now 34 spare levers. This was inspected by Colonel Von Donop who submitted his report on 27 November 1905. Outer home signals were also erected at Waterworks on the Up Scarborough line, and at Clifton on the Up line from Thirsk.(1)

Miscellaneous Other Works

A miscellany of minor works and alterations followed:

* At Copmanthorpe a new Horse Dock and points from the Up Normanton were inspected on 6 December 1906. By then the cabin had a 40-lever frame (eight spare levers).(2)

* In 1907 or thereabouts, a footbridge was built just south of Platform cabin to supplement the two subways at York

* At Clifton, it was reported in December 1908 that additional connections were brought into use to and from the Carriage Sidings on the Up side, worked from the existing cabin and frame.(3)

(1) TNA: MT 6/1426/3 and TNA: RAIL 527/411.
(2) TNA: MT 6/1536/6.
(3) TNA: MT 6/1768/1.

Zero Mileage Post

In 1905, the NER re-measured all of their lines (an exercise which became known as 'Re-miling') from set Zero posts, one of the largest being at the centre of York station.

	Name of Line	Location
LO. LP.	Longlands Loop	At Northallerton
M.W.& B.	Market Weighton and Beverley	From Market Weighton East
MIC. BR.	Micklefield Branch	From Church Fenton
R. CV.	Raskelf Curve	At Pilmoor
S. BR.	Sherburn Branch	To Gascoigne Wood
Y. & H.	York & Harrogate	From Poppleton Junction
Y. & M.W.	York & Market Weighton	From Bootham
Y. & N.	York & Newcastle	To Low Beaumont Hill signal cabin
Y. & N.M.	York & North Midland	To Altofts Junction
Y. & S.	York & Scarborough	From Waterworks Junction

Illustration 52. *Replica York Station Zero Post: this was erected at the centre of York station by the North Eastern Railway Association with financial assistance from the Railway Heritage Trust and the Ken Hoole Trust to mark the 150th nniversary of the formation of the NER on 31 July 1854. It was unveiled by Sir William McAlpine, Bt., Chairman of the Railway Heritage Trust on 31 July 2004. Photographed in 2013. (Richard Pulleyn)*

Chapter 7 : Developments in 1909 – Extending the Station

By 1909, traffic levels had increased to such an extent that even further expansion of the station became essential. Train lengths had also increased so expresses from the north could no longer be accommodated at the south end of Platform No 4; similarly, the trains of five 'foreign' companies (Great Northern, Great Eastern, Great Central, Midland and Lancashire & Yorkshire) could no longer be accommodated in the five bay platforms at the south end of York station. Furthermore, Platform No 4 was the only through platform for trains in the Up direction, and Bay Platforms Nos 6 and 7 were only signalled for arrivals, not departures.

The layout at the south end of the station was principally controlled from Locomotive Yard signal box on the west side, but traffic between it and Platform signal box was worked entirely by telephone, there being no block bells or instruments of any sort. Only a short distance further south was thc tall Holgate Bridge signal box, with a frame of 48 levers, which signalled the junction to and from York Goods Yards; working was by Absolute Block with both Locomotive Yard signal box to the north and South Points signal box to the south.

Consequently, a scheme was developed to extend Platforms Nos 1, 2, 3, 4, 5, and 6 at the south end and this received approval in 1906. The work was completed in stages:

* Platforms Nos 1 and 2 were extended.
* The crossover roads with double slips worked from Locomotive Yard signal box were replaced by facing and trailing connections. Consequently, trains could enter or leave any of the platforms from any of the running lines (except Down Leeds to Platform No 1, since that route was not needed).
* The Up Independent was converted into a passenger line, so that a train could depart via that route whilst another was leaving Platform No 4 towards the Up Leeds line.
* By making alterations at the north end, Platform No 14 was converted from a Down platform only so that it could be used also by trains from the north to the south, thus relieving some of the pressure on Platform No 4.
* Platform No 5 was also made bi-directional.
* Platform Nos 6 and 7 were signalled for departures as well as arrivals.
* Facilities for locomotives belonging to 'foreign' companies at the south end were moved from the west side to the east side.(1)

Locomotive Yard Signal Box

At the same time as these improvements were approved, it was proposed that a new signal box would replace both Locomotive Yard and Holgate Bridge signal boxes; given the extensive layout it was quite evident that the signal box would have to be large, so there was an investigation to help decide whether a power or mechanical interlocking frame should be provided. The NER had considerable experience of power signalling, with electro-pneumatic installations at Newcastle, Tyne Dock and Hull; whilst power signalling could produce a significant saving in the number of signalmen required, and hence reduce operating costs, at York, compared to many other locations, there was adequate space available for a large mechanical signal box. Furthermore, the cost of a power installation would have been so much higher:

(1) TNA: MT 6/1803/4 & MT 6/1803/5.

mechanical signalling was estimated to cost £16,761 whereas power signalling was estimated at £33,610 – more than twice as much – so the NER decided to construct a signal box with mechanical interlocking.

The new Locomotive Yard signal box (the third with that name) was opened on Sunday 6 June 1909, on which date Holgate Bridge signal box was taken out of use; it was estimated that the cost was £1,840, value of work recovered £100, and the annual saving £459 2*s* 4*d*. However, the 'old' Locomotive Yard signal box continued in use for a further week during the commissioning, not closing until Sunday 13 June 1909.

The design of the new signal box was Type S4; a balcony ran round the front and ends of the box with an outside covered shelter in the centre for the chargeman.

The new box contained a McKenzie & Holland (Pattern No.16) frame of 295 levers set in one continuous row, of which 43 levers were spare; to provide access to the chargeman's balcony there was a gap between levers 145 and 146 equivalent to five lever spaces, so the length of the actual frame itself was equivalent to 300 levers. This was the largest mechanical lever frame installation of its kind in the world, and the third largest of any sort, only the 374-lever power frame at Glasgow Central (Caledonian Railway) and the 488-lever Sykes' electro-mechanical installation at Glasgow St Enoch (Glasgow & South-Western Railway) being larger.

Because of the size and complexity of the frame, the tappet locking was fixed both in front and behind the levers which were placed further from the front wall of the box than would normally be the case when all of the locking was fixed behind the frame.

Illustration 53. *Locomotive Yard: opened on Sunday, 6 June 1909, the new signal box was the third with that name and was built to the NER Type S4 design – albeit of exceptional length. Behind the box part of the termination pole can be seen where electrical connections were brought into equipment within the building. (NRM Collection Reference 7157)*

Illustration 54. *Locomotive Yard: a balcony ran round the front and ends of the signal box with an outside covered shelter in the centre for the Chargeman. He is seen here, having attracted attention by banging the stick seen in his right hand, shouting instructions through the megaphone. (NRM Collection)*

Footnote : The name 'Loco Yard' or 'Locomotive Yard' derives from the site of the old round houses west of the line which were once used by visiting 'foreign' railway locomotives.

Illustration 55. *Locomotive Yard: the box contained a McKenzie & Holland (Pattern 16) frame of 295 levers set in one continuous row; to provide access to the Chargeman's balcony there was a gap between levers 145 and 146 equivalent to 5 lever spaces, so the length of the actual frame itself was equivalent to 300 levers. This was the largest mechanical lever frame installation of its kind in the world. (NRM 1997 7410_930_3_55Y)*

Illustration 56. *Locomotive Yard: another view of the signal box. (NRM 1997-7410_285_1_56Y)*

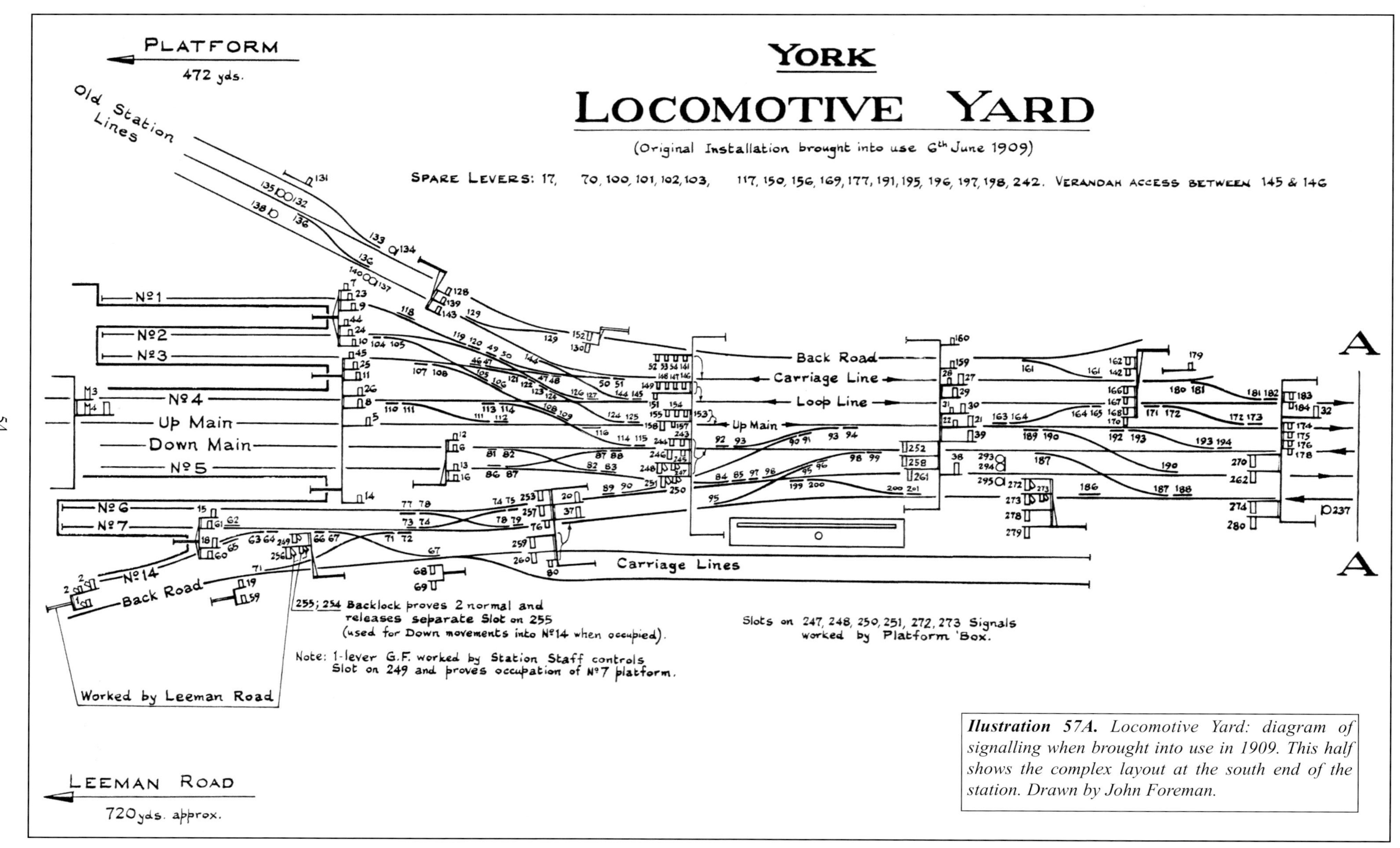

Ilustration* *57A. *Locomotive Yard: diagram of signalling when brought into use in 1909. This half shows the complex layout at the south end of the station. Drawn by John Foreman.*

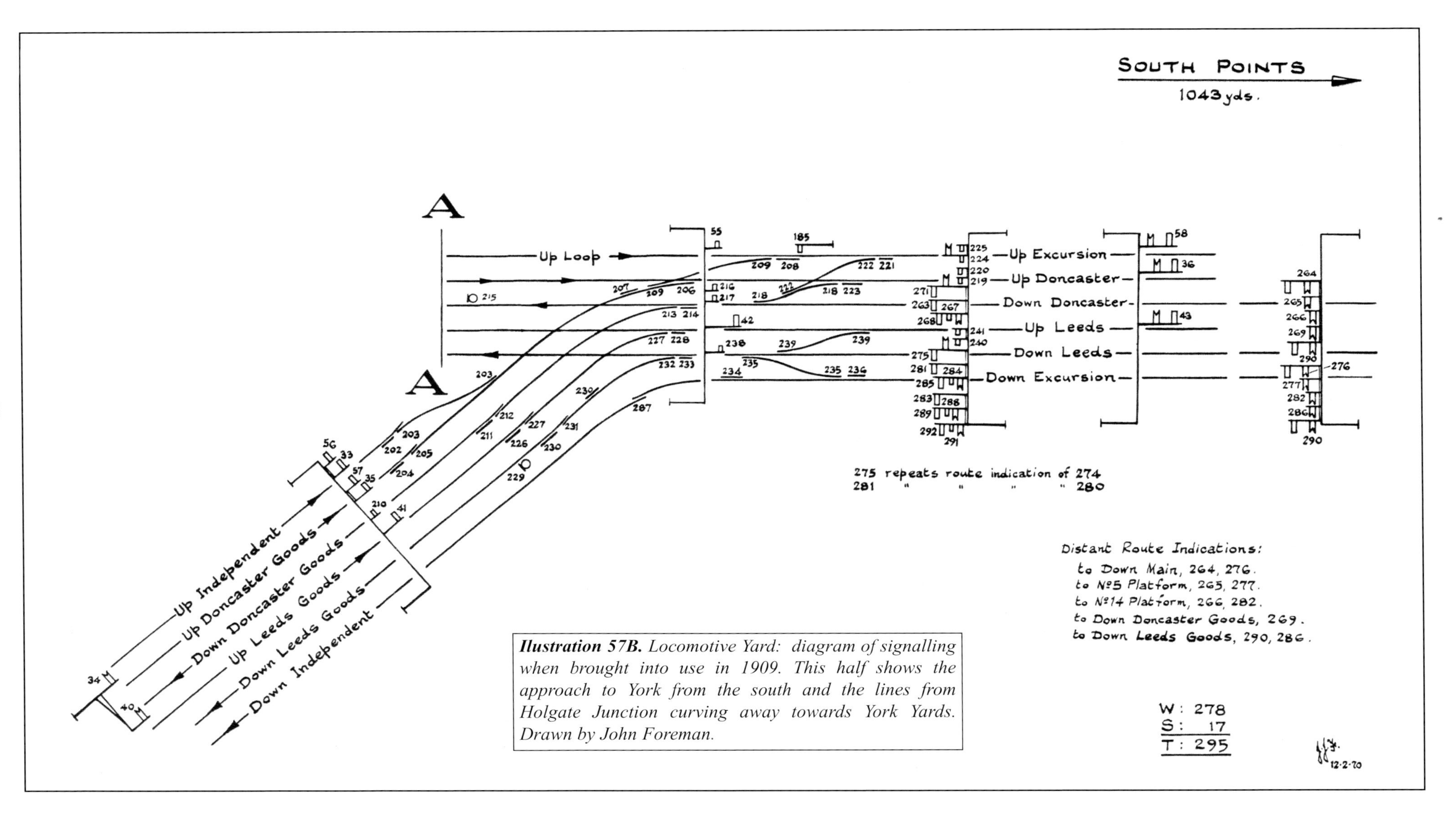

Illustration 57B. *Locomotive Yard: diagram of signalling when brought into use in 1909. This half shows the approach to York from the south and the lines from Holgate Junction curving away towards York Yards. Drawn by John Foreman.*

The signal bridge which formerly carried the home signals for the old Locomotive Yard signal box was moved further south to be directly outside the new Locomotive Yard signal box where it was re-used to form the largest signal bridge in the installation. Just north of the signal box a footbridge was erected for staff to access both sides of the line.

Locking bars were fitted inside the rail on all facing points over which passenger trains were run (*i.e.* whether running or shunting) and the levers had to be worked in rotation: when the road was being set the bars had to be pulled in sequence starting with the bar furthest from the train then, as soon as the engine got on to the first bar it locked the whole of the road as set. In addition, the switches of all facing points were fitted with 'wedges' or 'blocks' worked by the signal lever: the wire to the signal was attached to the wedge thereby ensuring that the switch was close up to the rail before the signal could be lowered. The rod working the wedge was slotted so that the wedge remained in place after the signal was returned to danger, and the wedge was only withdrawn by reversal of the locking bar, thus ensuring that the points remained locked until all of the vehicles had passed over.

Special Permissive Block working replaced telephone working at the south end of the station to and from Platform signal box. Separate bells and instruments were provided for each through line: Platform No 14, Platform No 5, Down Main, Up Main, and Platform No 4, from west to east respectively. Each of these lines could be worked in both directions (the main lines for shunting purposes only) and no movement could be made without acceptance from the

Illustration 58. *Locomotive Yard: locking bars were fitted inside the rail on all facing points over which passenger trains were moved, whether running or shunting. (NRM Collection)*

Illustration 59. *Although this 1981 photograph relates to an instrument in York Yard North signal box (formerly Severus Junction), it illustrates the type of instrument in use at Locomotive Yard signal box for signalling trains over bi-directional lines. The commutator on this instrument could be turned clockwise to accept a train in the Up direction; if the train was operating in the Down direction, the commutator on the instrument at the opposite end of the section would be turned anti-clockwise. (Christopher J Woolstenholmes, CJW148 30)*

opposite end of the section; trains could be accepted at 'Line Clear' or 'Caution' according to the state of the line. If a train for the north was accepted by the Platform signalman, the instrument was pegged to 'Down'; conversely, if a train for the south was accepted by the Locomotive Yard signalman it was pegged to 'Up'; those were the only two indications possible.

In addition, the relevant signals were electrically controlled from either end using a lever in the frame which was also connected to a 'plunger' instrument: to accept a train, the signalman reversed the lever and plunged his instrument to free the signal at the entrance to the section.

Block Working between Locomotive Yard box and South Points box was made more complicated as a consequence of Holgate Bridge box closing because the tail-lamp of trains from the south towards York Yards could not be seen; therefore, a wooden 'Groundsman's Signal Box' was built in place of the latter.

Absolute Block applied on the Up and Down Leeds and Doncaster lines, but with a separate bell between the Groundsman and Locomotive Yard signal boxes to advise the signalmen there as soon as a Down train had passed complete with tail-lamp which enabled them to send 'Train out of Section'. The Down line block instruments in Locomotive Yard box were specially adapted for this purpose: they were also controlled by the Holgate groundsman such that, after the Locomotive Yard signalman had pegged them to 'Train on Line', the instrument could not be 'unpegged' until the groundsman rang his bell.

The Main Goods Lines between North Junction and Locomotive Yard, also the Up and Down Excursion lines to and from South Points, were worked by Tyer's Recording (Permissive) instruments, as many as six non-passenger trains being allowed in each section (five of them being at caution). The Independent Goods Lines were worked by bell only.

When a train, whether goods or passenger, was accepted at caution only the calling-on signal was lowered; this negated the need to stop a train and show a green flag or light. See Illustration 61.

Unusually for such a large station with many movements being made throughout the day and night, there was very little whistling; instead, a system of electric push-buttons outside connected to bells and indicators installed in the signal box enabled drivers to inform signalmen which route they were to take. Similar arrangements were provided on the platforms so that station staff could advise the signalman when a train was ready to depart.(1) See Illustration 63.

(1) NERA JFM/8456: NER General Superintendent's Notice, 15 November 1909.

Illustration 60. *Locomotive Yard: one of the signalmen at Locomotive Yard signal box answers a block bell adjacent to what appear to be two Sykes indicators which are believed to have been part of the safety features for working the main platform lines in both directions. Painted on the sides of the levers are the numbers of levers which would have to be reversed before that particular lever could be operated.*

Illustration 61. *Holgate Tail Lamp signal box: on the right is the elevated cabin used to look out for tail lamps on trains heading towards North Junction as they did not pass Locomotive Yard signal box, which can be seen in the distance. (Colonel Thomas Preston / NRM Collection)*

Ten circuit telephones were provided, connecting Locomotive Yard signal box to the platforms, the Locomotive Foremen, the Station Master's Office, to all the boxes as far as Selby on the Doncaster line, and to all the boxes as far as Church Fenton on the Leeds and Normanton lines. See Illustration 64.

Locomotive Yard signal box was worked on each of three shifts by a Chargeman (officially titled the 'Traffic Regulator'), a First Leverman, a Second Leverman and two Signal-Lads (only one on the night-shift); during the busy summer timetable, an additional Leverman and Signal-Lad were employed on each shift. The chargeman was responsible for the smooth working of all of the traffic, a considerable responsibility given the number of trains and shunting movements taking place throughout the day; he spent most of his time on the balcony in constant communication with the shunters, and no running or shunting movement was allowed without his agreement, shouting out instructions to all concerned. The levermen were allocated to work defined parts of the frame such as the junction to York Yard and incoming signals, or the points and shunting signals in the centre of the frame, but each helped the other when necessary. Exceptionally, the lads worked the block bells and instruments, booked the trains in the Train Register and attended to the telephones, thereby keeping the Traffic Regulator informed.(1)

Illustration 62. *Locomotive Yard: the block instruments and bells were mounted on separate shelves at the back of the box. (NRM Collection)*

(1) RM Volume 29, 1911 and Volume 30, 1912.

Illustration 63. *Locomotive Yard: a system of electric push-buttons outside connected to bells and indicators installed in the signal box enabled drivers to inform signalmen which route they were to take. Similar arrangements were provided on the platforms so that station staff could advise the signalman when a train was ready to depart. (NRM Collection)*

Leeman Road and Waterworks Signal Boxes

On the north side of Waterworks signal box a double track crossed over the main lines to connect the Scarborough lines to and from York Yards. At the north end of the station in February 1909, an additional single line connection from Platform No 14, worked in both directions, was installed south of Waterworks signal box across the main lines to the Scarborough lines; this new connection was worked by both Leeman Road and Waterworks signal boxes using a system of releases and slotted signals.

New lever frames were commissioned in both signal boxes: an 85-lever frame (nine spare) in Leeman Road signal box, and in Waterworks signal box two new lever frames, Nos 1-66 and Nos 67-132 (19 spare).(1)

Upon completion of these works in May 1909, Platform signal box had a frame of 80 levers, 16 of which were spare; this frame had actually been installed in 1907 to replace the previous frame of 70 levers.(2)

Illustration 64. *Locomotive Yard: in addition to local telephones, circuit telephones were provided connecting the signal box to boxes as far as Selby on the Doncaster line, and to Church Fenton on the Leeds and Normanton lines. (NRM Collection)*

Askham Bog Signal Box and Chaloner Whin

As noted above, Askham Bog signal box closed on 14 August 1909 after outer home signals were erected at Chaloner Whin Junction on the Down Leeds, Down Normanton, and Down Doncaster lines. The estimated cost was £137, the value of work recovered £161, and the saving £134 2*s* 4*d p.a.*(3)

At the junction, a temporary contractor's siding was installed in February 1911 with a trailing connection into the Down Doncaster line just before junction; this was worked from a 1-lever ground frame locked by Annett's Key which was normally attached to the lever of the protecting signal, so removal of the key locked all necessary signals to danger. At this time, the contractor was undertaking earthworks to improve the main line curve towards Selby.(4)

A Midland Railway Traffic Notice for November 1911 states that the ground frame at Nelson's Brickyard Siding was temporarily converted into a block post on the Up Doncaster line only whilst the siding was being used as a ballast tip.

(1) TNA: MT 6/1812/2.
(2) TNA: MT 6/1857/1.
(3) TNA: RAIL 527/411.
(4) TNA: MT 6/1957/11.

Illustration 65. *Waterworks and Leeman Road: looking north over the station roof the Goods Lines are curving round from North Junction to run parallel with the mainlines as far as Clifton signal box, or taking the connection across the Main Lines towards Scarborough Bridge. (John Whitaker Collection)*

Locomotive Yard Signal Box

In 1911, new connections were installed at the south end of the station:

* Between Nos 1, 2 and 3 Platform lines and the Carriage Sidings on the Up side.
* Facing points on the Up Leeds line to Platform No 5 and to Down Main line.
* Facing points on the Down Main line to Platform No 5.
* Slips added to an existing through connection to form a cross-over road between the Up Main and Down Main lines.
* A facing cross-over road between the Up Leeds and Down Leeds lines.

All of these connections were controlled from the 295-lever frame in Locomotive Yard signal box, by which time only 17 levers were spare. The work was inspected by Colonel Von Donop and recommended for approval in his report dated 18 July 1911.(1)

South Points Signal Box

At South Points signal box a temporary trailing siding to an engineer's tip was connected to the Down Leeds Main worked from the existing frame of 29 levers (two spare); this was inspected by Colonel Von Donop and recommended for approval in his report dated 24 June 1912.(2)

Clifton Signal Box

In 1912, York North engine shed and the adjacent carriage sidings were much enlarged and a new crossover road was installed from the Down Sidings to the Up Independent / Shunting Neck; this was worked from the existing signal box but a new 120-lever frame (13 spare) was installed.(3) In order to minimise whistling by engines around Clifton when requiring to leave the shed, or when detained at signals, bell pushers had been installed at a number of locations in 1909 to operate indicators in the signal box; in 1913 the installation was extended to five locations.(4)

(1) TNA: MT 6/2007/7 & 8.
(2) TNA: MT 6/2108/4.
(3) TNA: MT 6/2134/4.
(4) NER Circular O.1037 1913.

Illustration 66. *Leeman Road: two signalmen on each shift operated the 85-lever frame. (NRM Collection)*

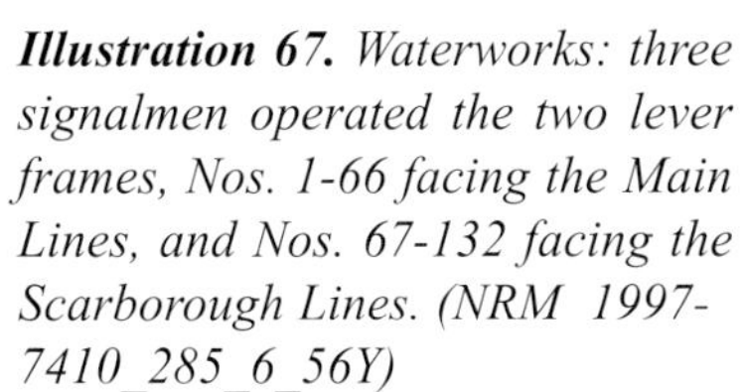

Illustration 67. *Waterworks: three signalmen operated the two lever frames, Nos. 1-66 facing the Main Lines, and Nos. 67-132 facing the Scarborough Lines. (NRM 1997-7410_285_6_56Y)*

Illustration 68. *(Below) Clifton: the timber-built signal box as photographed on 20 September 1937. (LNER / NERA Collection CE183-04)*

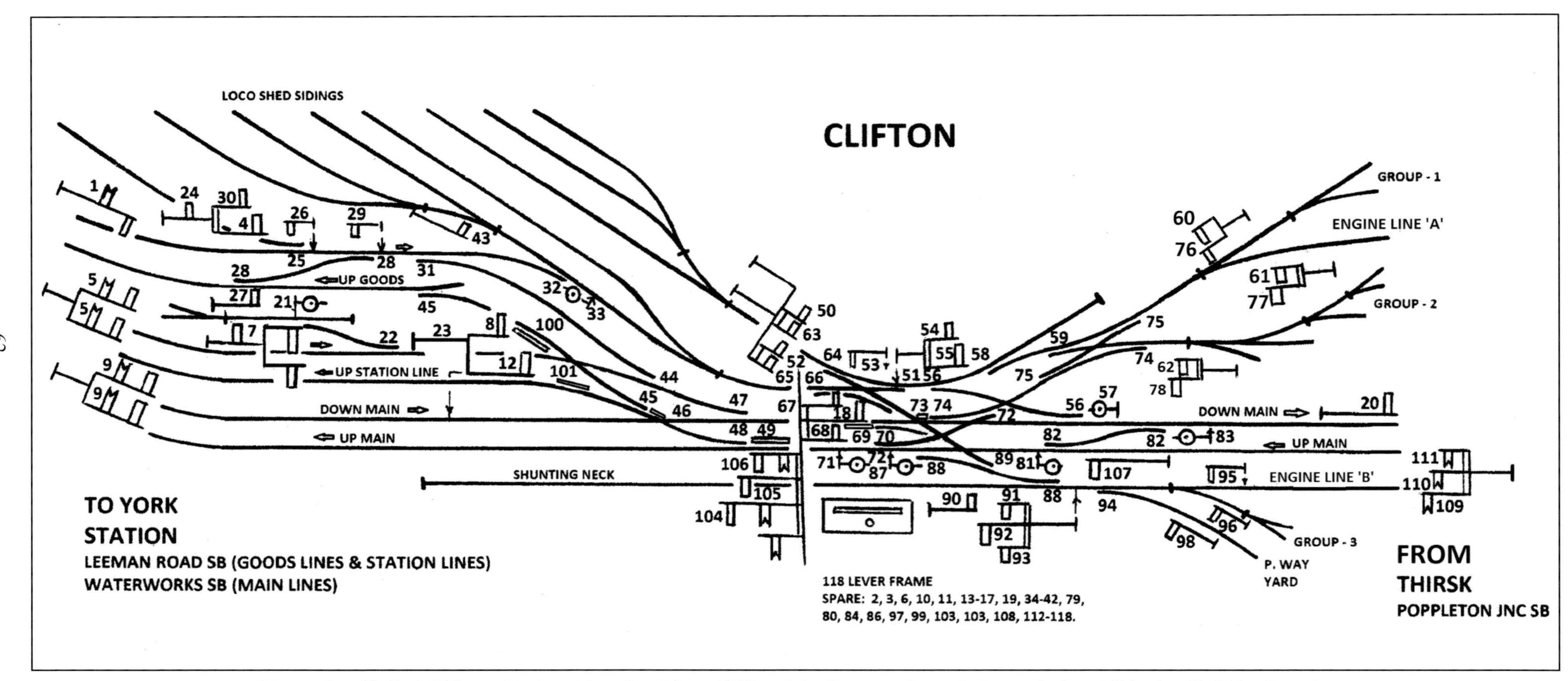

Illustration 69. *York Clifton: this signal box dated from 1900 and the diagram shows the layout before 1912 when York North engine shed and the adjacent carriage sidings were much enlarged and a new 120-lever frame was installed. (Richard Pulleyn)*

Chapter 8 : Impact of the First World War

Dringhouses

In 1918, the War Office required the NER to provide additional siding accommodation at both Darlington and at York in connection with the movement of coal from County Durham to London where it was required by public utilities; under normal circumstances, this coal would have been moved by coastal shipping. Sidings were provided on both the Up and the Down sides of the line between Dringhouses and Holgate Bridge and, included with the plans, a piece of land 30 feet x 6 feet is shown as required for a new signal box at Dringhouses. Land for the sidings and signal box were acquired under the Defence of the Realm Regulations and resulted in protracted correspondence with the previous occupier who sought (and received) compensation. The cost of the whole work was shared by the Treasury with the NER.(1)

A Midland Railway Traffic Notice dated 25 June 1918 states that the points at North Lane were to be worked by guards or shunters until the new signal box at Dringhouses was brought into use.

South Points Signal Box

On the Down side, four 'North Down Reception' through sidings were brought into use on 30 September 1918, controlled from South Points signal box which had to be extended 11 feet at the north end to accommodate a new 60-lever frame.

Holgate Bridge

At the exit from the North Down Reception lines, a new Holgate Outlet ground frame was brought into use on 1 December 1918. It was fitted with a 5-lever frame, released from Locomotive Yard signal box, and also took over responsibility from the Groundsman's signal box (see page 57) for reporting the passage of Down freight trains (complete with tail lamp) proceeding towards York Yards so that Locomotive Junction signal box could send 'Train Out of Section' to South Points.(2) See Illustration 71.

(1) TNA: MT 6/2546/7.
(2) TNA: MT 6/2511/1.

Illustration 70. *South Points: four 'North Down Reception' through sidings were brought into use on 30 September 1918, controlled from South Points signal box which had to be extended 11 feet at the north end to accommodate a new 60-lever frame. Careful examination of the brickwork reveals that the extension was at the north end; see also Illustration 78. (NERA Collection TS23)*

Illustration 71. *Holgate Outlet ground frame: located at the exit from the new North Down Reception lines, this ground frame was brought into use on 1 December 1918 (the photograph was taken on 20 September 1937). The ground frame also took over responsibility from Groundsman's signal box for reporting the passage of Down freight trains (complete with tail lamp) proceeding towards York Yards so that Locomotive Yard signal box could send 'Train Out of Section' to South Points. (LNER / NERA Collection CE183-09)*

Dringhouses Signal Box

At Dringhouses, sidings were constructed on both sides of the line: on the Down side there was a 'South Down Reception Line' and three 'South Down Reception' through sidings, but on the Up side a complete new Up Yard was brought into use on 2 September 1918; this incorporated an Up Reception Line, three through Up Reception Sidings, and four additional through sidings. At the north end, the sidings were controlled from South Points signal box, and at the south end a new Dringhouses signal box was commissioned on the Up side of the line, situated about 100 yards north of the former North Lane signal box. The NER Type S3 design of signal box was fitted with a 20-lever frame (two spare), and did not control the Up Leeds line.

Block Telegraph

According to the NER *Appendix to the Working Timetable* effective from 1 January 1918, Modified Block Telegraph Regulations applied between the following boxes and on the following lines to facilitate working of traffic:

Illustration 72. *Dringhouses: the signal box at Dringhouses lasted for just 10 years: it opened in 1918, by 1922 it was out of use, and in 1928 it was abolished. It is thus not surprising that few photographs exist, but at least it can be seen behind this express being hauled by NER Class Z No 733 on the Up Doncaster line. (NERA TS23)*

* Waterworks and Clifton: Up and Down – Modified Recording Regulations.
* Leeman Road to Clifton : Up and Down – Modified Recording Regulations.
* Locomotive Yard to Leeman Road: Platform No 14 Line.
* South Points to Locomotive Yard: Down Leeds and Down Doncaster.

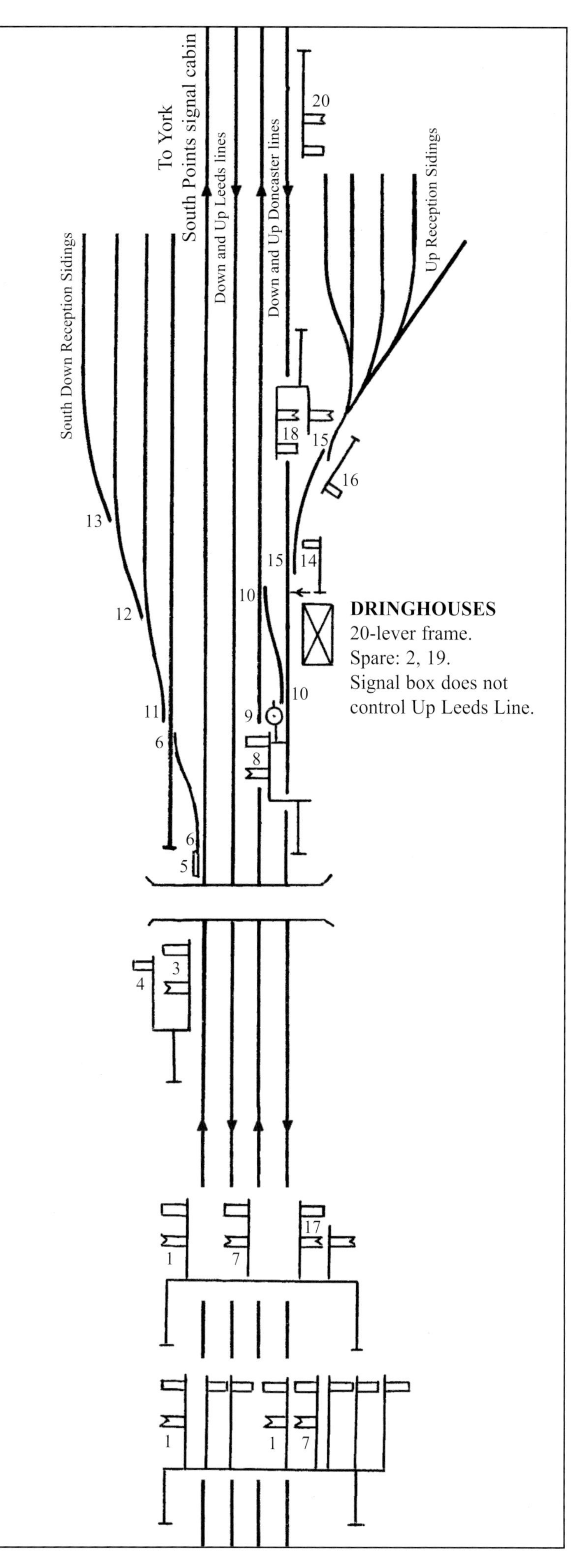

Illustration 73. *Dringhouses: during the First World War sidings were constructed on both sides of the line: on the Down side there was a 'South Down Reception Line' and three 'South Down Reception' through sidings, but on the Up side a complete new Up Yard was brought into use on 2 September 1918. At the south end, the sidings were controlled from a new Dringhouses signal box.*

There was extensive correspondence between the War Department and the NER emphasising that cost must be kept to a minimum so second-hand materials were to be used as far as possible. The signal box superstructure was to the NER S3 design with a frame of 20 levers and, although no records have been found to clarify where these were recovered from, it is speculated that the only likely box out of use at that time was Ringhay, on the line between Micklefield and Church Fenton.

Exceptionally, this diagram has been drawn vertically, a style favoured by the late John Bennett, who provided much useful information about the history of signalling around York. His sketch was based on TNA MT6.2511.1. (Richard Pulleyn)

Chapter 9 : Rationalisation by the LNER

After the First World War and the Grouping that followed, the LNER inherited a run-down railway which had been heavily used around York, with little maintenance or improvement during that time. Consequently, they introduced schemes to rectify the situation and, if possible, to reduce operating costs.

Severus Junction

The Crewe power frame at Severus Junction was the only example of its type on the NER, and it had proved most difficult and expensive to maintain. The NER had already decided to revert to a mechanical system so it was replaced on 9 April 1922 when a mechanical frame of 150 levers was installed at the back of the box – which had been extended at both ends to accommodate the extra length required. Placing the frame at the back of the box was not standard practice on the LNER at that time, so it is assumed that this was to assist with observing train movements.

Chaloners Whin

At Chaloners Whin a new lever frame was installed in 1926, reduced in length from 110 to 80 levers.

'Rowntree Halt'

Alongside the Foss Islands Branch, a loop was built in November 1927 on the north side of the Down branch with a platform for visitors and workers at the factory; originally, this was known as 'Rowntree's Cocoa Works' but later it was simply 'Rowntree Halt'. Up trains leaving the platform ran facing road across the Up Main to the Down Main then through the trailing mains crossover to gain the correct line. The platform was inspected and recommended for approval by Lieutenant-Colonel Anderson on 10 April 1929.

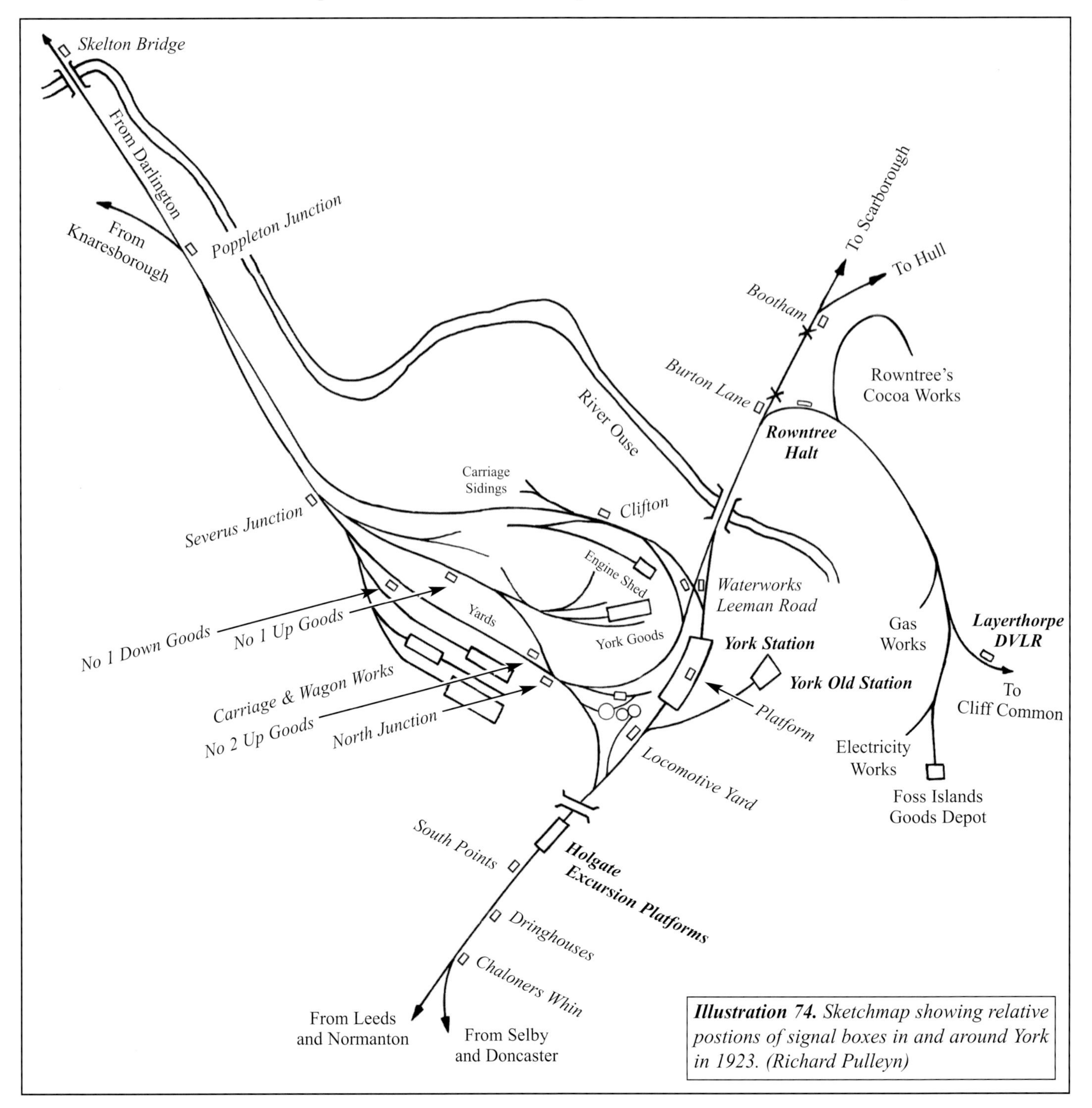

Illustration 74. *Sketchmap showing relative postions of signal boxes in and around York in 1923. (Richard Pulleyn)*

Illustration 75. *Chaloner Whin: a new lever frame was installed in 1926, reduced in length from 110 to 80 levers. (Richard Pulleyn Collection, per Signalman George Martin)*

(1)TNA MT 29/85.
(2) TNA: RAIL 390/1617.

Burton Lane Level Crossing

In 1933 Burton Lane level crossing was replaced by Crichton Avenue overbridge.(1)

Naburn Swing Bridge

In 1926, George Davidson (Divisional General Manager, LNER North-Eastern Area) presented a paper to the LNER Traffic Committee and Works Committee proposing closure of North and South signal boxes and the conversion of Naburn Swing Bridge box into a block post. The alterations would enable the services of five men and one lad to be dispensed with, resulting in a saving of wages of £1075 per annum; there would also be a saving of £44 *p.a.* in respect of coal and clothing, making a total saving of £1119 *p.a.* There would be an additional charge of £65 for maintenance, leaving a net saving of £1054 *p.a.* The cost of the new works was estimated at £2067, and the saving of £1054 *p.a.* represented an equivalent return of 50.9% on the outlay, so it was recommended that the expenditure be authorised. Westinghouse Brake & Saxby Signalling Company Limited submitted a tender of £1210 which was accepted, to include two ground frames (one 2-lever GF and one 5-lever GF) to replace control of points previously worked from Naburn South signal box.(2)

Illustration 76. *Chaloner Whin: looking south towards the junction, the Doncaster lines curve off beyond the signal box whilst the Normanton lines continue towards Church Fenton, accompanied by the Leeds lines on the right. A series of double junctions provided great flexibility when regulating traffic. (Christopher J Woolstenholmes Collection)*

The works were inspected by Lieutenant-Colonel Anderson on 10 April 1929. Anderson reported that the lines were fully track circuited and all signals were motor operated: on the Up line these were No 1, No 2 and No 3 block homes, each with repeater distant signals working automatically; on the Down, home, starter and distant were all located south of the bridge. The signal box had two frames: the main frame had 11 levers, working the signals and ground frame controls, and the Bridge frame of four levers (two to control the bridge locking, and two to work emergency detonator placers below the signal box in the middle of the bridge). The two frames were interlocked so that the bridge locking gear could not be released unless all approach signals were at danger, and unlocking of the bridge disconnected all electrical connections for working signals. In addition, at each end of the bridge existing double arm signals were retained; these were worked by the bridge mechanism, and stood at 'Clear' when the bridge was locked in position for rail traffic.

The Special Instructions provided that in clear weather Down passenger trains not booked to stop at Naburn must not be accepted at 'Line Clear' unless the bridge was locked normal for the railway and all track circuits on the Down line were clear. Down passenger trains booked to stop at Naburn station could be accepted at 'Line Clear' when the bridge was open to river traffic provided that the track circuits were clear to the Down starter. Down goods trains could be accepted, in clear weather only, under the 'Warning' arrangements with the bridge open to river traffic. On the Up line, no passenger train could be accepted unless the bridge was locked normal, but goods trains only could be accepted under the 'Warning' arrangement in clear weather with the bridge open to river traffic.

Lieutenant-Colonel Anderson recommended these works for approval but, given the heavy, fast traffic, he asked the company to consider additional safeguards such as controlling the block working in each direction by the bridge bolts, controlling the starting signals of boxes in rear by the bridge lock, or providing facing sand drags on either side of the bridge. However, unlike Goole Bridge where sand drags were installed, this was not the case at Naburn and no evidence has been found that any other safeguards were introduced at that time.(1)

The procedure for operating the bridge after closure of the North and South 'outpost' boxes was described in LNER Circular O.1744 dated 15 November 1926, and can be summarised as follows:(2)

Opening (for River Traffic)

1. Pull No.2 Lever to release locking bolt of wedge blocks and disconnect protecting signals.
2. Pull No.1 Lever which released the steering column and levers for both lifting the bridge and withdrawing blocks.
3. Push over the Knuckle Lever to lift the bridge off the blocks.
4. Pull over the Wedge Block Lever to withdraw the blocks.
5. Pull back the Knuckle Lever and secure by trigger which was fastened to the floor.
6. Press down the foot treadle to withdraw the Locking Bolts, and secure the treadle down in notch.
7. Proceed to swing the bridge by turning the Steering Lever steadily to the right hand, until the bridge is sufficiently open when the Steering Lever could be turned back to the Shut position. (The bridge could be swung to the Left Hand if required, but had to be swung to the right to start with).

(1) TNA: MT29.85.
(2) NERA 0554.

Illustration 77. *Naburn: during the 1920s, the LNER carried out a number of signalling projects to rationalise signalling and thus reduce costs, in particular where technology such as motor points and track circuiting now made that possible. At Naburn, the Swing Bridge signal box became a full block post in 1929 resulting in closure of Naburn North and South signal boxes. (NERA Collection NERA.2821)*

Closing to River Traffic

1. Check that all is clear before starting to close.
2. Turn the Steering Lever steadily to the left hand and, when the bridge has come to a stand not more than three inches past normal position, sharply kick out the foot treadle from the notch, which will put in the locking bolts, then finish closing in a left hand direction.
3. Release the Knuckle Lever and push it over to lift the bridge.
4. Push over the Wedge Block lever to put in the blocks.
5. Pull over the Knuckle Lever to lower the bridge on to the blocks
6. Push back No.1 Lever to lock the steering gear.
7. Push back No.2 Lever to lock the wedges and connect the protecting signals.

Dringhouses Signal Box

Dringhouses signal box was shown as closed in the Appendix dated May 1922, and was abolished at 6 pm 30 September 1928 when all points and signals were transferred to South Points signal box; this work required power-operated points into the Down Reception lines and extensive track circuiting.

At South Points an extra five levers were added to the frame, making a total of 65 levers. The works were inspected and recommended for approval by Lieutenant-Colonel Anderson on 12 November 1929.(1)

Locomotive Yard to Leeman Road Accident

On 30 August 1931 a light engine collided with a loaded passenger coach which had been left standing on the Up Engine Line on the west side of the station whilst the train engine was turned. That line was not worked by the block system, the signalman at Leeman Road signal box simply making a note in the Train Register when the line was obstructed by shunting moves; until cleared by the shunter direct or via a telephone call from Locomotive Yard signal box, a reminder advice was also placed on the levers of protecting signals. On this occasion here was confusion because a number of vehicles were removed from the south end of the Engine Line but that did not include the remaining passenger coach.

Poppleton Junction

On 11 June 1933, as stage-work for the East Coast Main Line Widening Scheme being progressed by the LNER, additional Up and Down Slow lines were brought into use north of the River Ouse bridge; Skelton Bridge and Hunting Bridge signal boxes were closed and Poppleton Junction signal box, working to Beningbrough station signal box, took over control of the new lines north of the bridge, as well as the existing Independents south of the bridge. All lines were fully track circuited and colour-light (searchlight) signals were installed north of Poppleton Junction. An early form of Track Circuit Block applied on both the Fast (centre) and Slow (outside) lines.

(1) TNA: RAIL 401/86 and TNA: MT 29/85

Illustration 78. *South Points: when Dringhouses signal box was abolished in 1928 all points and signals formerly controlled from there were transferred to South Points signal box; an extra five levers were added to the frame, making a total of 65 levers. (BR / NERA Collection CE183-06)*

Illustration 79. *Poppleton Junction: looking north towards the junction for Harrogate, after the introduction of colour light signalling in 1933 when Skelton Bridge signal box was closed. The signal bridge includes 'D.1' searchlight 'Repeater for D.2' installed under No.11 Down Inner Home to Main. The photograph was taken in September 1937. An oddity is that the signal arms on the dolls third and fourth from the left appear to have been painted incorrectly; no other explanation is known. (LNER / Mick Nicholson Collection)*

Illustration 80. *Skelton Bridge: after closure of Skelton Bridge signal box, a ground frame, released by Poppleton Junction signal box, was installed to work a crossover. (Richard Pulleyn Collection)*

A new 2-lever Skelton Bridge ground frame was brought into use to control a Main to Main crossover.

Special Instructions

Signal Boxes between Clifton and Locomotive Yard

The LNER (NE Area) issued a full set of Special Instructions (Reference O.2919 and dated 11 March 1935) for each of the signal boxes between Clifton and Locomotive Yard signal boxes. A selection of key features can be summarised as follows:

Clifton The Absolute Block Regulations applied between Poppleton Junction and Clifton boxes. On the Up Main in clear weather, Clifton could accept a train under Regulation 4 to the Outer Home provided that the line was clear as far as the Inner Home. On the Down Main, a train could be accepted at Line Clear to the Down Main Home signal provided that Train Out of Section had been given for the previous train and the block indicator was in the normal position; however, when a train had been accepted the points were not to be set from Up Main to Up Station Line. Similarly, on the Down Station Line, a train could be accepted at Line Clear to the Down Station Line Home signal provided that Train Out of Section had been given for the previous train and the block indicator was in the normal position. On both Down lines, Train Out of Section could be sent as soon as a train with tail-lamp attached had passed the signal box.

Leeman Road The Regulations for Train Signalling by Recording Instruments applied between Clifton and Leeman Road on the Up and Down Station Lines; more than one train was only allowed where no train conveying passengers was concerned. Facing line working was also allowed on the Down Station Line for engines and trains not conveying passengers. A train could be accepted to the Outer Home on the Up Station Line at Line Clear provided that the line was clear as far as the signal box. Instructions for working Platform No 14 Line and the Engine Line are included below.

The Up and Down Goods Lines between Leeman Road and Clifton signal boxes were worked in accordance with the following code of bell signals:

	Bell Signal
Call Attention	1
Obstruction Danger	6
Up Line	
Light Engine for Engine Line	2
Light Engine for Marshalling Yard	3
Freight Train (of any description)	4
Pilot Engine or Engines with vehicles, loaded or empty	1 - 1 - 1
Down Line	
Light Engine for Shed	2
Pilot or Empty Train for Nos.1 or 2 Groups	3
Pilot or Empty Train for Nos.3 or 4 Groups, or Fish Stage	4
Light Engine requiring to return Main Line to Station	5

Waterworks The Regulations for Train Signalling by Recording Instruments applied between Clifton and Waterworks on the Up and Down Main Lines; more than one train was only allowed on the Up Main where no train conveying passengers was concerned. On the Down Main more than one train was allowed except in the case of two trains conveying passengers; also a Goods Train (but not including engines or engines and brake vans coupled) was not to be allowed to enter a section already occupied by a train conveying passengers. Facing line working was also allowed on the Down Main Line for engines and trains not conveying passengers.

The Regulations for Train Signalling by Recording Instruments also applied between Waterworks and Platform signal box on the Up and Down Main Lines, and Platform Nos 4 and 5 Lines; special indicator instruments were provided in place of Recording Instruments which had to remain pegged in the appropriate position as long as the line was occupied. Platform No 4 Line could be used in both directions; facing line working was also authorised on the Up and Down Main and Platform No 5 Line for shunting movements.

Illustration 81. *Platform signal box: at the 70-lever frame there are two signalmen on duty. The diagram shows that the area was mostly track circuited; this work was commenced before the Second World War in preparation for the major resignalling that was already planned. (NRM Collection)*

The Absolute Block Regulations applied between Waterworks and Burton Lane signal boxes. The Blocking Back Outside Home signal (3 - 3) only needed to be sent when the Up Line in the direction of Bootham required to be occupied outside the 'Limit of Shunt' indicator.

The Train Out of Section could be sent as soon as a train with tail-lamp attached had passed the signal box.

Platform The Regulations for Train Signalling by Recording Instruments applied on the Up and Down Main Lines between Platform and Locomotive Yard signal boxes. Platform No 4 Line could be used in both directions; facing line working was also authorised on the Up and Down Main and Platform No 5 Line for shunting movements.

Locomotive Yard The Absolute Block Regulations applied between Locomotive Yard and South Points signal boxes on the Up and Down Doncaster and the Up and Down Leeds lines.

The Regulations for Train Signalling by Recording Instruments applied on the Up and Down Excursion Lines between Locomotive Yard and South Points signal boxes, also on the Up and Down Goods Lines between Locomotive Yard and North Junction signal boxes (so far as they were applicable where such instruments are not provided).

The Regulations for Train Signalling by Recording Instruments also applied on Platform No 14 Line, which was used in both directions. When a train was accepted the signalman at the advance box was required to pull over a release lever to free the appropriate signal at the rear box. If it was then necessary to allow a shunting movement to be made into Platform No 14 Line when it was already occupied a special bell code and plunger instrument was used:

	Beats on Bell
Call Attention	1
Release Required for Leeman Road SB Calling-On signal	2
Release required for Locomotive Yard SB Calling-On signal	3
Return Release	4

The Engine Line was only to be used in the Up Direction and only for trains not conveying passengers. Movements over the line between Leeman Road and Locomotive Yard signal boxes were arranged by telephone. Whenever any vehicle or vehicles were left on the Engine Line the shunter was required to advise the traffic regulator at Locomotive Yard signal box or the signalman at Leeman Road box; the signalman then had to place a clip on the lever controlling the protecting signal. The shunter also had to advise when vehicles were removed.

Unfortunately, as outlined above, an accident occurred on 30 August 1931 when a light engine collided with a passenger coach conveying a theatrical

Illustration 82. *Platform signal box: viewed from the concourse side. The base of the signal box is occupied by the bookstall and a footbridge has been erected at the south end. (NERA Collection NERA TS23)*

Illustration 83. *Platform signal box: viewed from the platform side, looking south through the station on 20 September 1937. By this date the footbridge has been moved a few feet further north and is now opposite the centre of Platform signal box. Closer to the camera, note the bracket supporting the signal gantry incorporates decorative cast-iron with the letters 'NER' prominent. The bracket has been extended to take four dolls instead of the original two; the weight is taken partially by a stay connected to the roof. (LNER / NERA Collection CE183-02)*

company travelling from Rhyl to Scarborough. Although the rules prohibited the use of the Engine Line by passenger trains, the company's officers had no objection to a loaded coach entering the line during shunting operations provided that it was removed forthwith. In this instance there was a misunderstanding between the two shunters and the signalmen involved.

The Train Out of Section could be sent for Down trains when advised by the groundsman at Holgate Bridge; when he was not on duty it could be sent as soon as a train with tail-lamp attached had passed the signal box.

Applicable at all of the above Signal Boxes

* In all cases signalmen were required to treat bay platform lines as occupied unless informed by the person-in-charge that the line was clear to the buffer stops.

* When shunting movements were being made by pilot engines and there was no tail-lamp on the rear vehicle, signalmen were required to satisfy themselves that the line was clear before sending the Train Out of Section bell signal.

* When a pilot engine went behind a train to attach, detach or perform shunting operations within sight of the signalmen at Platform, Waterworks or Locomotive Yard signal boxes (except Platform No 14 Line) it was not necessary for that engine to be signalled to the box in advance.

* Pilot engines with or without vehicles, loaded or empty, were all signalled as '1 - 1 - 1'.

Renaming of Signal Boxes

In October 1938: Poppleton Junction was renamed Skelton; Severus Junction (post-Grouping, 'Severus' on the LNER standard signal box nameboard and in such as the 1927 Working Time Table) was renamed York Yard North; North Junction was renamed York Yard South. However, 'old habits die hard'. The names of locations had been passed down from one generation to the next, and many railwaymen had long memories so it was not uncommon even in the 1960s and 1970s to hear railwaymen refer to Severus and even South View as locations.

Chapter 10 : Extending the Station – 1938

Throughout 1938 and 1939, preparations were being made for installation of a single power box planned to control all of the passenger lines in the area. Working the station with so many signal boxes had almost inevitably caused problems; for example, in 1924 the following instruction had been issued to the signalmen at Clifton signal box:

> We are often experiencing difficulty in the station owing to not being aware of the approach of certain express trains from the North, with the result that the possible chance of diverting the train to another platform without causing delay has been lost. Therefore, on all busy Saturdays, Platform SB should be well informed as express trains approach your box from the North.(1)

Westinghouse proposed installation of a Style L miniature power frame as an option, but Nock (2) states that experience with that type of frame at Darlington South convinced the LNER to install an OCS panel at York. A contract had been placed with Westinghouse before the outbreak of the Second World War. If war had not broken out in 1939, it was more than likely that this new box would have been commissioned in the period 1940 - 1942. Indeed, the new signal box at Northallerton controlling an important part of the ECML actually opened on the day that war was declared – 3 September 1939. Further examples of the preparatory works follow.

Leeman Road

In March 1938 alterations were made at the north end of Platform No 14, bringing into use a new line on the Down side of a new island platform, terminating in an engine siding between the Goods line and Platform No 14; this line was named Engine Line No 2, the previous Engine Line becoming Engine Line No 1.(3)

Locomotive Yard Signal Box

Platform No 15 was brought into use on 2 April 1938 with connections to and from Up and Down Leeds lines; this was track circuited throughout between Leeman Road and Locomotive Yard.

Platform No 14 was temporarily out of use for rebuilding as a permanent structure. At this stage, Platform No 16 was worked as a bay platform from the north end only.(4)

York Station Platform Re-numbering

On and from 12:1 am on Monday 26 September, the platforms at York station were renumbered as follows:

1894 Number		1938 Number
1	Up side, south end Bay	1
2	Up side, south end Bay	2
3	Up side, south end Bay	3
4	Up side, Main Through	8
5	Down side, Main Through	9
6	Down side, south end Bay	10
7	Down side, south end Bay	11
8	Down side, north end Bay	13
9	Down side, north end Bay	12
10	Up side, north end Bay	7
11	Up side, north end Bay	6
12	Up side, north end Bay	5
13	Up side, north end Bay	4
-	Down side, Through (New in 1900)	14
-	Down side Island (New in 1938)	15
-	Down side Island (New in 1938)	16

(1) Letter from York SM Office, 21 August 1924.
(2) OS Nock, *British Railway Signalling*, page 113.
(3) LNER WON No. 7 - 12 / 13 March 1938.
(4) LNER Supplementary Notice No. 9, 2 to 6 April 1938.

Illustrations 84 and 85. *York Power Signal Box: these photographs show the box under construction before the outbreak of war in August 1939. The operating floor, at the south end, was small compared with the massive relay room that was required at that time. (LNER / NERA Collection CE124 and CE123)*

Clifton Signal Box

In the period Saturday 22 to Monday 24 October 1938, preparatory alterations were also made to the layout at Clifton which was simplified and route indicators were installed such that many of the signals could be dispensed with.

New Signal Box at the Waterworks Crossing

Waterworks crossing was redesigned so that two passenger lines crossed the main lines south of the box to connect the Scarborough lines to those west of the station; the goods lines continued to pass on the north side of the signal box. Consequently, at 11 pm on Saturday, 19 November 1938 all signals and most of the release levers at the existing Waterworks signal box were disconnected.

The new Waterworks signal box was available for control of traffic at 6 am on Sunday, 20 November 1938, located just 27 yards north of its predecessor; it was fitted with a 110-lever frame, positioned at the back of the signal box, and extensive track circuiting was installed. It was intended that this new signal box should only be a temporary measure but, in the event, it remained in use for almost 13 years; the old Waterworks box had to be demolished to enable the redesigned Scarborough line crossings to be installed.(1)

Leeman Road, Waterworks, Clifton

An additional island platform was built to the west of Platform No 14; this became Platform Nos 15 and 16. New Station Lines W and X gave access from the north to Platforms 14, 15 and 16 (used as a bay). The Up and Down station lines (leading to Platform Nos 12 and 13) were renamed Up Station Line Z and Down Station Line Y respectively. At the same time, the new Waterworks crossing was brought into use to connect the Scarborough lines to and from Platforms Nos 14, 15 and 16, also to the Goods Yards as described above.

LNER Supplementary Notice No 6 included an explanation of how subsidiary signals should be read:

All subsidiary signals exhibited WITHOUT A ROUTE INDICATOR, whether under a running signal or elsewhere, authorise movements at 'Caution' only as far as the line is clear towards the next signal whether the latter is a subsidiary or a running signal. When a subsidiary signal is exhibited under a running signal together WITH A ROUTE INDICATION all intervening subsidiary signal ahead (where provided) will be at 'Proceed', but the line immediately in rear of the next running signal ahead, or platform line as the case may be, will be occupied at the time the signal is exhibited, but the intervening section of the line will be clear.(2)

(1) LNER (NE Area) Programme No. 27 (12 to 25 November 1938.
(2) LNER Supplementary Notice No 6 (3 to 9 March 1939.

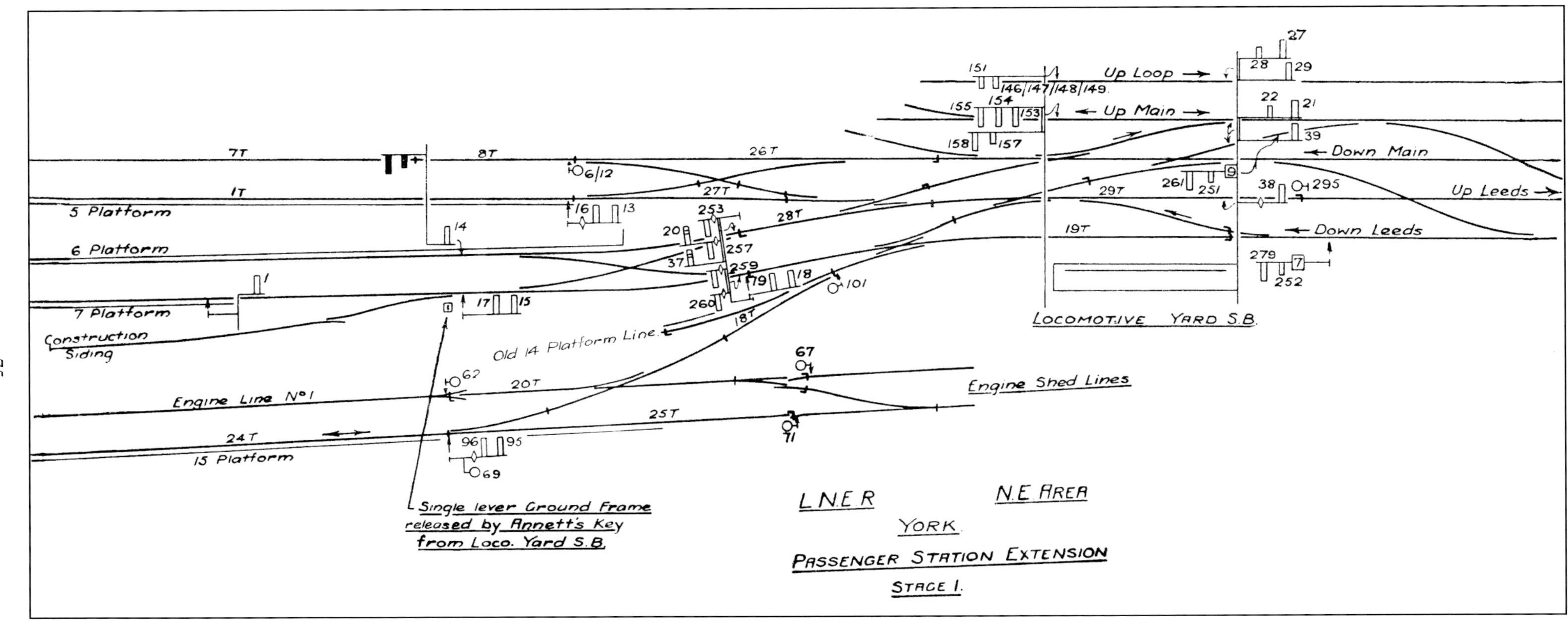

Illustration 86. *York Locomotive Yard, April 1938: this was the first stage in a further extension of the station by the addition of platforms on the west side. An additional island platform was constructed to the west of Platform 14 to be known as Platform 15; Platform 16, at the opposite side of Platform 15, was brought into use as a temporary bay platform accessible only from the north end at this stage. At the north end of the station, alterations were also being made at Waterworks signal box including a new crossing; see also Illustrations 87 and 90. (LNER (NE Area) Supplementary Notice of Signalling Arrangements dated 2nd to 6th April 1938)*

__Illustration 87.__ (Right) Taken at the south end of York station, this view shows the new Platforms 15 and 16 under construction in 1938. (Mick Nicholson Collection)

__Illustration 88.__ (Below right) An undated view of the interior of Locomotive Yard signal box at about the start of the Second World War. A number of spare levers have been removed and track circuits have been installed. The lever at the front of the photograph is in the reverse position and it will be noticed that the top half has white tape affixed; this was a trick employed by many signalmen, especially in boxes with large frames, so that they could look along the levers and check immediately whether that lever was correctly set for a route. (NRM Collection)

__Illustration 89.__ (Below) A derailment at Waterworks Crossing in 1938; exceptionally, this shows both the corner of the original signal box on the right and new Waterworks signal box in the middle background. (NERA RW Taylor Collection, NERA.063)

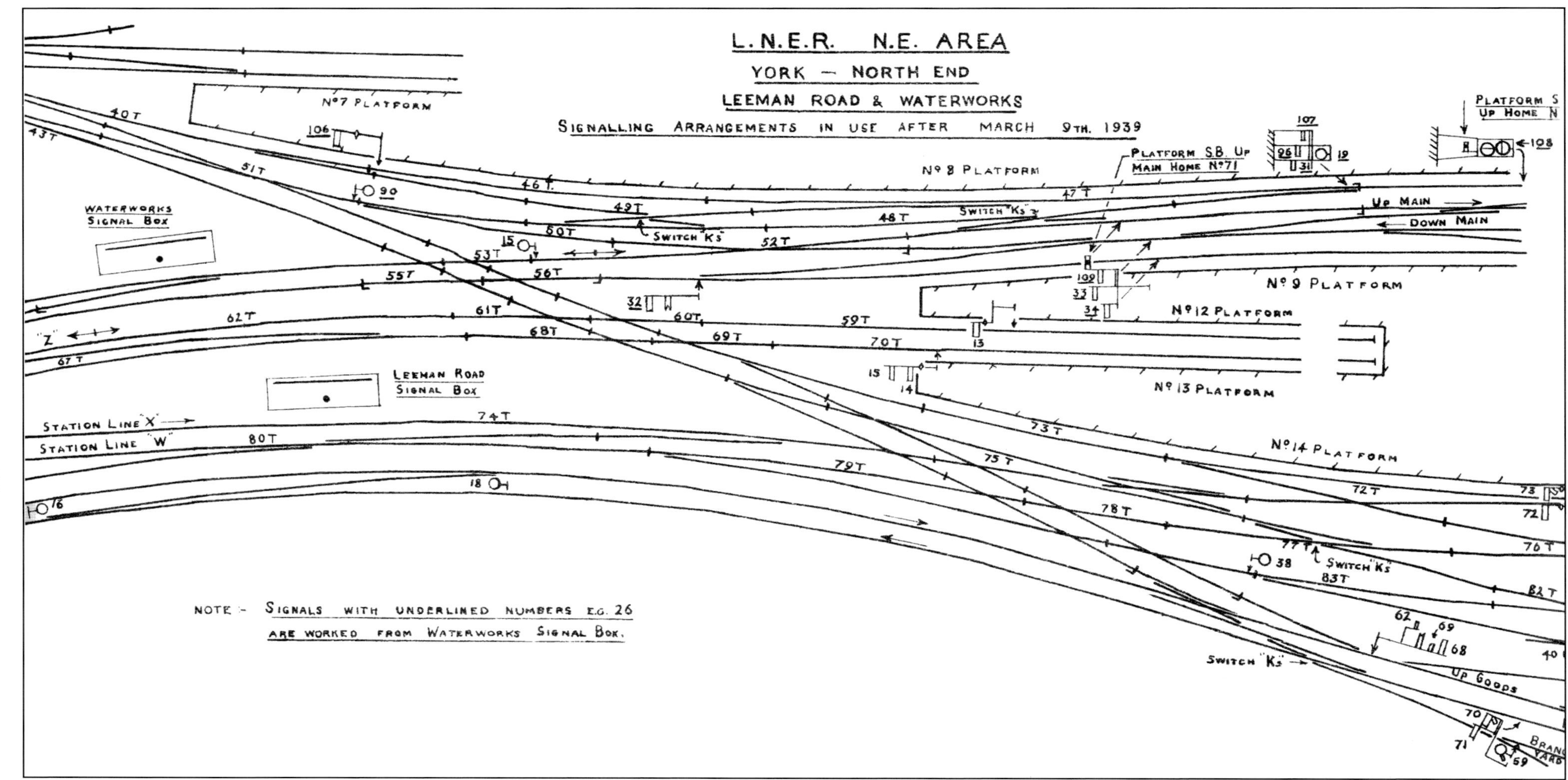

Illustration 90. *York Waterworks and Leeman Road: as referred to in Illustration 86, an additional island platform was constructed to the west of Platform 14 to be known as Platform 15; Platform 16, at the opposite side of Platform 15, was brought into use as a temporary bay platform accessible only from the north end at this stage. At the north end of the station, alterations were also being made at Waterworks signal box where new Station Lines W and X gave access from the north to Platforms 14, 15 and 16. The Up and Down station lines (leading to Platform Nos 12 and 13) were renamed Up Station Line Z and Down Station Line Y respectively. At the same time, the new Waterworks crossing was brought into use to connect the Scarborough lines to and from Platforms Nos 14, 15 and 16, also to the Goods Yards. (LNER (NE Area) Supplementary Notice of Signalling Arrangements dated 3rd to 9th March 1939)*

Chapter 11
Impact of the Second World War – 1939 and Beyond

Precautions

Although the colour-light signalling installed by the LNER north from Skelton in the 1930s was a great help to locomotive crews, especially during fog which was common across the Vale of York, it was recognised that it created two vulnerabilities.

Firstly, there were just four main lengths of cable between York and Darlington supplying current direct from the electricity undertakings to signalling equipment including signals, points, track circuits, controls *etc*. In case any of these supplies were lost, emergency generating machinery was provided in each of the areas, but if the cables were damaged special signalling arrangements were prepared: if telephones were available then Block Regulation 25(a)iii would apply except that an over-run of 440 yards need not be maintained, but a train must not be allowed to leave the box in rear until the preceding train had passed the handsignalman and was continuing its journey. However, if telephones were not available then time interval working (Regulation 25(a)iv) would apply. To shorten the sections, the signal boxes at Beningbrough, Tollerton, Raskelf, Pilmoor and Otterington would be opened when necessary. Furthermore, Temporary Block Posts could be provided at Skelton Bridge (in a temporary hut on the Down side south of the bridge) but also at Sessay (in the station master's office on the platform) and in the old signal boxes at Wiske Moor, Danby Wiske, Cowton, Croft Spa and Croft.(1)

Secondly, it was anticipated that the colour-light signals could act as navigation lights by enemy aircraft so switches were provided in signal boxes for the purpose of reducing the intensity of these signals to approximately the same power as oil signal lamps. Signalmen were instructed that 'they must operate these switches at the commencement of the blackout period, and restore them to full intensity at its termination, except that full intensity may be maintained during fog or falling snow.'(2)

Traffic Levels

By way of introduction to this period, Major Wilson from the Ministry of War Transport commented about a journey he made from Northallerton to York on the afternoon of Thursday 6 November 1941:

> Occupation of the lines by freight trains was remarkable; we passed no less than 17 Down and 14 Up freight trains in the 28 miles between Northallerton and Skelton signal box. Between Thirsk and Northallerton there was a freight train standing on the Down Slow line at every colour light signal (9 in all) waiting for an express on the Down Fast line to clear the outlet from the Slow line at Northallerton. Over this distance I also noted 5 freight trains on the Up Slow and 2 in the Thirsk Up Yard Reception Sidings. There is thus considerable congestion in both directions…It is obvious that the necessity for relief is urgent.

Major Wilson correctly identified that one of the main problem arose at Skelton Bridge where the Independent lines joined the Main lines to pass over the bridge which could only accommodate two tracks; furthermore, the four lines north and south of the river were (and are) are in different order on the formation: south of the river the lines were paired Down and Up Independent, Down and Up Main, whereas north of the river they were paired Down Slow and Down Fast, Up Fast and Up Slow.

Before the outbreak of the Second World War, the LNER had planned to construct a modernised marshalling yard at York; they had concluded that an additional bridge would be required for Down traffic (heading north) but for Up traffic this was not practicable without constructing an elaborate fly-over junction. Nevertheless, the following works formed the nucleus of a much grander proposal, even though that may have to be considered as a post-war project.(3)

Skelton

At 5 pm on Sunday 8 June 1941 a new signal box was brought into use immediately north of the old box which had closed at 5 am that morning. Colour-light signalling replaced the semaphores, with track circuited running lines throughout; at Skelton Bridge the points were motor operated; the ground frame was retained to work the mains crossover, but elsewhere points remained mechanical, worked from a new 75-lever frame at the back of the box.(4)

The new box was part inspected on 14 November 1941 (in connection with the new Up Independent Clifton Loop – see below) and, to quote Major Wilson:

> The box was constructed recently when the colour light signalling from Northallerton was extended southwards, and will eventually form part of the extensive York Resignalling Scheme, now in abeyance for the duration of the war. This is a fine new brick and concrete signal box which has been built to ARP standards. It is commodious and well arranged.

South of Skelton signal box the connection from the Up Main to the York City Waterworks siding was worked by 2-lever ground frame, electrically released from the signal box.

(1) L&NER (NE Area) Notice No.19 dated 14 to 27 September 1940.
(2) L&NER (NE Area) Notice No.19 dated 1 to 14 February 1941.
(3) TNA: MT 6/2752.
(4) LNER (NE Area) Programme No. 12 dated 6 to 8 June 1941.

Illustration 91. *Skelton signal box: built to meet ARP requirements, the signal box had few windows as built but in later years more were installed at operating floor level as seen here. The large relay room is located alongside. In the right background, the large white building is the filter house at York water works. (Richard Pulleyn)*

Illustration 92. *Skelton Junction: this August 1960 view looks north from the Up side where the junction to and from Harrogate meets the ECML. The impressive rodding run is evidence that the points towards York Yard North are all mechanically operated. (John F Mallon / Joint NERA - Ken Hoole Study Centre Collection, JFM_3260)*

Skelton to Clifton

Owing to congestion in the Up Goods Yard it had become increasingly necessary to find paths through York station for Up freight trains; consequently, as part of a programme of new works (on Ministry of War Transport account) to facilitate wartime traffic between Glasgow – Edinburgh – York – London, an Up Independent line from Skelton to Clifton (known as the Clifton Loop) was completed in August 1941 and brought into use in mid-September 1941. At approximately 875 yards long, it could hold two freight trains to await a path through the station; train crews could also be relieved while trains were standing on the Independent outside the engine shed, and any defective wagons could be shunted off into adjacent sidings. The facing connection from the Up Main was located opposite York Yard North signal box but worked by motor from Skelton Junction signal box; the trailing connection at the south end was worked from Clifton signal box. These works were finally inspected on 6 November 1941 and recommended for approval by Major Wilson.(1)

Skelton Bridge

An improvement for traffic on the Down line was approved by the Treasury on 20 June 1941; this consisted of an additional single line bridge over the River Ouse thereby reducing congestion in York yards by enabling freight trains to leave more freely whilst keeping traffic clear of the Fast line. The new line was approximately 560 yards long; unworked spring points provided a trailing connection with the Down Slow. The new bridge was built about 50 feet upstream from the masonry arch bridge carrying the main lines, in order to lessen the risk of both bridges being damaged by a single bomb in the event of enemy attack. The bridge and connections were finally brought into use on 18 October 1942 worked from Skelton signal box. See Illustration 94.

Harrogate Branch

The resignalling at Skelton also impacted on the Harrogate Branch. Nether Poppleton gate box had previously controlled its own signals on both the Up

(1) TNA: MT 29/94 and TNA: MT 6/2752.

and Down lines; as part of the resignalling, it retained its own signals on the Down line, but a new Up starting signal for Poppleton station replaced Nether Poppleton's signals on the Up line and the gate box became electrically released from Poppleton for that line only. The gates remained hand worked with key-locks and the 5-lever ground frame located in the crossing signal box was retained.

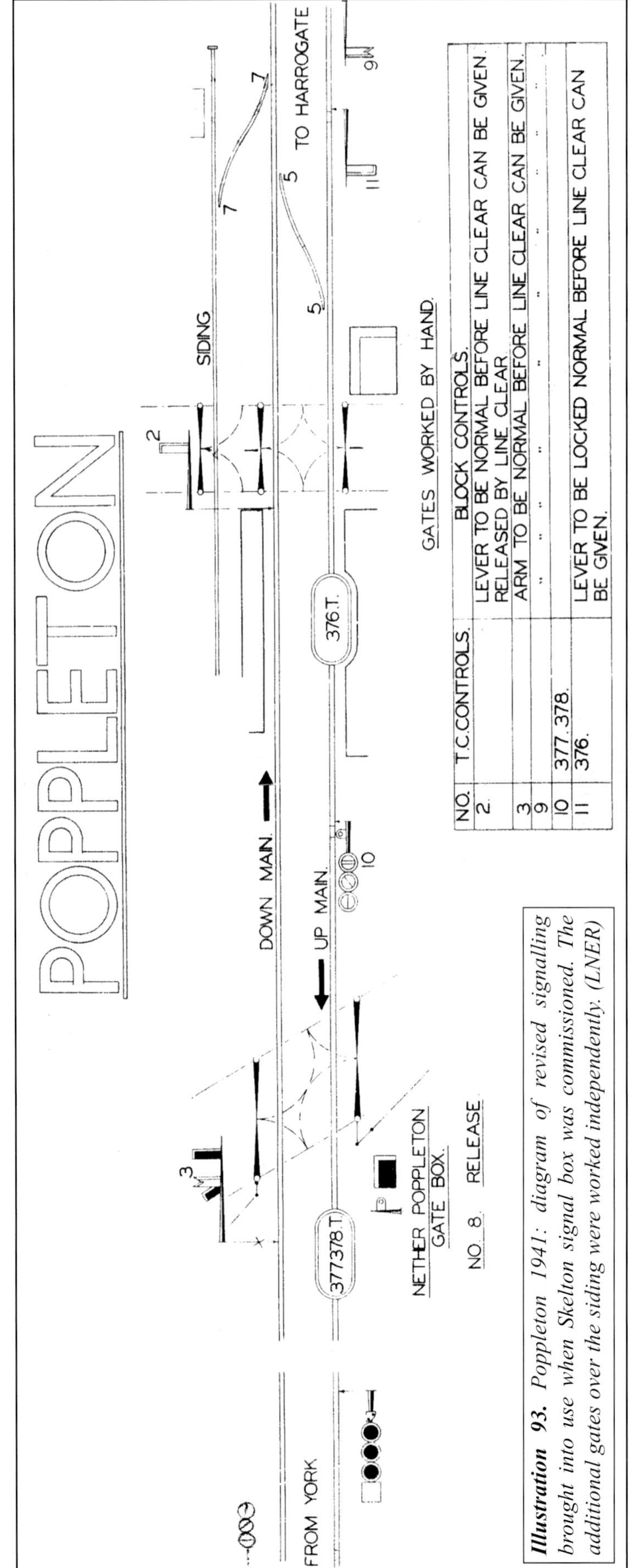

Illustration 93. *Poppleton 1941: diagram of revised signalling brought into use when Skelton signal box was commissioned. The additional gates over the siding were worked independently. (LNER)*

At Poppleton station signal box, the 8-lever frame was replaced by an 11-lever McK&H frame. The Down line continued to be worked by Absolute Block, but Track Circuit Block applied on the Up line towards Skelton signal box. At that time, there were four gates at the level crossing, two on either side, which worked sympathetically by rods under the crossing, so the signalman only had to move one gate and the others followed.

Skelton Yard

As part of the extensive works designed to supplement existing facilities which by the summer and autumn of 1941 had become inadequate to handle the heavy increases in war time traffic, a submission was made to the Treasury for finance in connection with the proposed installation of reception and departure sidings between Skelton Junction and Skelton Bridge:

> To avoid the occupation of running lines by trains waiting to enter the marshalling yard which now occurs, and to make their engines available for a return trip as soon as possible after their arrival with an Up train. For this purpose, a turntable is to be provided adjacent to the new sidings. It is proposed to provide a group of 6 additional Up Reception lines and 6 Down Departure lines. This will form the nucleus of a modernised marshalling yard which the Company intend to construct after the war as part of a scheme of general improvements at York. The cost is estimated at £60,000; about 8 acres of additional land will be required to be purchased by the Company, works expected to take about 7 months to complete.

Illustration 94 is extracted from a sketch submitted in connection with proposals submitted in January 1942 for a New Yard at Skelton; this includes the new bridge for the Down Independent and (in dotted lines) the possible future flyover at Skelton Bridge.(1)

Built on the west side of the ECML, immediately north of the junction with the Harrogate line at Skelton, the new sidings were not used for marshalling but acted as a reservoir to clear the running lines and to feed the York marshalling yards from the north; they also acted as a departure yard for north-bound traffic. Traffic between the new yard and York yards was worked by trips as required.

(1) TNA: MT 29/94.

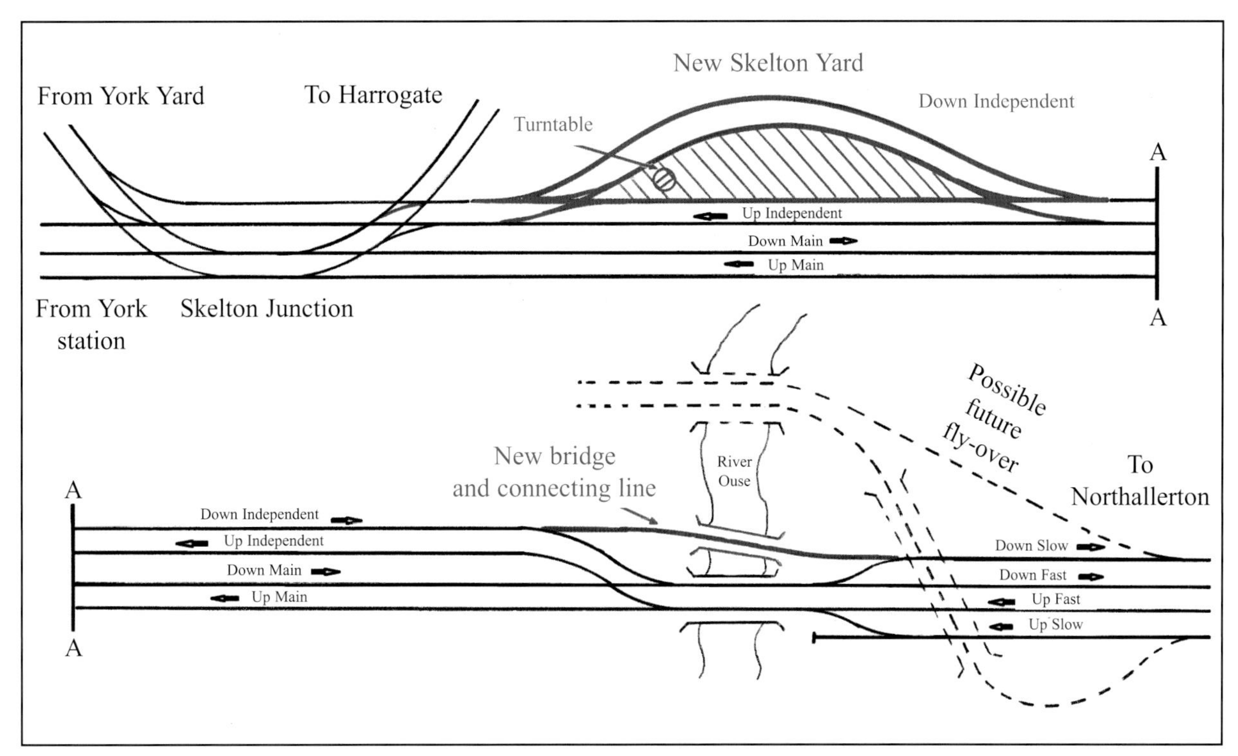

Illustration 94. *Skelton, 1942: wartime works. (Richard Pulleyn Collection)*

The new yard became operational in October 1942. Formed from a group of six looped sidings for each direction, each siding was capable of holding a 70-wagon train. Engine lines ran between the two groups of sidings, with a turntable and locomotive facilities at the south end. The Up Independent ran between the ECML and the yard; the Down Independent was diverted to run outside the yard on the west side. Connections at the south end of the yard were worked mechanically from Skelton signal box; those at the north end worked from switches on the panel integrated in the diagram above the lever frame, and from a new Skelton Yard ground frame at the north end of the yard, released from Skelton signal box and worked by the yard inspector.(1) See Illustrations 95 and 97.

An inspection of Skelton New Sidings (as they became known) took place on 19 August 1943 when Major Wilson also further inspected the signal box, both of which were recommended for approval. After installation of the new sidings, the 75-lever frame had eight spare levers but an additional 17 switches were mounted on the panel diagram to work signalling in the Skelton Bridge area.(2)

York Air-Raid:

During the early hours of Wednesday 29 April 1942, an air-raid took place across and around this part of the city when the station and yards were heavily bombed.

One of the high-explosive bombs fell close to Skelton signal box blocking the Up and Down Main goods lines in the York Yard North section, the Up and Down Main lines in the Clifton section, and the Up and Down Branch (Harrogate) lines. Yard Foreman Albert Cade and a colleague were on duty as fire watchers near the yard master's office (alongside York Yard South signal box) when they received a call from York Yard North signal box asking them to help extinguish incendiaries. Cade made his way through the yard and just beyond No 1 Down Goods he had to deal with many of these bombs which were falling all around. He then continued towards Skelton where wagons on the Down Departure lines were burning. Subsequently, he was given a 'Merit Award' for his actions in the midst of the raid.

Further towards the station, Clifton sidings (both Up and Down), Leeman Road Shops, the Central Store and Branches Yard were all out of action, and over 50 locomotives were trapped in the North Shed area. At the station itself, Platform Nos 1, 2 and 3 were badly damaged, as were many of the administrative offices, and a large part of the station roof had been destroyed by incendiary bombs. A train standing in Platform No 9 was damaged by explosions and then gutted by fire, some passengers making their way to Locomotive Yard signal box where they were given tea and their wounds temporarily dressed.

Meanwhile, Albert Simpson was on duty as a signalman at Leeman Road signal box when it was badly damaged by a bomb blast; he managed to get away from the signal box and went on foot to examine the line towards Clifton. Finding that it was possible for a train to pass, he then worked with a driver and fireman to remove a train of 20 vehicles from Platform No 15, extinguishing the flames as they passed. He then returned to his box and tried to set the route to allow an empty coal train from Platform No 15, but the points could not be moved so he worked his way along the train putting out fires. He too gained a 'Merit Award' in recognition of his efforts.

(1) LNER (NE Area) Programme No. 23, 24 October to 6 November 1942.
(2) TNA: MT 29/94.

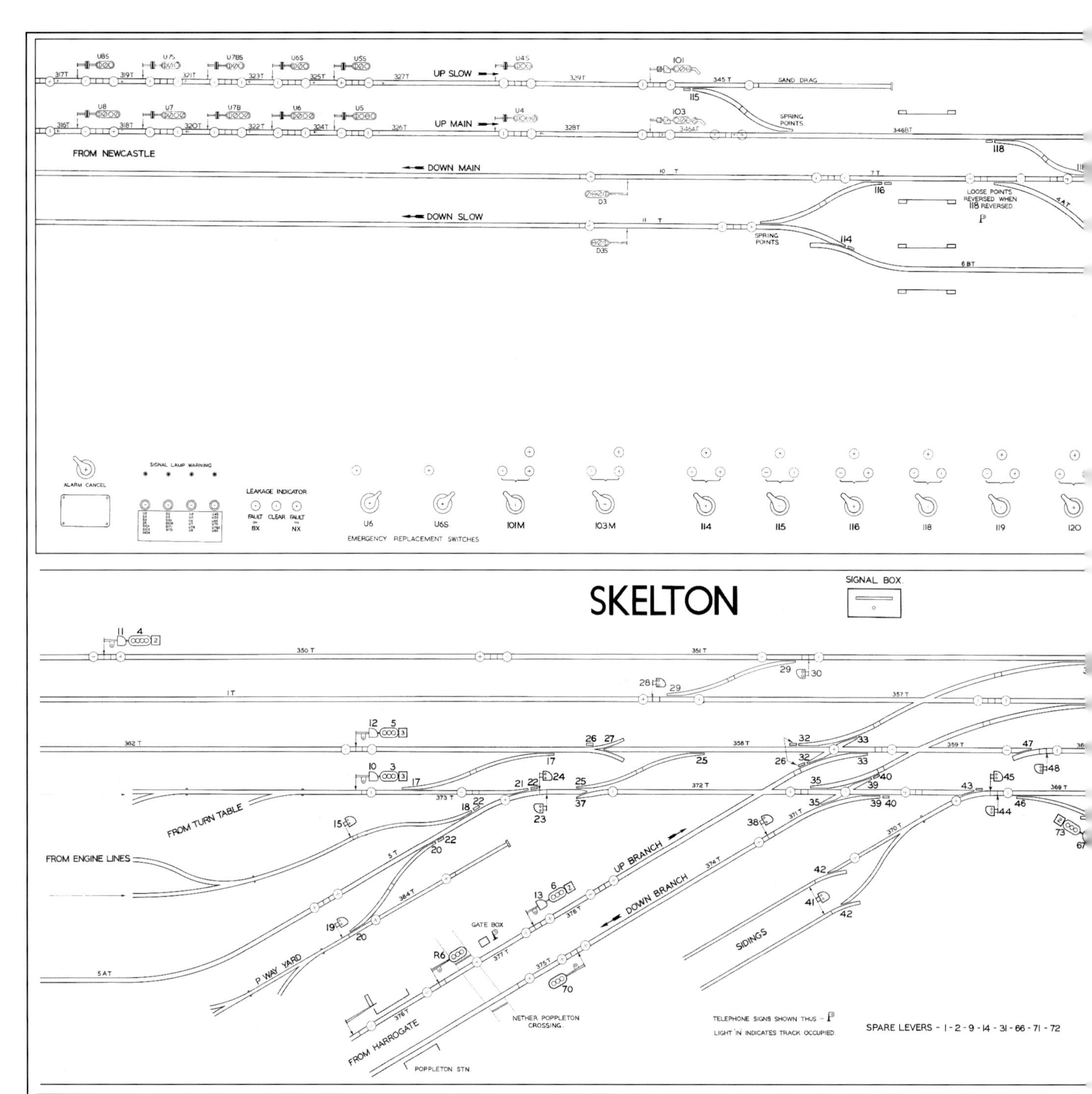

Illustration 95. *Skelton: a representation of the actual diagram in the signal box after Skelton New Sidings opened in 1942, togther the switch panel at the north end working the connections at Skelton Bridge and the north end of Skelton Yard. (LNER)*

Platform signal box was badly affected with broken windows, damage to doors, furniture and fittings *etc*; signal and point connections and track circuits were all out of order. As mentioned above, Leeman Road box was severely damaged and Waterworks less so, but telephone, telegraph and block wires were destroyed over much of the area. At Skelton a 660 volt main cable was severed by debris; signalling location boxes and other equipment was put out of action. Within four days, however, block working was fully restored and all semaphore signalling was back in action. Since the Control telephone circuits to the north were out of action, temporary Control Offices were set up at Beningbrough station and at Bilton Junction (north of Harrogate).(1)

It is sobering to think what might have happened had the York re-signalling been completed and York power signal box had been hit. A few miles further north, the power box at Northallerton had been commissioned on 3 September 1939, the day that war broke out.

Dringhouses

During the war a government cold store was built adjacent to Dringhouses Down Reception Sidings, from which a rail connection was made at the north end towards South Points signal box. See Illustration 152.

(1) *Back Track*, August 2000.

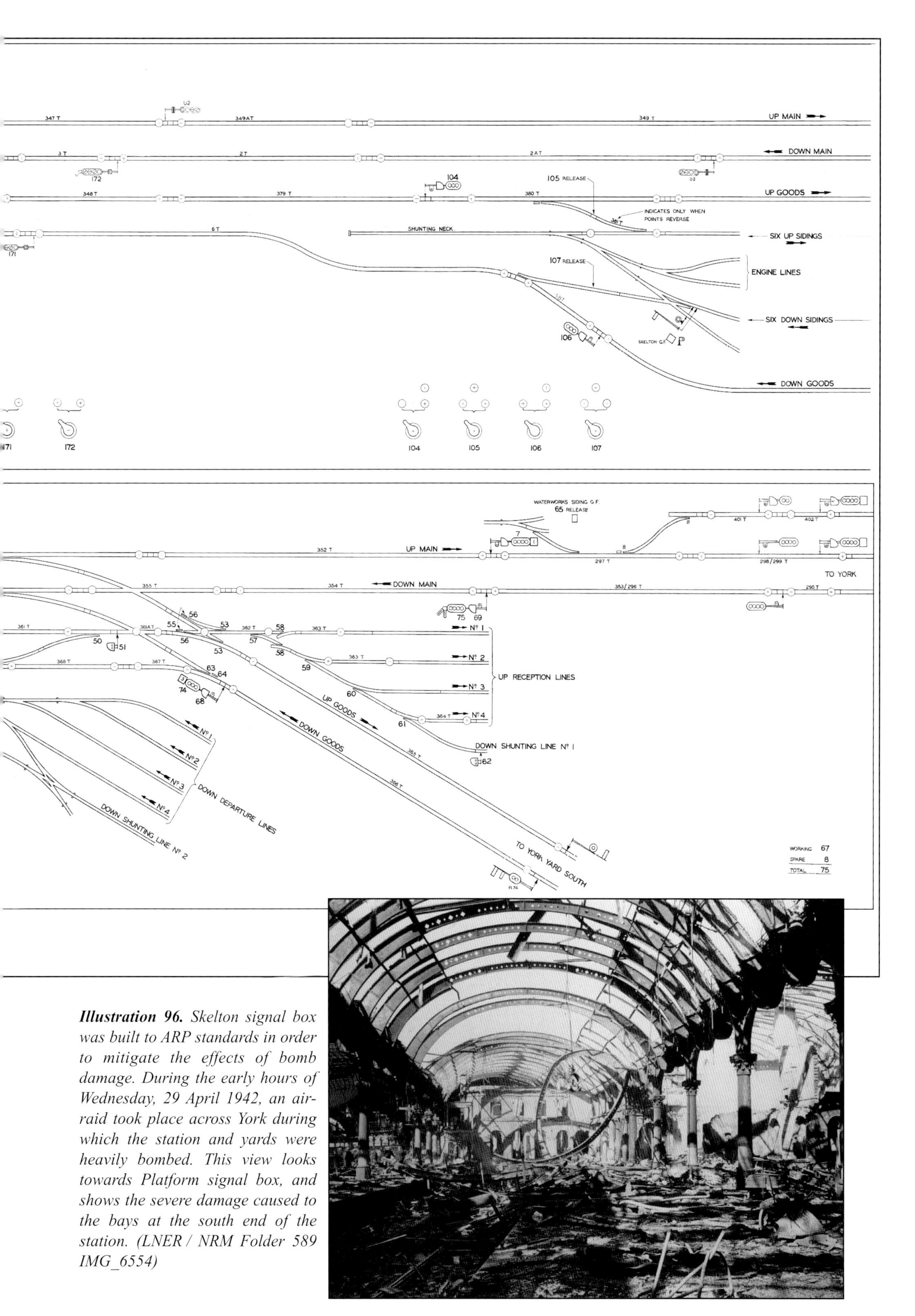

Illustration 96. *Skelton signal box was built to ARP standards in order to mitigate the effects of bomb damage. During the early hours of Wednesday, 29 April 1942, an air-raid took place across York during which the station and yards were heavily bombed. This view looks towards Platform signal box, and shows the severe damage caused to the bays at the south end of the station. (LNER / NRM Folder 589 IMG_6554)*

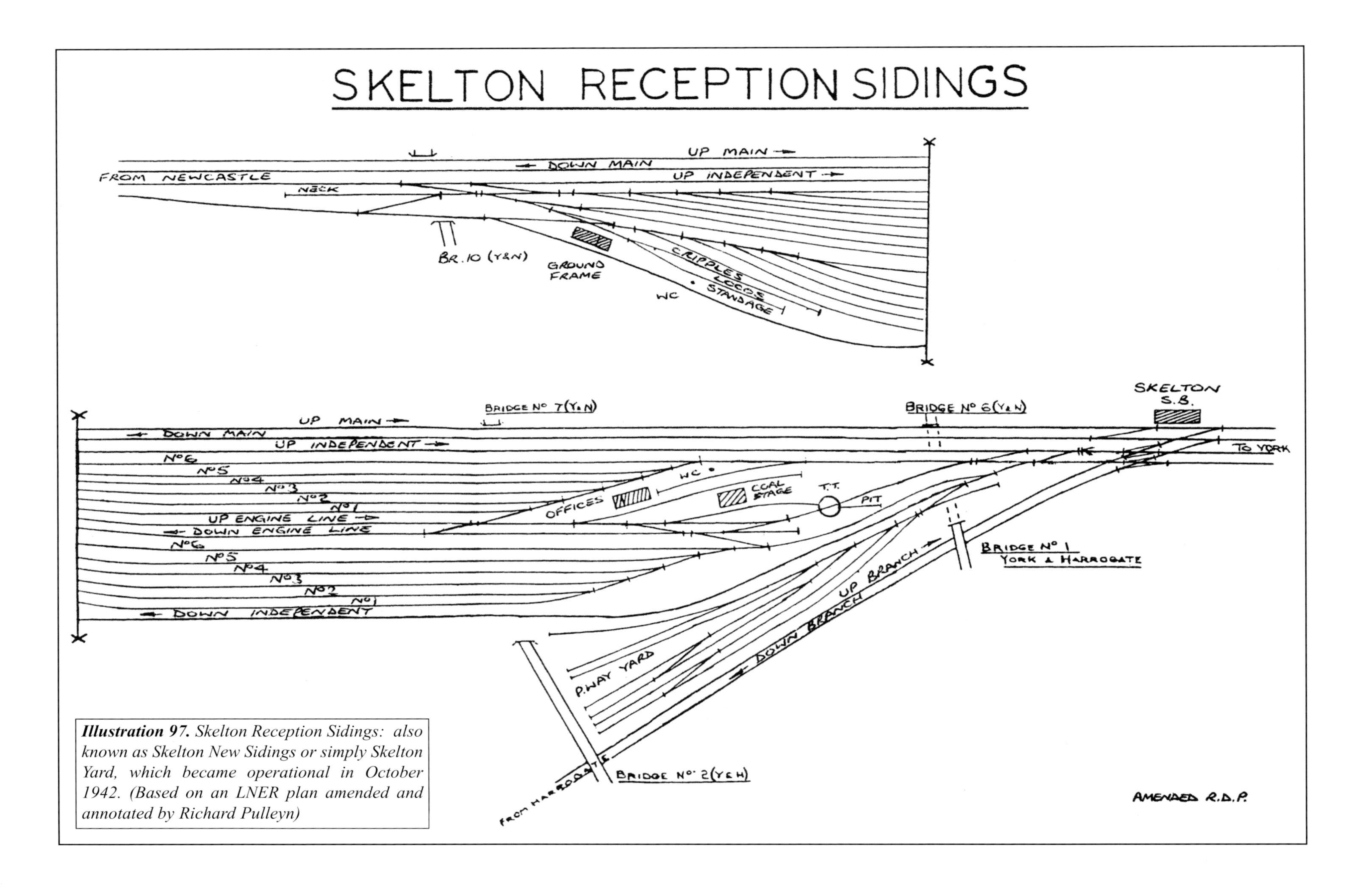

Illustration 97. *Skelton Reception Sidings: also known as Skelton New Sidings or simply Skelton Yard, which became operational in October 1942. (Based on an LNER plan amended and annotated by Richard Pulleyn)*

Chapter 12 : Major Resignalling Scheme – 1946 to 1951

Although the Second World War came to a close in 1945, it was not until the following year that the LNER and Westinghouse were able to recommence work on the York Resignalling scheme. Initially, that work was limited to track circuiting all running lines and converting mechanical points to power operation, both of which greatly facilitated transfer to the power box.

From the outset York power signal box (PSB) was simply referred to as 'York Box' so that term will be used below.

York New Signalling 1951

Introduction of the new colour-light signalling was undertaken in three stages by Westinghouse, working alongside former LNER S&T Staff who had become BR S&T Staff on 1 January 1948:

Stage 1 Sunday, 8 April 1951 – Closing of Chaloners Whin and South Points signal boxes and transfer of control to Outer South Panel of York Box. As a temporary measure, Locomotive Yard signal box worked to York Box by Absolute Block over the Down Leeds and Down Doncaster lines, and Permissive Block on the Down Holgate Excursion line. To the south, Naburn (towards Selby and Doncaster) and Copmanthorpe (towards Leeds and Normanton) became established as the fringe boxes.

Stage 2 Sunday / Monday, 20/21 May 1951 – Closing of Locomotive Yard, Platform, Leeman Road, Waterworks and Clifton signal boxess with transfer of control to York Box.

Both of the above stages being complete, York Box became fully operational at 11:59 pm Monday 20 May 1951.(1)

Stage 3 Sunday, 27 May 1951 – After demolition of Locomotive Yard signal box, laying in south end connections to Platform Nos 15 and 16 and provision of relevant signals could be completed.

The completed signalling was inspected by Lieutenant-Colonel Wilson and Brigadier Langley on 15 / 16 March and again on 5 / 6 December 1951. They stated in their report dated 22 January 1952 (2) that 'This is by far the largest route relay interlocking in the world.' The new signal box was located over Platform Nos 13 and 14, the main operating room and the relay room being at first floor level; it was over 200 feet long and about 40 feet wide. The signalmen were expected to work entirely from indications on the panel although there were small bay windows which provided a very limited outlook over parts of the station.

Illustration 98. *Waterworks and Leeman Road signal boxes: the view from the north end of the station circa 1950, with Leeman Road box on the left opposite the 'temporary' Waterworks box which finally lasted some 13 years. Note that the lower part of the timber-built Waterworks box has been encased in thick brickwork as a wartime precationary measure; Clifton signal box was treated in the same fashion. Note also that colour light signals have already been installed. (Richard Pulleyn Collection)*

Illustration 99. *Locomotive Yard signal box: immediately outside the signal box, work is underway to install altered connections to Platforms 15 and 16. (NERA Collection TS23_7)*

(1) BR (NE Operating Area) Circular O.3905.
(2) TNA: MT 29/58.

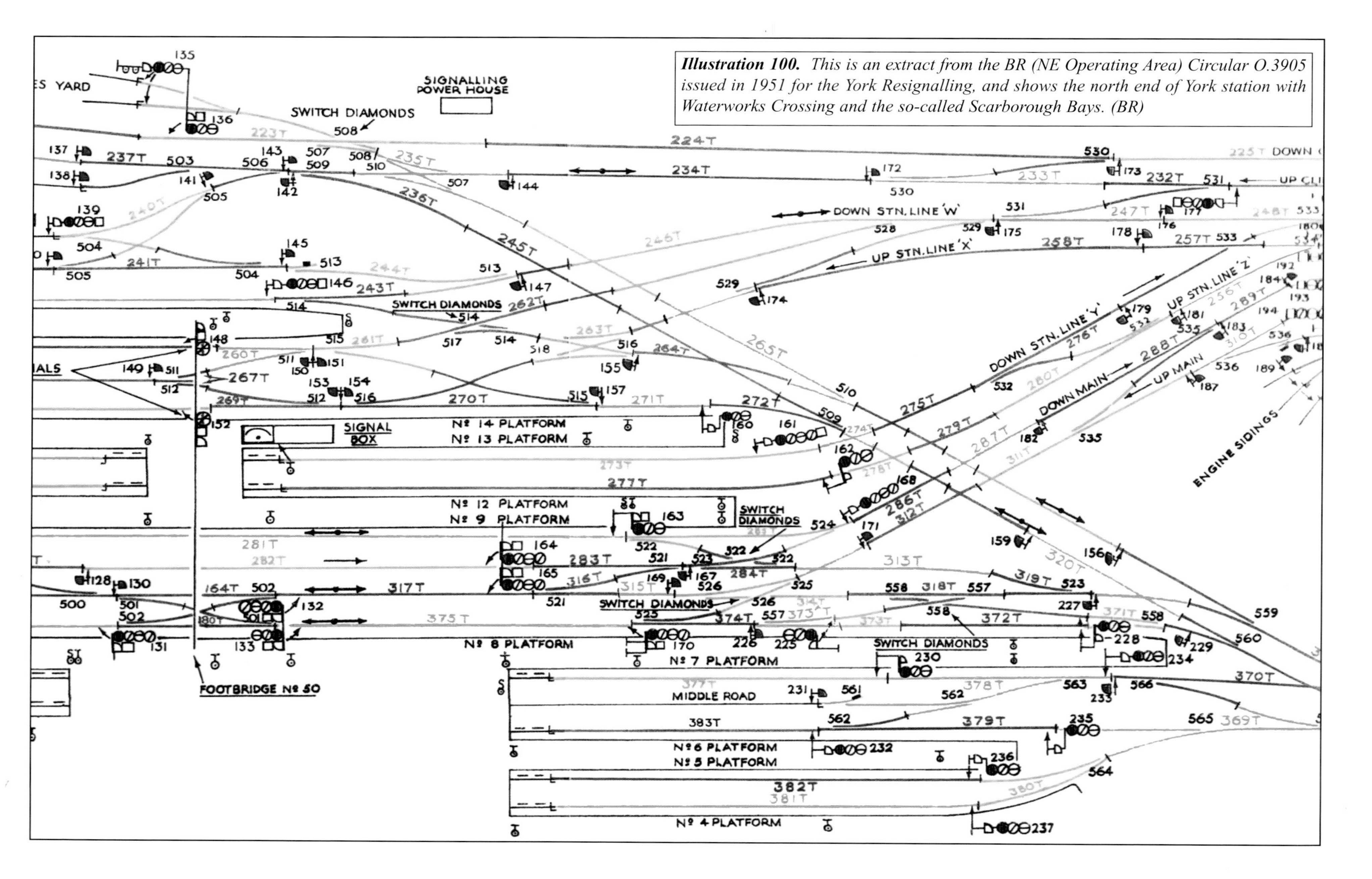

Illustration 100. *This is an extract from the BR (NE Operating Area) Circular O.3905 issued in 1951 for the York Resignalling, and shows the north end of York station with Waterworks Crossing and the so-called Scarborough Bays. (BR)*

The panel had four sections or 'facets', arranged in an arc, with a console below on which groups of turn buttons were mounted, together with signal post telephone connections and transmitting controls for the train describers. An Inspector (normally referred to as the Traffic Regulator) regulated traffic from a central desk, assisted alongside by a Desk Signalman who concentrated on telephone work but was also able to provide temporary relief to the Panel Signalmen for meal breaks *etc*. A public address system had first been installed in the mid-1930s when the station announcer was located in Platform signal box, so this was moved to a separate booth on the operating floor of the PSB.

On the console there were 827 'Route Setting' switches, all grouped according to the signal number; provided that the route was clear, operating these red switches set the points in the correct position, cleared intervening shunting signals, and then cleared the appropriate main running signal. The route was proved clear by a row of white lights indicated on the diagram then, as a train proceeded over the set route a row of red lights indicated occupation of the track circuits. When passed, signals were restored to danger automatically and, provided that the route switch had been returned to normal, the points in the route were then freed progressively and panel indications extinguished – a Westinghouse system known as 'Sectional Release Route Locking'. For shunting purposes, subsidiary signals were operated by white switches; 171 black switches were also provided for working points individually in case of need, for example for maintenance.

Illustration 101. *York Box: as seen in latter years showing its massive bulk, mostly comprising accommodation for the relay room. The small look-out porch was located at one corner of the operating floor, with staff facilities to the right. (ChristopherJ Woolstenholmes, CJW384 21)*

Illustration 102. *York Box: an overview of the station layout, this view was taken on 6 October 1962. (John M Boyes, Armstrong Railway Photographic Trust JMBT434)*

Illustration 103. *York Box: examples of the Route Setting switches on the One Control Switch panel at York, built and installed by Westinghouse Brake & Signal Company. Red switches set the main running routes, whereas the white switches operated subsidiary signals for shunting purposes. Above the Route Setting switches on this section of the panel are some of the black individual point operation switches which were normally set in the centre (Locked) position but could be operated left (Normal) or right (Reverse); the indicator lights show the position of the points as set. (British Railways / Richard Pulleyn Collection)*

The illuminated diagram was mounted on columns behind the control desk although an article in *Westinghouse Review* magazine shows that the original design would have had the illuminated diagram attached to the control desk, which was standard practice at that time for a Westinghouse 'One Control Switch' (OCS) installation, so it is believed that York was the first installation in what became the predominant style going forward. No explanation has been found for this design change, but presumably Westinghouse had decided to redesign their products during the Second World War and agreed the change with BR who had taken over from LNER by that date. It may be surmised, therefore, that if it had not been for the war the panel would have looked somewhat different.

Movements on the running lines to Naburn, Copmanthorpe, York Yard South and Skelton were advised in both directions by train describers mounted directly above the relevant section of the diagram: information displayed by stencil lights included class, destination and position by signal number This system was developed by STC (Standard Telephones and Cables Limited); one of the main features was that, not only did the describer indicate the order in which trains were approaching, but the indication then 'stepped up' as the train progressively operated the track circuits using the STC Polaridex System. Manual intervention allowed interposing of descriptions from one line to another or stepping up.

When a description was set up and transmitted it flashed at both the transmitting and receiving ends, and a buzzer sounded at the receiving end until the signalman there pressed an acknowledgement button. The class of train was displayed according to the train classification descriptions then in use (A, B, C1, C2, C3, D, E, F, G, and H), and both the Route and Destination were displayed as a code *e.g.* L for Leeds, N for North, NR for Normanton, YD for York Yard, SC for Scarborough; a full list is shown in Illustration 104. See also Illustrations 105 and 106.

Interpretation of Codes.	**Display Code.**
Class A	A
,, B	B
,, C1	C1
,, C2	C2
,, C3	C3
,, D	D
,, E	E
,, F	F
,, G	G
,, H	H
Spare	SP
Leeds	L
Normanton	NR
Doncaster	D
Harrogate	H
York Yard	YD
Terminating York Station	YK
York and North	YN
North	N
York and East	YE
East	E
Dringhouses Down Yard	DD
Holgate Sidings	HO
Clifton Loco.	CL
York and South	YS
York and West	YW
Dringhouses Up Yard	DU
Skelton	SK
Clifton Sidings	CS
South	S
West	W
Foss Islands	F
Hull	HL
Scarborough	SC
South Shed	SS

Illustration 104. *Codes used for the train describers linked to York Box. (BR / Richard Pulleyn Collection)*

A train describer was also in use on the Up Scarborough line, but the Down Scarborough line was worked by Absolute Block to Burton Lane signal box (or to Bootham when Burton Lane signal box was switched out). Shunting movements along the Up Scarborough line towards a Limit of Shunt board required permission from the signalman at Burton Lane; the York signalman sent the special bell signal '5 - 2' and, provided that no movement had been authorised towards York, a release lever at Burton Lane could be reversed (which controlled the relevant subsidiary signals at York) then the bell signal was acknowledged by repetition. After the shunting movement was completed, the York signalman sent the special bell signal '2 - 5', the release lever could be restored and the bell signal acknowledged again. See Illustration 135.

On the lines to and from York Yard South, the equivalent to Permissive Working on Track Circuit Block applied provided that none of the trains involved conveyed passengers.

External equipment included the following:

* 74 controlled running signals, with 53 route and junction indicators.
* 215 subsidiary signals (including 154 ground signals).
* Intensified lights fitted to semaphore signals reading towards the colour-light signalling.
* 330 point mechanisms – from Clifton to the north end of Dringhouses, points were electro-pneumatic; south to Chaloner Whin points were electrically operated using Style M3 Point Machines.
* 'Train Ready' platform signalling equipment was provided because of the length and curvature of the platforms.
* Electrical power was obtained from the BEA Generating Station at Foss Islands, with a back-up stand-by diesel alternator set available if required.
* Two air compressors (one in use and the other on stand-bay) were provided in the Power House (see diagram extract below), which cut in when the mains air pressure dropped to 55 psi or cut out when it reached 65 psi.

A 24-hour traffic count was undertaken on 13 December 1951 (when passenger traffic was at a low winter level) with the following results:

Train Movements	**Sub-Total**	**Total**
Through Passenger	98	
Terminating or Starting Passenger	237	
Total Passenger Trains		325
Through Freight	236	
Terminating or Starting Freight	83	
Total Freight Trains		319
Light Engine Moves	635	
Shunting Moves	877	
Grand Total		2156

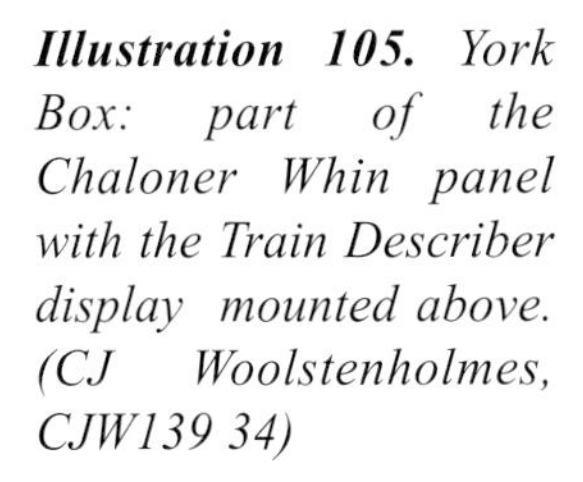

Illustration 105. *York Box: part of the Chaloner Whin panel with the Train Describer display mounted above. (CJ Woolstenholmes, CJW139 34)*

Illustration 106. *York Box: part of the panel showing the train describer set-up buttons. (CJ Woolstenholmes, CJW139 29)*

The north and south ends of the station were recorded separately, so a movement which passed over both was counted twice; however, shunt moves were counted by task, some of which required only one switch operation, but others which required up to as many as 10 operations.

At outlying locations such as Chaloner Whin junction, operating handles for working the points in case of failure, were located in lineside cabinets fitted with 'Hepper's Releases'; these were controlled from the panel by the signalman in York Box, enabling staff to obtain the handles when released.

Although Locomotive Yard, Waterworks, Leeman Road and Clifton signal boxes were all demolished, the operating floor of Platform signal box was retained in use for station staff, and known as the 'Inner Office' (as opposed to 'Outer Office' which was behind the Booking and Ticket Office) until it was later converted into a cafe. The ground floor of Platform signal box had been a bookstall for many years, latterly operated by WH Smiths and that continues in use in 2020.

Copmanthorpe

In preparation to become a fringe box to York, a new signal box was opened at Copmanthorpe on 12 November 1950; this was situated at Moor Lane level crossing, the new signal box replacing both Copmanthorpe station signal box and Copmanthorpe Moor gate box. This had 17 working and five spare levers, together with two sets of gates worked by separate 'involved' wheels – one each for the Leeds and Normanton lines.

Naburn and Bishopthorpe Lane

On 9 April 1951, in connection with the resignalling south of Chaloner Whin to the fringe box at Naburn, an electric release operated from the latter signal box was installed at Bishopthorpe Lane level crossing; however, attendance was withdrawn subsequently in November 1958.

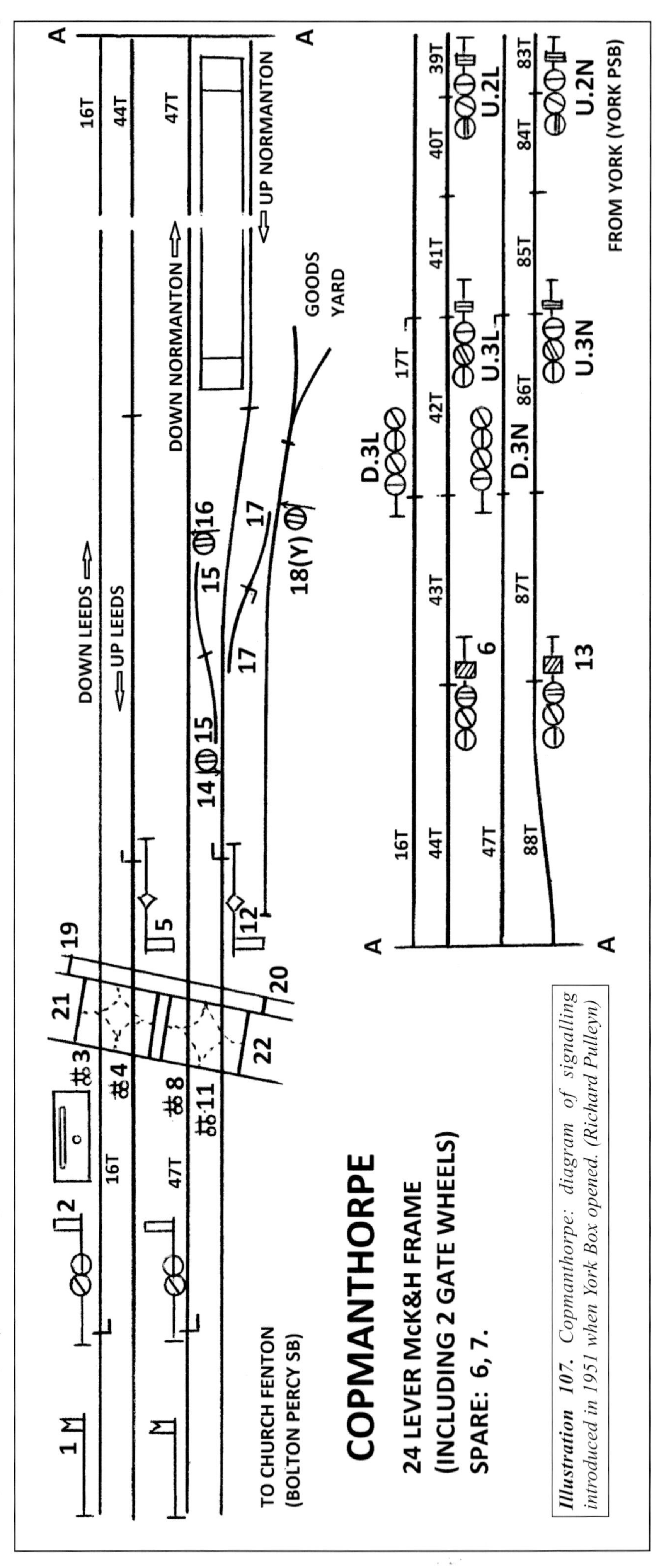

Illustration 107. Copmanthorpe: diagram of signalling introduced in 1951 when York Box opened. (Richard Pulleyn)

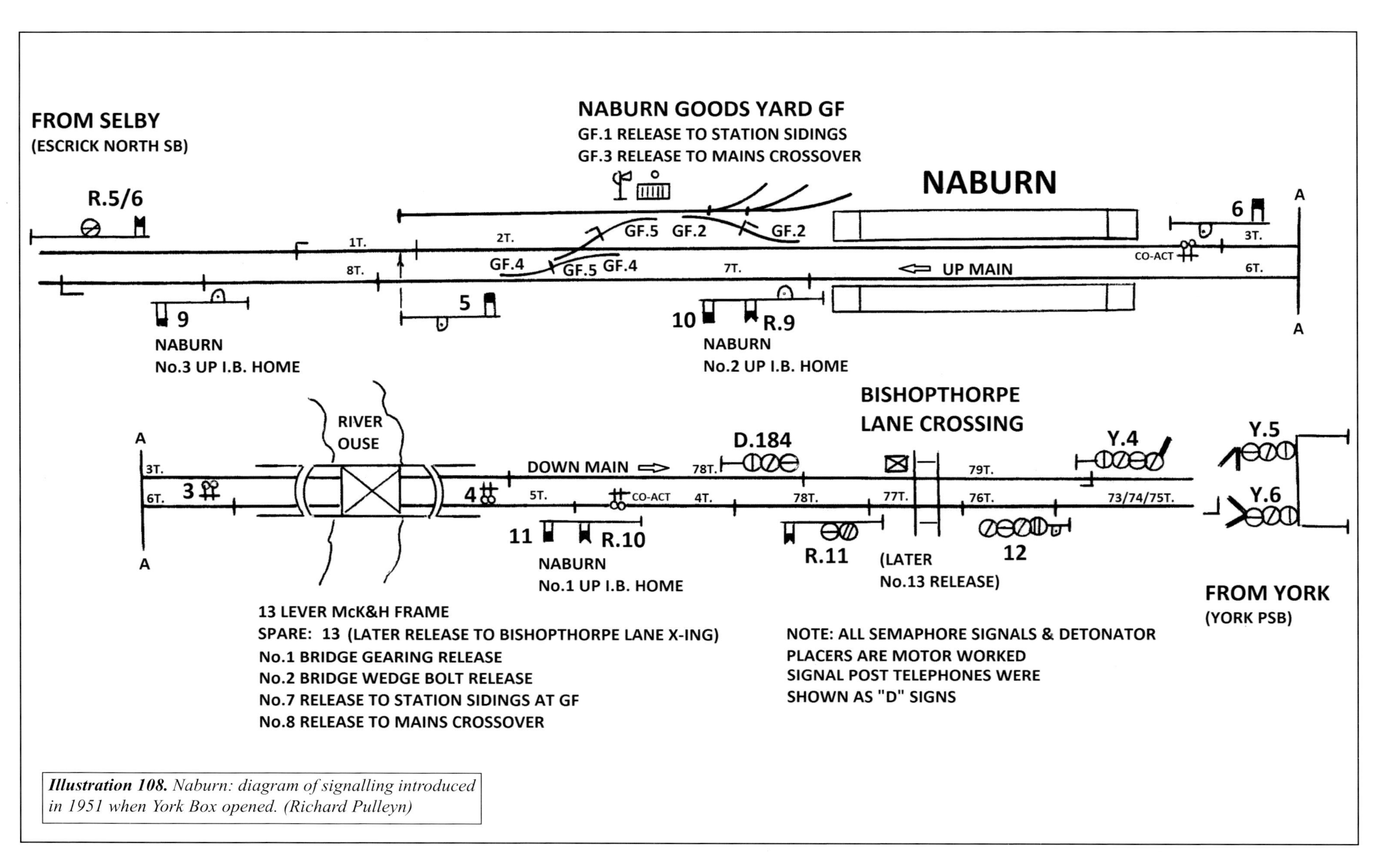

Illustration 108. *Naburn: diagram of signalling introduced in 1951 when York Box opened. (Richard Pulleyn)*

Chapter 13 : Through York Yards Post Second World War

York Yards between Severus and Holgate Bridge had been used intensively during the Second World War but the basic layout was very little changed from the turn of the century as shown in Illustration 22 on page 29.

York Yard South, 1950s

The 125-lever McK&H frame installed in 1903 continued in use, although 28 levers were spare by February 1961.

Fortunately, the Special Instructions for York Yard South (1) issued when York Box opened in 1951 were preserved in the RJ Talbot Collection and these give some indication of the complexity of working the lines controlled by York Yard South:

* Down Main Goods to No 1 Down Goods signal box – Permissive Block.
* Up Main Goods from York Yard North signal box – Permissive Block.
* Up Goods to York Box – No Block Regulations.
* Down Mineral to York Yard North signal box – No Block Regulations (Telephone), recorded in Train Register.
* Nos 1 and 2 Down Reception Lines to No 1 Down Goods signal box – No Block Regulations.
* Down lines between York Box and York Yard South signal box – Permissive Block as modified for Train Describer Working:

  Down Goods
  Down Leeds Goods
  Down Doncaster Goods
  Down Scarborough Goods

* Up Lines between York Yard South signal box and York Box – Permissive Block as modified for Train Describer Working:

  Up Scarborough Goods
  Up Doncaster Goods
  Up Leeds Goods

* Up Goods and Up Mineral lines from No 2 Up Goods signal box – Regulations for 'Electric Bell' working:

	How Beats to be Given
Call Attention	1
For Up Trains or Engines towards Leeds	2
For Up Trains or Engines towards Doncaster	3
For Up Trains or Engines towards Scarborough	4
For Up Trains or Engines drawing up to make a shunt	5
Engine Assisting in Rear of Train	2 - 2

As soon as the bell signals were acknowledged by York Yard South to No 2 Up Goods signal box, the signalman there described the train by giving the appropriate 'Is Line Clear' signal. The 'Engine Assisting in Rear of Train' to be given after the signal describing the train where appropriate.

* Up Goods and Up Mineral Lines towards No 2 Up Goods signal box – Regulations for 'Working in Wrong Direction': Two Block Bells and Two Block Indicators were provided:

	How Beats to be Given
Call Attention	1
To No 1 Up Goods	1 - 5
To No 2 Up Goods	2 - 4
To No 3 Up Goods	3 - 3
To No 4 Up Goods	4 - 1 - 1
To Midland Yard	5 - 1
To Van Siding	2 - 2 - 2
Train Out of Section	3 - 4

Illustration 109. *York Yard South: formerly known as 'North Junction' this signal box controlled traffic at the south end of York Yards. Dating from 1903, it is to the NER Type 2 design as evidenced by the weather-boarded gable ends without bargeboards and the semi-circular-arched locking room windows which have later been bricked up. There are three large ventilators on the apex of the roof and, unusually, a short balcony with external access steps at the north end. When photographed in 1953, Signalman Syd Alison was sitting behind the open window at this near end. (Frank Archer)*

The signalman at York Yard South was required to give the 'Call Attention' signal and on receiving an acknowledgement, then pass the proper signal on the bell; if the signalman at No 2 Up Goods signal box was in a position to accept the train or engine, he then acknowledged the bell signal and placed the block indicator to 'Train on Line'. When the train or engine had cleared the fouling point he gave the 'Call Attention' signal and, on receiving an acknowledgement, gave the 'Train Out of Section' bell signal and placed the Block Indicator to 'Line Blocked'.

'Working in Wrong Direction' was also authorised for light engines proceeding from York Yard South on the Down Goods or Down Leeds Goods lines to Holgate Down Reception Lines.

(1) BR NE Operating Area, Circular O.3927.

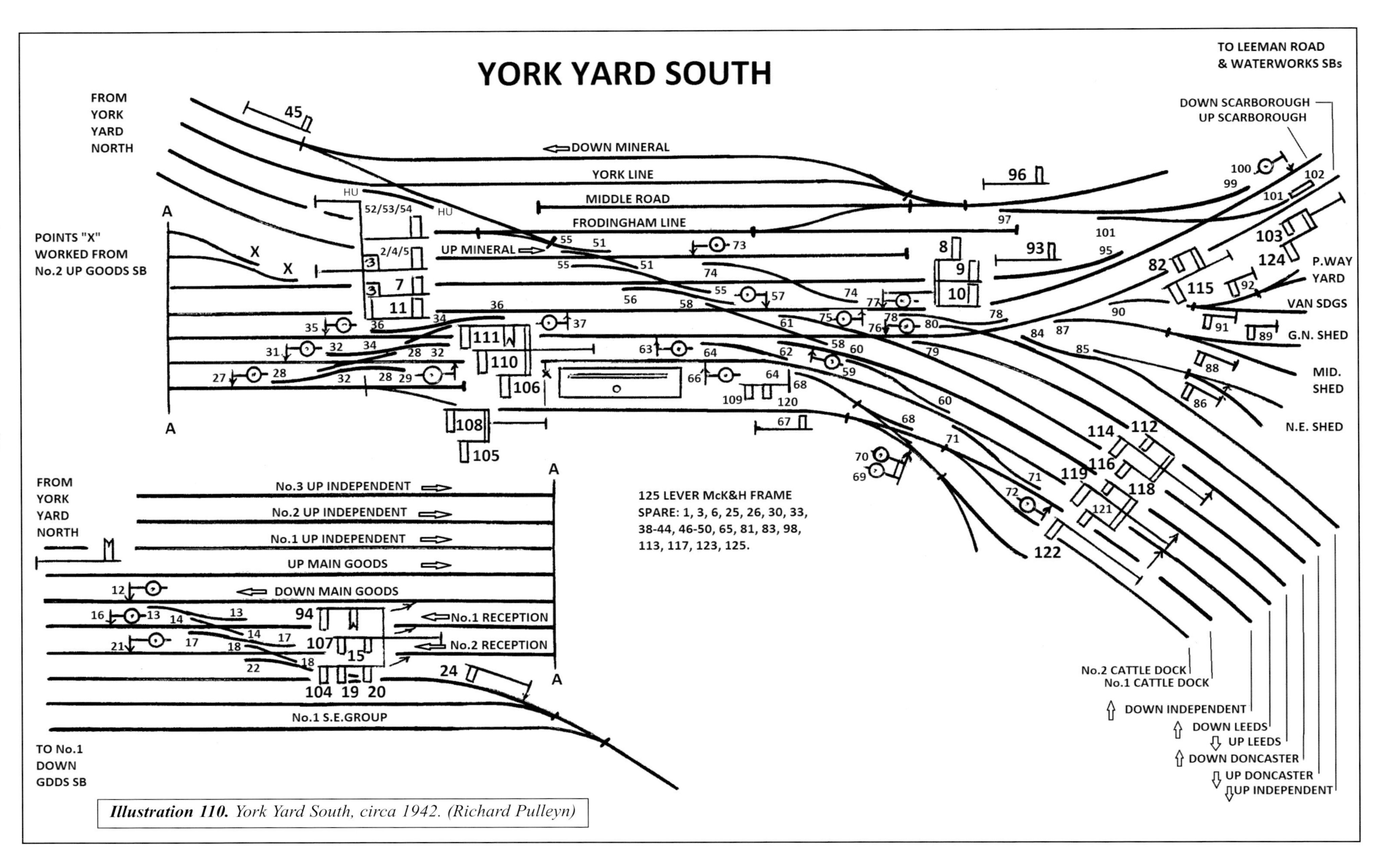

Illustration 110. *York Yard South, circa 1942. (Richard Pulleyn)*

Illustration 111. *York Yard South: in 1953, Signalman Alf McClean stands at his 125-lever McK&H frame. (Frank Archer)*

Illustration 112. *York Yard South: behind the box were two shunting lines for propelling wagons over the low hump into one of the Down yards. On the steps of the hump shunter is a young Frank Archer who started his railway career as a Train Recorder at Skelton signal box before transferring to the Goods Guard Links when he reached the required age. (Frank Archer Collection)*

Semaphore signals controlled from York Yard South signal box which applied to lines worked from York Box (with colour-light signals) were fitted with Intensified Electric Lights which had to be switched on as soon as visibility was reduced such that it was not possible to see the fog sighting object.

Single-stroke bells were also provided between York Yard South and the yard foreman's office in Branches Yard, where the following Code of Bells applied:

	How Beats to be Given
Call Attention	1
For Engines to Enter Branches Yard	
From Up Scarborough Goods	2
From Down Scarborough Goods	3
For Engines or Trains to leave Branches Yard for Down Scarborough Goods	4
For Points to be put back to Normal	2 - 2
Down Scarborough Goods Clear	3 - 1

And again between York Yard South and the shunters' cabin at the south end of No 1 Down Yard, with the following Code of Bells:

	How Beats to be Given
Call Attention	1
From Hump to Down Main	1 - 2
From Down Main to Hump	3
From Down Main to Locomotive Road	2 - 1
Train or portion of train removed from Down Main	2
From Hump to No 1 Down Reception Line	2 - 2
From No 1 Down Reception Line to Hump	1 - 3
From No 1 Down Reception Line to Low Road	3 - 1

Illustration 113. *York Yard South: the Train Describers in this box were used by Standard Telephones and Cables Limited to illustrate their product in a marketing brochure. The company's 'Polaridex System' not only indicated the order in which trains were approaching, but those indications then 'stepped up' as trains progressively operated the track circuits. On the left here is the Transmitter Cabinet, and on the right the Receiver Cabinet. (ST&C Limited)*

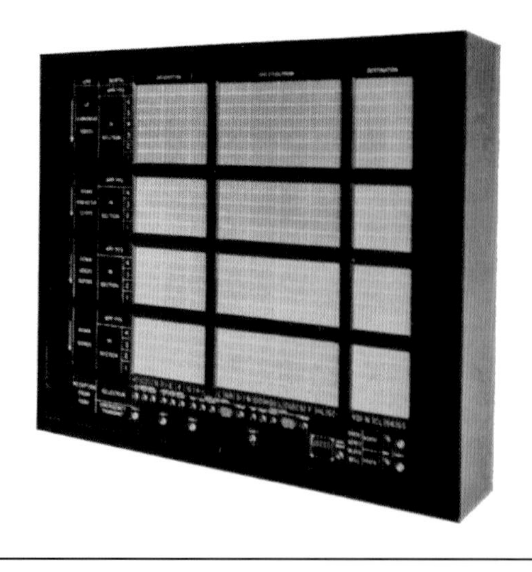

Train or portion of train removed from No 1 Down Reception Line	4
From Hump to No 2 Down Reception Line	1 - 4
From No 2 Down Reception Line to Hump	2 - 3
From No 2 Down Reception Line to Low Road	3 - 2
Train or portion of train removed from No 2 Down Reception Line	5
Close Points leading from Hump	4 - 1

In 1960 the Down direction block section was to No 1 Down Goods signal box (634 yards), whereas the Up direction block section was from York Yard North (1017 yards); by that time York Yard South signal box was open from 3 am on Mondays until 2 pm on Sundays.

No 1 Down Goods Signal Box

The box was fitted with a 40-lever McK&H Frame (of which six levers were spare). It controlled the exit from No 1 Down Yard / No 1 Group (Sidings 1 to 6), No 2 Down Yard ('Klondyke') / No 2 Group (Sidings 7 to 11), and No 3 Group (Sidings 12 and 13), Locomotive Sidings (with turntable and coaling stage), and No 4 Group.

As implied by its name, No 1 Down Goods signal box only controlled traffic in the Down direction. By 1960 it was open from 6 am on Mondays until the yard closed on Sundays.

The running lines from York Yard South (634 yards) were:

* Down Main Goods (Permissive).
* No 1 Down Reception (Bell only – No Block).
* No 2 Down Reception (Bell Only – No Block).

Towards York Yard North (570 yards), the running lines were worked as follows:

* Down Main Goods (Permissive).
* No 1 Down Independent / Exchange Line – used in Down Direction only (Bell Only – No Block – using bell for Down Main Goods without 'Call Attention').
* Special bell codes were also used for both Down and Up trains, *e.g.* '2 - 2 - 2 for Train or Engine from York Yard North to No 1 Down Goods Box on No 4 Exchange Line'.
* Nos 2, 3 and 4 Independents / Exchange Lines – used in both directions – Special working with one bell and instruments that could be placed at 'Train on Line' by the signalman at York Yard North (for a train in the Down direction) or by the signalman at No 1 Down Goods signal box (for a train in the Up direction); after the train or engine had arrived the special bell signal '3 - 4' was given. (1) For a photograph of the type of instrument used, see Illustration 59 on page 56.

Many of the signalmen in the York District trained initially as 'Booking Lads' (keeping an accurate Train Register, making and receiving telephone messages *etc.*) at such locations as Skelton and York Yard North; when ready to take control of their own signal box they were frequently initiated at No1 Down signal box . Those who worked at '1 Down' (as it was known locally) related how busy it could be, especially with shunting moves between siding Groups; taking meals was impossible even during the night shift. Furthermore, the 'Spur' behind the box was used to stable the pilot locos between activities so there was always smoke, soot and ash around with loco crew and shunting staff walking in and out, so it was not a clean environment and newly appointed signalmen were always keen to move on to much more attractive locations at stations elsewhere in the district.

No 1 Down Goods signal box was still in use in 1962 when the new York Yard South signal box was opened, and is believed to have closed 2 October 1966.(2)

Illustration 114. *No.1 Down Goods: being situated in York Yards with no public access, it is not surprising that very few photographs of the York Yard boxes were taken, so it is extremely fortunate that Frank Archer, who was working as a Train Recorder and then a Goods Guard in the 1950s, was sufficiently interested to make sure that they were recorded. No.1 Down Goods lasted longer than any of the other Yard boxes and did not close until October 1966. (Frank Archer)*

(1) BR(NER) Operating Instruction O.4346, dated 1 May 1959.
(2) NERA JF Mallon Register.

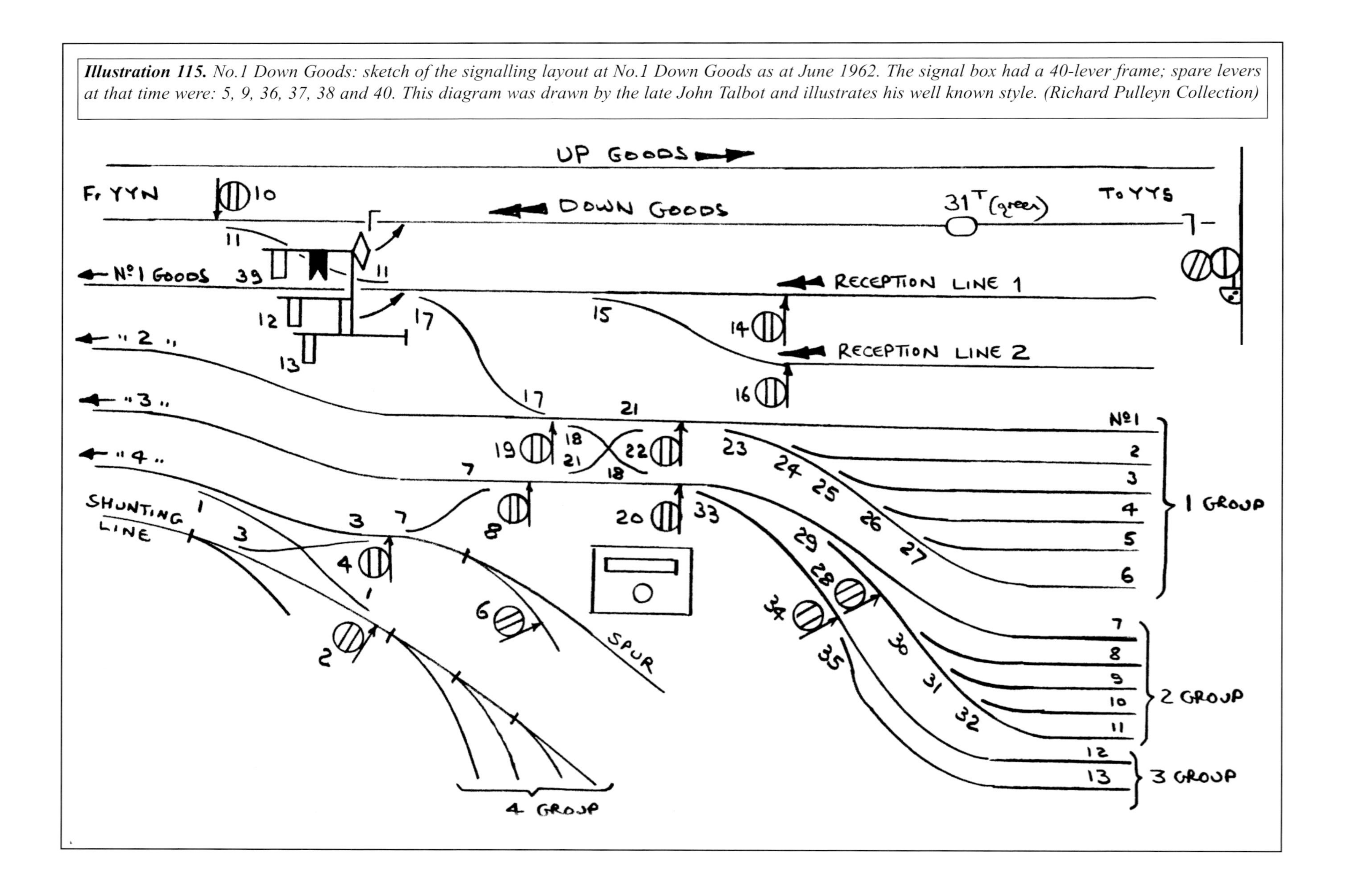

Illustration 115. *No.1 Down Goods: sketch of the signalling layout at No.1 Down Goods as at June 1962. The signal box had a 40-lever frame; spare levers at that time were: 5, 9, 36, 37, 38 and 40. This diagram was drawn by the late John Talbot and illustrates his well known style. (Richard Pulleyn Collection)*

No 1 Up Goods Signal Box

No 1 Up Goods signal box was located at the north end of the Up Yard, where Nos 2 and 3 Loops ran through from York Yard North. It had a 20-lever frame, later renewed at the back of the box, working connections towards York Yard South on the No 1 Independent (known locally as 'Tasher'), also the Nos 3 and 4 Independents.

Illustration 116. No.1 Up Goods: this box was located at the north end of the Up Yard, where Nos2 and 3 Reception Lines ran through from York Yard North. (Frank Archer)

Illustration 117. No.2 Up Goods: the configuration of the windows, and the boarding above the main windows in particular, show that this box was to the NER Type 2 design dating from the early 1900s. (Frank Archer)

The yard consisted of 14 sorting sidings: Nos 1 and 14 were through roads but Nos 2-13 were single ended, each of which was allocated traffic for the following:

	Destination
1 Through Road	
2	GNR
3	GCR
4	Branches Yard
5	North
6	Milford
7	Hull
8	North
9	Selby
10	Coal Tubs
11	Leeds
12	Vans and 'Hold Ups'
13	Conflats
14 Through Road –	Warehouse Wagons

No 2 Up Goods Signal Box

No 2 Up Goods signal box was located at the south end of the Up Yard where No 1 Up Goods Independent ('Tasher'), and No 2 Up Goods Independent ('Through') – which came from York Yard North signal box – converged with No 3 Up Goods Independent and No 4 Up Goods Independent – which came from No 1 Up Goods signal box. The box controlled West Sidings – which consisted of 4 single ended sidings (Sidings 1 to 4) – but also Nos 1 to 4 Receptions, and No 4 Group. It had a 35-lever frame (including four spare levers) at the back of the box, replacing an earlier 37-lever McK&H No.4 pattern frame on 30 January 1928.

In 1905 it had a 37-lever Mck&H No.4 pattern frame which had been recovered from Barkston Junction (Church Fenton); this was replaced on 30 January 1928 by a 35-lever frame (including 4 spare) at the back of the box.

In 1955, a plan was prepared proposing changes be made to the Up Marshalling Yard and in June 1958, after the yard had been redesigned, both No 1 and No 2 Up signal boxes closed.(1)

(1) Reference: 55 – YS -320.

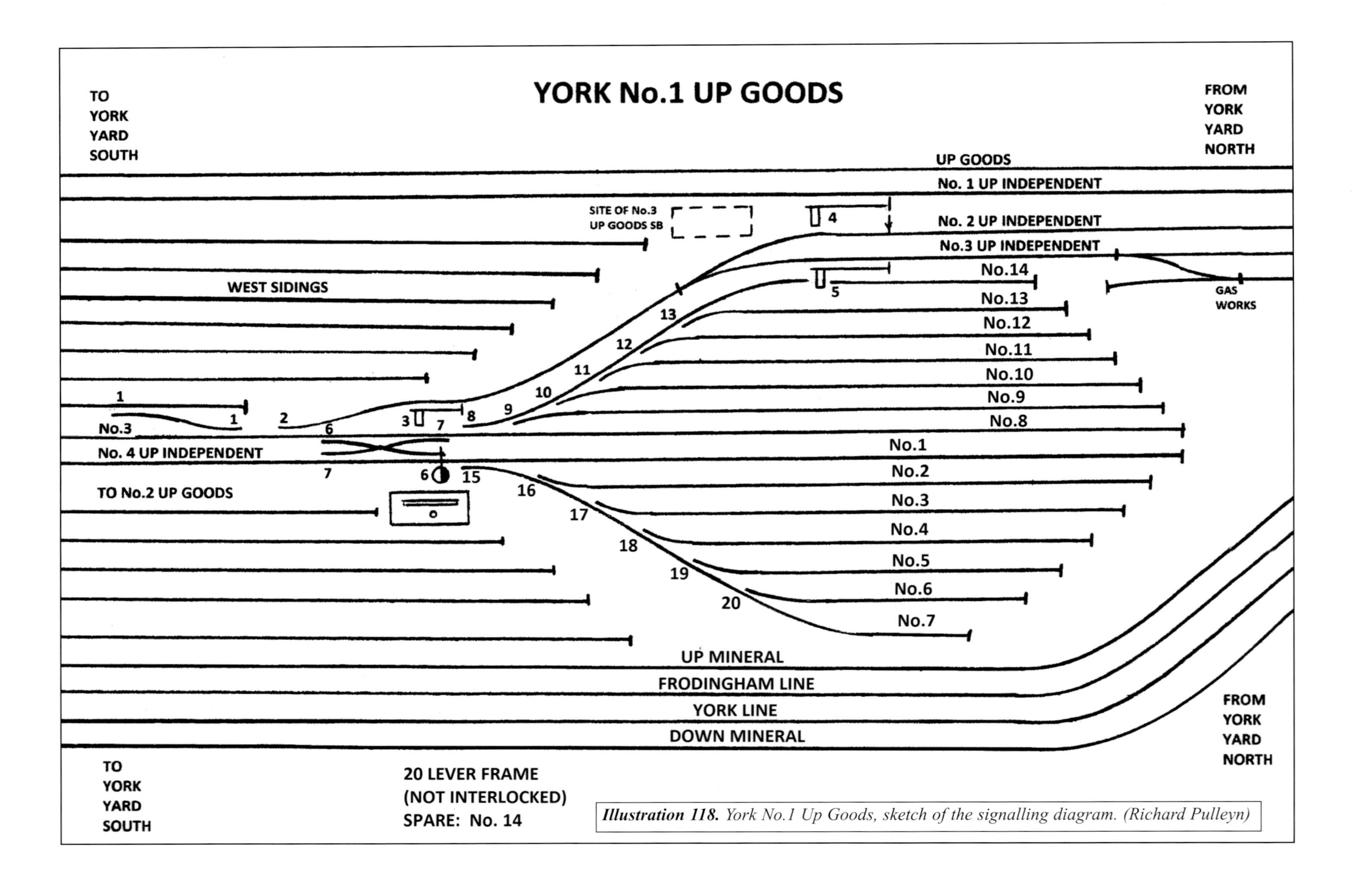

Illustration 118. *York No.1 Up Goods, sketch of the signalling diagram. (Richard Pulleyn)*

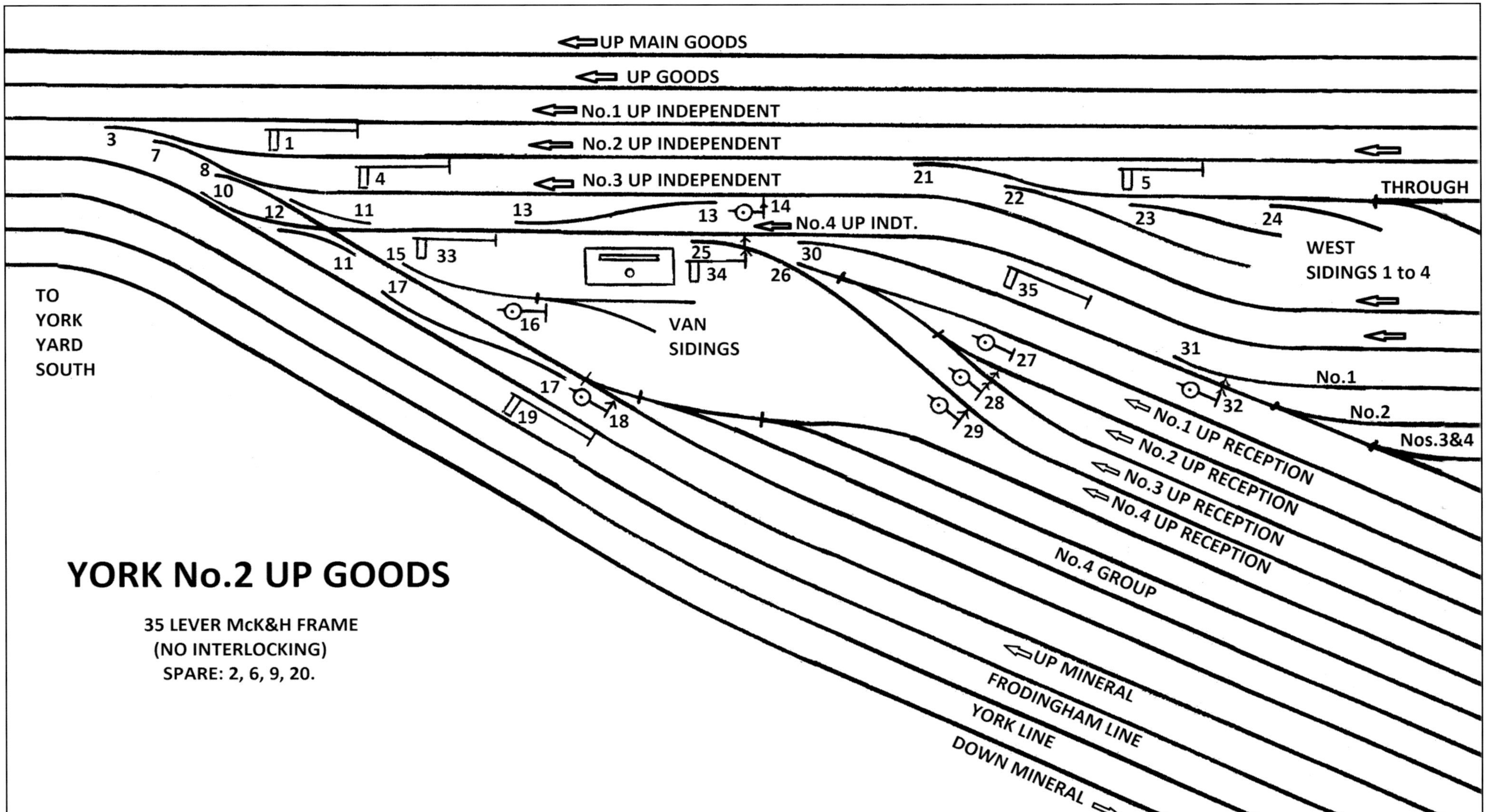

YORK No.2 UP GOODS

35 LEVER McK&H FRAME
(NO INTERLOCKING)
SPARE: 2, 6, 9, 20.

Illustration 119. *York No.2 Up Goods, sketch of the signalling diagram. (Richard Pulleyn)*

York Yard North Signal box

As noted above, Severus Junction had been renamed York Yard North in October 1938, at the same time that North Junction became York Yard South and Poppleton Junction was renamed Skelton. With a 150-lever McK&H frame York Yard North was an impressive sight from the main line, although it had no connection with the ECML. By 1960 York Yard North was open from 4 am on Mondays until 2 pm on Sundays.

After closure of the intermediate Yard boxes by the mid-1960s, it controlled the following lines in the Down direction from York Yard South (1204 yards):
* Connection to and from York Carriage Works.
* Exit from Nos 1, 2 and 3 Down Yards.
* Nos 1 to 3 Independent / Exchange Lines.
* Down Main Goods(Permissive Block).

Illustration 120. *York Yard North: photographed on 16 October 1966, a couple of years before the superb signal bridge was replaced by a colour light on the Up Main Goods. The view is across the Up Clifton Loop and the Up and Down Main lines, none of which were controlled from York Yard North signal box. (CJB Sanderson / Armstrong Railway Photographic Trust)*

Illustration 121. *York Yard North: on 9 May 1964, a Class F freight hauled by K1 No 62007 photographed on the Up Main Goods line from Skelton. The Up Shunting Line and Up Arrival Lines are between the train and the ECML; the Down Departure lines are seen to the left. (John Foreman)*

Illustration 122. *York Yard North: photographed in 1964, the block shelf includes a Tyers Permissive instrument for the Main Goods lines to and from York Yard South, a single-stroke bell for the Main Goods lines to and from Skelton (worked by TCB) and the remaining instrument with bell for working the Up Shunting Line in either direction. (John Talbot)*

Towards York Yard South (in the Up direction), it controlled:
* Up Main Goods (Permissive Block).
* Up Goods ('Tasher') (Telephone Block).
* North Arrival Line (to Up Yard) – shunting moves.
* No 1 Frodingham Line (Telephone Block).
* York Line (Telephone Block).
* Down Mineral (Telephone Block).
* Connection to & from York Wagon Shops – shunting moves.
* Up and Down Warehouse Lines – shunting moves.
* Leeman Road Permanent Way Yard ground frame – a 5-lever covered frame, electrically released from York Yard North signal box to control connections between the Up and Down Warehouse lines and the Permanent Way Yard.

On the Up from Skelton (1017 yards), it controlled:
* Up Main Goods (Permissive Block).
* Up Shunting Line (Up and Down Shunting Line No 1) – special Block Instrument (see below).
* Exit from Up Arrival Lines Nos 1 to 4 (Telephone Block).

Towards Skelton (on the Down), it controlled:
* Down Main Goods (TCB Permissive).
* Entrance to Down Departure Lines Nos 1 to 8 (Telephone Block), also No 9 which also gave access to British Sugar Corporation Private Sidings.

Illustration 123. *York Yard North: the 150-lever frame was still in use in 1964 when Signalman 'Johnny' Johnson was setting a route. At the desk a new recruit Train Recorder is being trained by a more experienced Lad, often the first step in a signalling career. (John Talbot)*

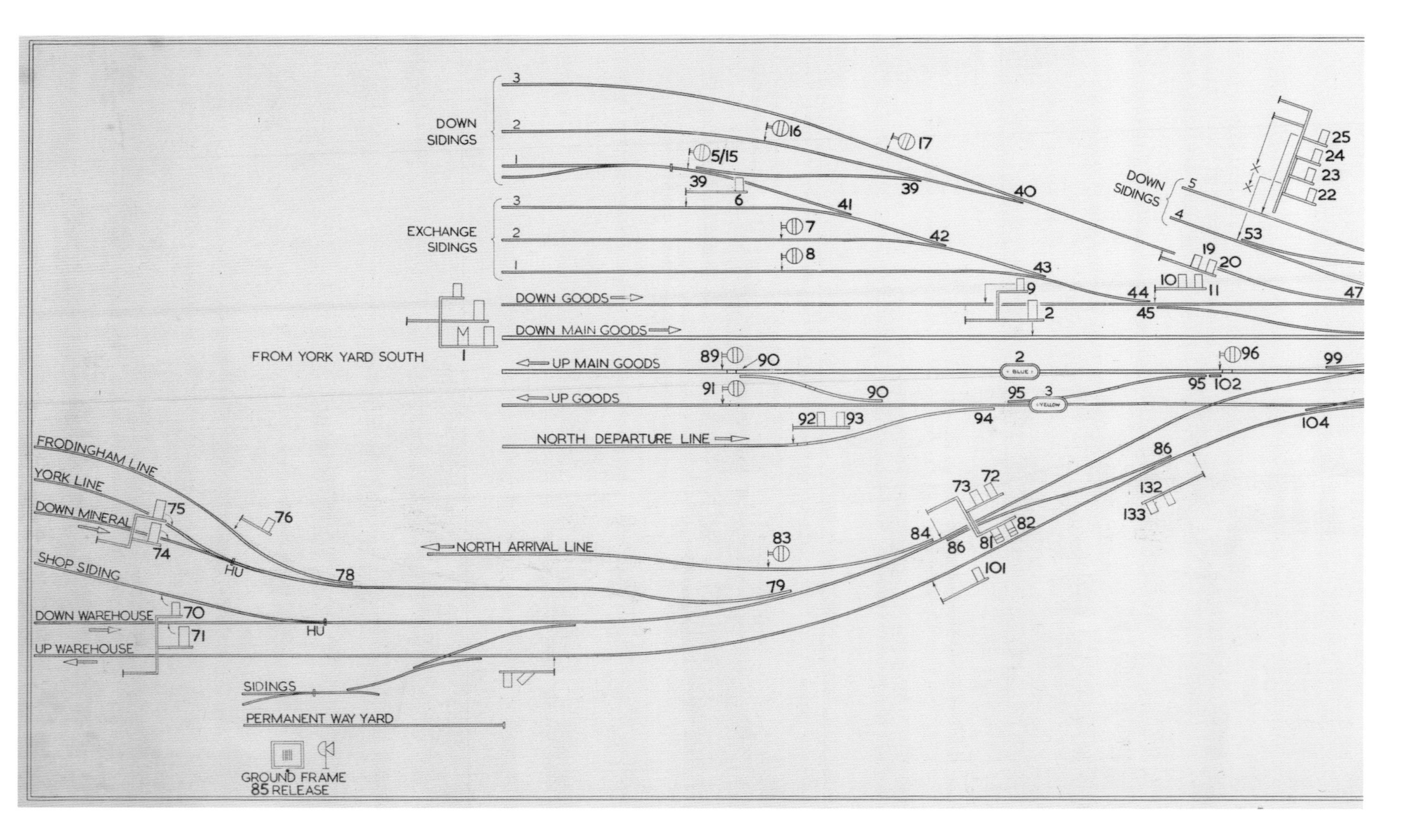

DOWN SIDINGS
EXCHANGE SIDINGS
DOWN SIDINGS
DOWN GOODS
DOWN MAIN GOODS
FROM YORK YARD SOUTH
UP MAIN GOODS
UP GOODS
BLUE
YELLOW
NORTH DEPARTURE LINE
FRODINGHAM LINE
YORK LINE
DOWN MINERAL
NORTH ARRIVAL LINE
SHOP SIDING
HU
DOWN WAREHOUSE
HU
UP WAREHOUSE
SIDINGS
PERMANENT WAY YARD
GROUND FRAME
85 RELEASE

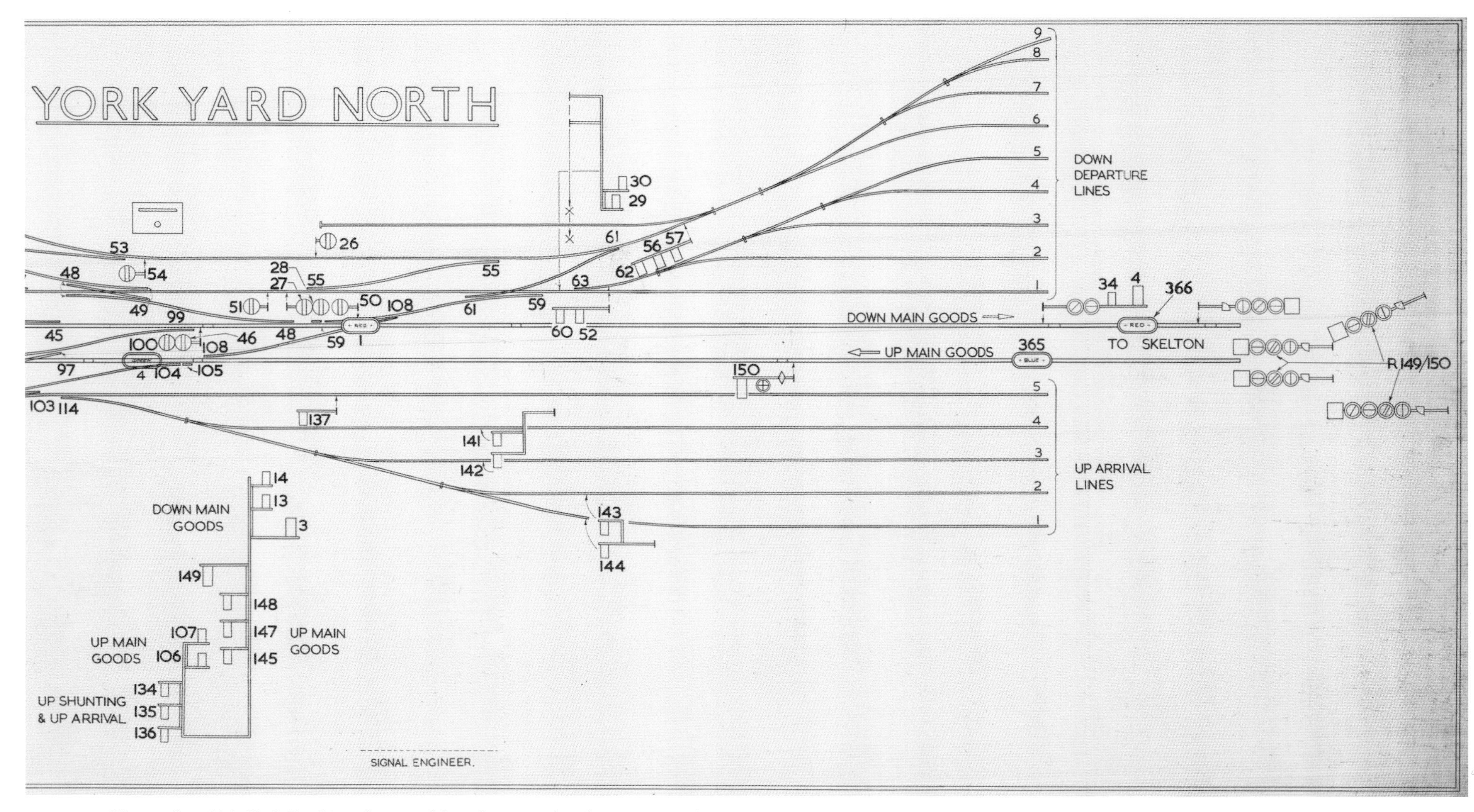

Illustration 124. *York Yard North: signal box diagram dated circa 1966 showing the extent of the layout controlled. It will be seen that there were very few track circuits so great care was required before any points were changed, despite the fact that traffic levels were heavy and many shunting moves were required. (BR)*

Illustration 125. *Leeman Road Permanent Way Yard Ground Frame: the 5-lever covered ground frame was sited alongside the Warehouse Lines and released from York Yard North signal box. Immediately behind was the Down ECML between York station and Skelton where York shed's V2 No 60981 heads a Down express on 28 March 1959. (NW Skinner / Armstrong Railway Photographic Trust)*

As a 'Goods Only' box, York Yard North was often used at a training location for 'Booking Lads'; frequently, they were new entrants to the railway, and many were in their first employment after leaving school. With trainee signalmen next door at No 1 Down Goods, as explained above, and trainee booking lads in the box, it was often referred to as 'the nursery end' of the Yard; that was unfortunate because it was also the busiest end in many ways, but it was always taken in good spirit by those who worked there. Indeed, during the mid to late 1960s, the author was employed as a temporary York District Relief Train Recorder and 'Yard North' was a regular place of work, often covering vacancies as lads moved on to become signalmen; he also enjoyed training new recruits, some of whom even had to learn the 24 hour clock. Originally, the signal box had been double manned and with lads on all three shifts, but by the mid 1960s there was only one man and a lad on early and late turns, and a man on his own on nights. The Rule Book dictated that only signalmen were to work the lever frame and operate the block bells but the yard master and his assistants took a 'blind eye' to the booking lads helping out, initially under the strict guidance and supervision of the signalman but, as the lads became more proficient, it was not unusual for the signalman and the lad to share the work between them; this was all good training for the lads who then moved on to become signalmen themselves.

A narrow road over-bridge carrying Landing Lane was situated immediately north of the signal box, with the north end yard foreman based in a cabin just beyond, although he spent most of his time outside supervising moves. The box had a useful small balcony, adjacent to which the Train Register desk was placed, so the booking lad had to be ready to jump off his stool and go to the open window to listen to the instructions being issued by the yard foreman which he then passed on to the signalman. Typically, a whole list of moves would be shouted out so the lad had to be sharp and quickly jot them down on a pad of scrap paper, often made from out of date notices torn to size; they might include, for example, 'Loco off 3 Up Arrival to Shed, Yard Pilot from 1 Group to Warehouse, P Way Pilot from Top Yard through the frame, then out for Fenton.' The latter referred to the locomotive allocated to the Permanent Way Engineer (in the mid 1960s that was often 65894) which had come Up the Main Goods line from the Top Yard situated at Skelton Junction alongside the Harrogate Branch; 'Through the frame' meant using the ground frame to access Leeman Road Yard, then 'out for Fenton' would mean taking the train it had collected to Church Fenton. The lad then had to ring Control to consult them about the train and ask when it might have a 'path' so that the signalman could regulate its departure.

Chapter 14 : Freight Modernisation

York Up Yard

In 1955, a plan was prepared to simplify and modernise York Yards between Skelton and York Yard South, although financial justification was difficult given that little traffic was originating in the York area (other than from Rowntree's), and that massive new yards were already planned north of York (the Tyne and Tees Yards) and in West Yorkshire (Healey Mills and Stourton). Nevertheless, some modest improvements were made: York Up Yard was remodelled during 1958 when a small hump was constructed.

Dringhouses

Dringhouses Up Yard was also converted from a flat installation into a hump yard; the hump was constructed at the north end; after passing over the hump wagons ran through automatic retarders into groups of sorting sidings. The capacity of the yard was expanded by extending existing sidings and adding nine new through sidings on the east side thereby providing two groups of 11 sidings. Consequently, in 1962, Dringhouses became the first marshalling yard in the country to deal exclusively with fully-braked freight trains; about 800 wagons were arriving each day to be sorted into night trains leaving for different parts of the country.

A control tower was erected at the north end of the yard adjacent to the hump with the operating floor 26 feet above rail level to give a good view of the whole yard. The control desk was designed for operation by one person and was divided into three sections: the left-hand panel contained all the telecommunications equipment; the centre section had an engraved diagram depicting the layout of the yard, with point and signal switches mounted in their geographical positions; the right-hand section had three rotary switches to select the appropriate pump units to operate the retarders and select the braking pressure at each retarder. Adjacent to the control desk were pneumatic tubes by means of which the yard staff passed data to the operator.

Movements over the hump were controlled by standard double-sided three-aspect position-light hump signals which displayed: three vertical white lights for normal speed, three oblique white lights for slow speed, and three horizontal white lights for stop. These signals were operated from a three-position switch on the control panel. Points were operated by Model 'Y' electro-pneumatic point motors controlled by means of two-position switches on the panel, but no track circuits were provided to protect the points. Signalling equipment was provided by AEI-GRS Limited.(1)

(1) *Railway Gazette*, 26 October 1962.

Illustration 126. *Dringhouses Yard: a view of the control tower at about the time it was first commissioned. (David J Williamson Collection)*

Illustration 127. *Dringhouses Yard: a view of the control tower from the rear, 2 May 1986. (Claire E Williamson)*

Following the 'Beeching Era', however, traditional wagon load traffic declined significantly, especially that connected with the once extensive branch lines around York. Consequently rationalisation became necessary: Dringhouses Up Yard was sufficient to handle traffic in both directions, north and south, so 1966 saw closure of Dringhouses Down Yard, Branches Yard, and Warehouse Yard; York No 2 Down Yard was handed over for Civil Engineering use, and York Up Yard was largely used for staging and storage purposes. Any remaining full load traffic (some livestock, domestic coal and sand for Redfearn's National Glass Works) was concentrated at Foss Islands.

Illustration 128. *Dringhouses Yard: these photographs were taken in 1962 when the Up Yard control tower and hump were commissioned. (AEI-GRS Limited)*

Chapter 15 : Skelton Junction in the 1960s

Some recollections by the author who was employed as a temporary Train Recorder or 'Box Lad' at Skelton signal box during the mid to late 1960s, covering holidays for the regular lads and vacancies which had arisen after the incumbents had moved on, often to become signalmen, crossing keepers or guards. For a view of the box, see Illustration 91 on page 79.

It was with some trepidation that I approached the box for the first time since access was by crossing the junction including both Independents, Branch and Main lines; fortunately, visibility in each direction was good, besides which the signalmen always kept a careful look out, especially for visitors, and would shout out a warning if there was a train approaching. When I arrived I was asked to show my ID which in those days was a 'Wages Card' and to my youthful consternation it prompted a lot of laughter from both signalmen on duty, so why the mirth? The nearest signalman, a tall imposing character, saw my concern so he shook me warmly by the hand and said 'Welcome Mr R Pulleyn – that's my name too!'. He then explained that he was Reg Pulleyn. So it came about that my Christian name 'Richard' was heavily underlined on the wages card to avoid confusion with 'Reg' when I went to collect wages for us both from the Outer Office at York station – there were no wage deliveries in those days – they were collected from 'Home Station'. Happily, after that extremely nervous introduction on my part, we got on really well and whenever his regular lad was booked off he would ask for me as relief lad so we often worked together on the same shift. We never managed to establish whether we were related because there are so many branches of the Pulleyn family in York and the surrounding area.

Returning to my first shift at Skelton, when I arrived there was no lad on duty to help train me but Reg was a good mentor and I was keen to learn so I picked up the routine fairly quickly, although the wide variety of block working was quite an eye-opener:

To and from Tollerton:

* the Main and Slow lines were worked by Track Circuit Block (TCB) with a bell for the Main and a gong for the Slow.

To and from York Box:

* the Main lines and the Clifton Loop were worked by Track Circuit Block using a Train Describer.

To and from York Yard North:

* Up Main Goods = Permissive Block ;
* Down Main Goods = TCB Permissive;
* Up Shunting Line (Up and Down Shunting Line No. 1) = bi-directional block using a special instrument;
* Up Arrival Lines Nos 1 to 4 = Telephone Block;
* Down Departure Lines Nos. 1 to 8 = Telephone Block, also applied to No 9 DDL which also gave access to British Sugar Corporation Private Sidings.

To and from Poppleton:

* Up Branch = TCB
* Down Branch = Absolute Block

Illustration 129. *Skelton: as photographed on 22 January 1977, most of the 75-lever frame can be seen with the dark green illuminated track diagram above. The train describer for working to and from York Box is at the right hand end of the block shelf with the special block instrument alongside for working the bi-directional Up Shunting Line. (Christopher J Woolstenholmes, CJW56)*

The train describer that can be seen in Illustrations 129 and 130 was used for signalling trains on the Up and Down Main and the Clifton Loop to and from York Box; it would buzz loudly to announce the next train approaching, the buzzer being silenced by the train recorder pressing a 'Receive' button. A Down express would be described as Class 'A' alongside destination 'N' so the lad then had to shout out 'A for the North'. A local train to Harrogate was described as Class 'B' alongside destination 'H' announced as 'One for the Branch', and so on. A full list of the codes is included in the description of York Box.

Setting up a description to transmit to York Box was a little more complicated because it required description (Class of Train), direction (*i.e.* where the train originated such as SK for Skelton New Sidings) as well as destination, so we were provided with a copy of the York station simplifier which was marked up with the required information to input. Besides recording all bell signals and train descriptions in the Train Register there were two further important duties for the box lad, both of which required a lot of telephone work so a telephone concentrator was placed alongside his Train Register desk; this concentrator had two handsets and a bank of switches to connect to a whole range of locations. Firstly, York Control had to be contacted to establish the identity of trains approaching from the north because these lines were worked by Track Circuit Block using a single stroke bell for the Fast (or Main) lines and a gong for the Slow lines; once established, that information had to be passed on to the signalman working the switch panel for Skelton Bridge and the north end of the Yard so that he could route trains correctly. Secondly, the yard inspector for Skelton New Sidings had to be advised about any trains entering the yard, and he contacted the box when a train was ready to depart so those details had to be passed on to the appropriate signalman.

Illustration 130. *Skelton: a closer view of the train describer for working to and from York Box, with the special block instrument alongside for working the bi-directional Up Shunting Line. (Christopher J Woolstenholmes, CJW56 23)*

Because I was only a temporary member of staff initially I was not provided with a railway uniform. It was quite innocently, therefore, that I arrived for duty that first week wearing a red anorak with a beautifully knitted red jumper underneath. As soon as I walked in the door I was instructed to remove both items of clothing and never to wear anything like that again for work since drivers could easily mistake the coloured garments for a red flag. So I spent the whole shift shivering in my shirt sleeves, but a lesson had been learned.

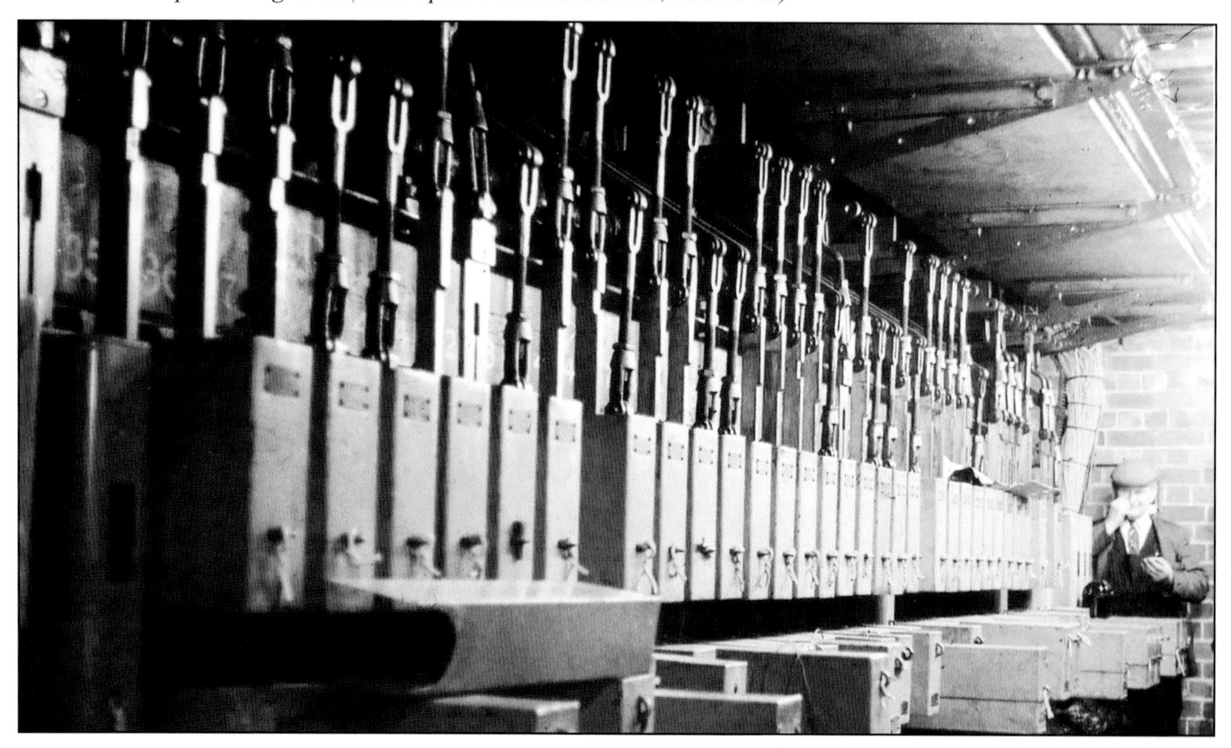

Illustration 131. *Skelton: under the lever frame, with the locking boxes above, this is the impressive array of combined lever locks and circuit controllers in the locking room. Christopher J Woolstenholmes, CJW56 16)*

A couple of weeks later it was my first night shift, something I had never experienced before, although I would never show my excitement; furthermore, I was working with a different set of signalmen, both of whom were known as 'old hands' meaning that they had years of experience – and were referred to as 'Mister'. One of the men 'Mr Robinson' had worked many of the signal boxes in the York area and had moved to Skelton after his previous job at Beningbrough (the next box to the north) had closed. He had a fund of interesting stories which I thoroughly enjoyed listening to – and we were both keen gardeners so we got on well together. His partner on the shift was 'Mr Eden' who was very keen on Signalling Rules & Regulations; since I had shared that interest myself for many years, he was another most influential man to be working alongside. Fortunately for me both men were quite prepared to share not only their knowledge, but also their experiences; I was well aware of the requirement for signalmen to keep a close watch on trains for anything untoward such as an open carriage door but also for something called a 'hot box' which I had heard signalmen mention but I knew nothing about so I asked them to explain. Remarkably, that very night I was leaning on the windowsill watching a Down fitted freight heading north when I spotted wisps of smoke coming from the side of a wagon and there was the telltale smell that Mr Eden had mentioned. He was stood at the opposite end of the box and spotted the same defect as I shouted out so he quickly restored the next controlled stop signal which the driver spotted and brought his train to a stand. By then there was a light drizzle but the driver dismounted and came on the telephone when it was agreed to detach the wagon; the whole train was backed into one of the Down Departure lines to clear the Down Main which was still quite busy with traffic. The shunter in Skelton New Sidings was already occupied at the north end of the yard so Mr Robinson, a conscientious railwayman, went out with a shunting pole 'to keep the job running' by helping the guard detach the defective wagon; by the time he came back in the box the rain was pouring down so he was soaked through and decide to return home for a change of clothing. When he came back an hour or so later he also had a parcel for me – a new, unused BR uniform which was exactly the right size – he had heard from Reg about my youthful error but there would be no more red jumpers for me!

At that time, the box was manned by two signalmen and a lad on all three shifts, except on Saturday nights and Sundays when one signalman had to work the job without assistance. The second signalman at Skelton on Reg's shift was known as 'Rigor' (as in rigor mortis) because he was said to be reluctant to answer a bell and even more reluctant to start heaving the mechanical points for the junction; once my interest had become established, however, it suited me because he was quite content to sit at the desk and 'do the book' whilst I attempted his role under close supervision. We later heard that he had an incurable health problem so felt rather bad about his nickname especially since he had been so kind to me.

Having explained that the signalman had to work the job without assistance on Sundays, it came as quite a shock as I finished late turn on the first Saturday when Reg told me to be back in good time in the morning – that's when I learned that the lad was booked on for the Sunday morning to clean the signal box. So, instead of having what I thought would be a well deserved lie in bed I had to cycle home, try to catch some sleep then get up again at 5 am to be back at the box by 6 am; this was what we called 'doubling back'. The next shock was when my cleaning duties were explained; although we had mains water the toilet was an 'Elsan', it was not much better than a seat on a bucket and my first job was to empty the contents into a pit which had been dug a few yards north of the box on the embankment. The pit was covered by a paving slab which I had great difficulty in shifting, then I went back to collect the toilet but I didn't realise that the bucket was a separate item so instead I heaved the whole thing out – until I was quickly corrected amidst great hilarity at my youthful ignorance.

The toilet having been duly emptied and returned to its rightful place in the cupboard under the box steps I went back inside to be greeted by the delicious smell of sausages and bacon cooking on the gas stove – it was Reg's habit to treat himself to a full cooked breakfast on Sunday mornings, but that was not for me and I was instructed to make a start at sweeping up. Now that is a quite simple process but I went about it with far too much enthusiasm, sending clouds of dust swirling about and, worse still, landing on Reg's fried eggs which were gently bubbling in the pan. The language was rather blue so I was taken off that duty and told instead to dust the block shelf and clean the 75 levers in the frame. That was when I discovered a large electrical switch on the end of the block shelf; it looked like the sort of switch that might be used to turn off a domestic electricity supply so I asked about its function to be told that it was a relic from the war which was used to dim all of the colour-light signals between York and Tollerton in the event of an air raid as described above (see *Chapter 11 : Impact of the Second World War – Precautions*).

All the traffic working at Skelton held my interest but there were a few activities which I especially remember. One was a regular move from the Carriage Works to bring into service new stock or stock which had been repaired; this was strung together into a massive length of mixed carriages and vans which were propelled out from the connections at York Yard North along the Down Main Goods past Skelton box on to the Down Independent alongside Skelton Yard before being routed Up the Main and on to Clifton Loop where it could be re-marshalled as required. Clifton Loop was also used for another memorable train, the 'Red Bank Empties' which was returning newspaper vans to Manchester from numerous destinations throughout the north; consequently its length was quite extraordinary, generally requiring double heading. Another move of interest was reversing the order of a whole train by 'sending it round the handle', a reference the layout which enabled a train to run from the Up Main or

Clifton Loop on to the Scarborough Goods lines to York Yard South, then round via York Yard North back to Skelton Yard.

Traffic in and out of the New Sidings was extremely varied but mainly comprised of company trains, for example conveying iron ore to Teesside and finished steel in return. Some trains had to be split and worked to other yards in York which were described as Trip Workings and signalled at '3' beats on the bell made slowly almost like '1 - 1 - 1'. These trains were not required to convey a guard's van but should still have had a tail lamp to signify that they were complete; however, in practice, there was often a shortage of these lamps when and where they were required so it was not unusual to see a fire bucket or similar hooked on to the last wagon in which case we telephoned ahead to let the next man know what to look out for.

A number of locomotives from the north were detached, turned and watered before collecting a return trip. In between these moves, the Permanent Way pilot loco would be shuffling in and out of the their yard alongside the Harrogate branch with trips to and from Leeman Road. Trains placed in the Departure lines were heading north and held there awaiting suitable locomotives, which had often hauled trains into the Up Arrival lines; the bi-directional Up and Down Shunting Line No 1 could be used for transferring the locomotives but this was not popular at Skelton because it required all of the heavy points to be reversed at the north end so it was only when I was allowed 'on the frame' that this occurred.

Illustration 132. *Signalman Reg Pulleyn was also a prominent local politician. Seen here with Sir Christopher Collett, Lord Mayor of the City of London on the left, Reg Pulleyn, Lord Mayor of the City of York stands proudly to the right in April 1989. (Richard Pulleyn Collection)*

Finally, a few more words about my signalling mentor Reg Pulleyn. Reg devoted a large part of his life to the City of York and its people, so it is not surprising that he became heavily involved in local politics: during a 30-year career in local government, he held a number of prestigious positions in the city, having represented the Holgate ward and the Beckfield Ward on York City Council, he was elected to North Yorkshire County Council in 1973, becoming the Sheriff of York first in 1974 - 1975, then again in 1995 - 1996. In between, he was Lord Mayor in 1988 and 1989, proudly greeting Her Majesty the Queen when she visited York Minster in November 1988, following completion of repairs after the 1984 fire. In fact Reg was the third member of the Pulleyn family to become Lord Mayor of York, being preceded by Ralph Pulleyn in 1537 and Robert Pulleyn in 1939 – coincidentally all having the initial 'R'. He was appointed an honorary Alderman of York City in 1993, honorary Alderman of North Yorkshire County Council a year later, and was a recipient of the British Empire Medal.

As a member of the then National Union of Railwaymen, Reg was also a life-long trade unionist, as was Keith Brining, another of his partners at Skelton; working with them both could lead to some fascinating discussions and debates which fired my enthusiasm almost as much as the skills of railway signalling, to the extent that I subsequently went on to study industrial relations at business school and made that my career, but that is another story.

Reg went on from Skelton to work in York Box, although it was a regular jibe that he spent more time in politics or on union business than he did at work – British Railways was extremely supportive of those who contributed to their communities in that way. One benefit of working in York Box for Reg was that he met Molly, one of the York station announcers and in 1983 she became his second wife, enjoying many happy years together. Reg and Molly both retired from the railway in 1989, in Reg's case after 46 years service, and they continued to live in their NER Cottage Home in the Tang Hall area of York. Sadly, after a long battle against cancer, Molly passed away in 2009 and Reg died suddenly in 2015 age 87.

Illustration 133. *Signalman Reg Pulleyn with his wife Molly Pulleyn who was the 'Voice of York Station' where she worked as a Train Announcer. (Richard Pulleyn Collection)*

Chapter 16 : Around York from the 1960s to the 1980s

Burton Lane

As briefly explained when describing the commissioning of York Box, the Up Scarborough line was worked by Track Circuit Block with a train describer, but the Down Scarborough line was worked by Absolute Block to Burton Lane signal box. Shunting movements occupying the Up Scarborough line between signals Y.245 and Y.244 towards a Limit of Shunt board required permission from the signalman at Burton Lane; the York signalman sent the special bell signal '5 - 2' and, provided that no movement had been authorised towards York, a release lever at Burton Lane could be reversed (which controlled the relevant subsidiary signals) and the bell signal acknowledged by repetition. After the shunting movement was completed, the York signalman sent the special bell signal '2 - 5', then the release lever could be restored and the bell signal acknowledged.

Bootham

The Down Scarborough line from Burton Lane signal box was worked by Absolute Block, and the Up Scarborough line was worked by Track Circuit Block (Bell). However, when Burton Lane signal box was switched out the arrangements described above then applied at Bootham so an additional train describer was provided at Bootham together with a release for the shunting movement at York.

York to Market Weighton CTC

The route from York to Hull via Market Weighton included 23 manually-operated level crossings between Bootham and Beverley North signal boxes – a distance of just over 30 miles – and the cost of manning them adversely affected the economic viability of the line. The British Transport Commission modernisation plan called for significant improvements so, early in 1961, the North Eastern Region placed a contract with Westinghouse Brake and Signal Company Limited for the provision and installation of colour-light signalling operated by Centralised Traffic Control (CTC).

Illustration 134. *Bootham: on 10 February 1961, two locking fitters undertake routine examination and maintenance to the lever frame; the floorboard hatches have been removed to reveal the locking trays. (NRM Fastline Collection Reference F13655)*

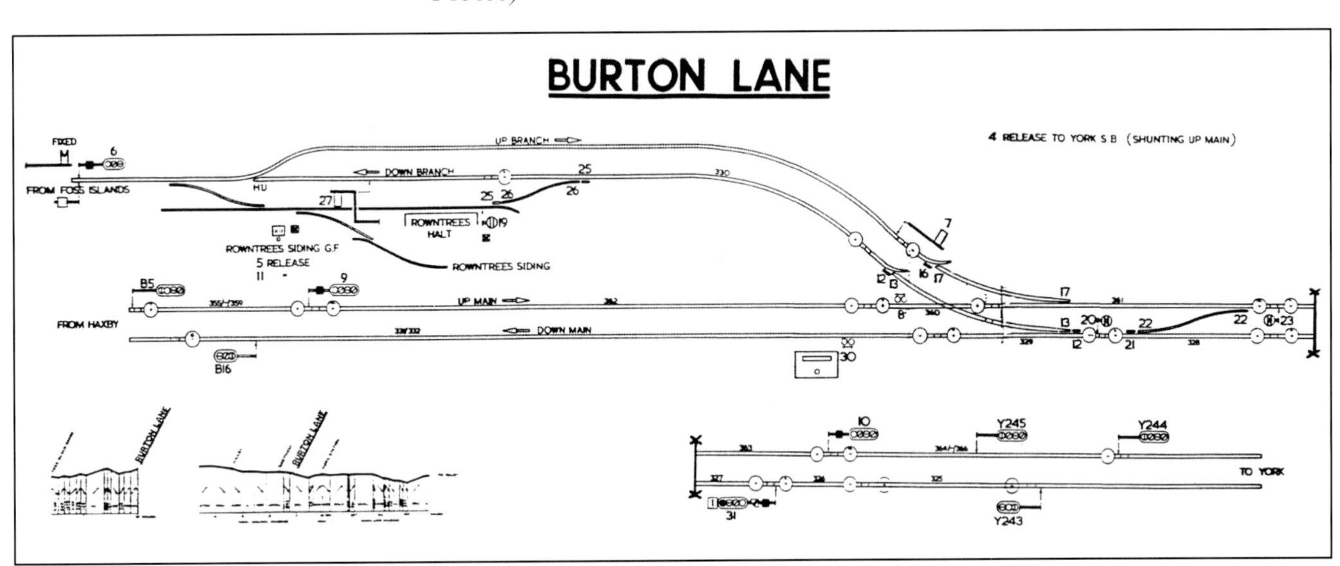

Illustration 135. *Burton Lane: facsimile of the signal box diagram in 1969 after the Outer Home signal from Foss Islands had been replaced by a colour light signal. This also shows the platform for Rowntree Halt and the ground frame-worked connection into the works. 'Hold Up' points, worked by hand, were used for the connection from the single to double line because they were on a freight only line, too far from the signal box to be worked, and because guards frequently had to use all of the layout to marshall traffic from Rowntree's Cocoa Works.*

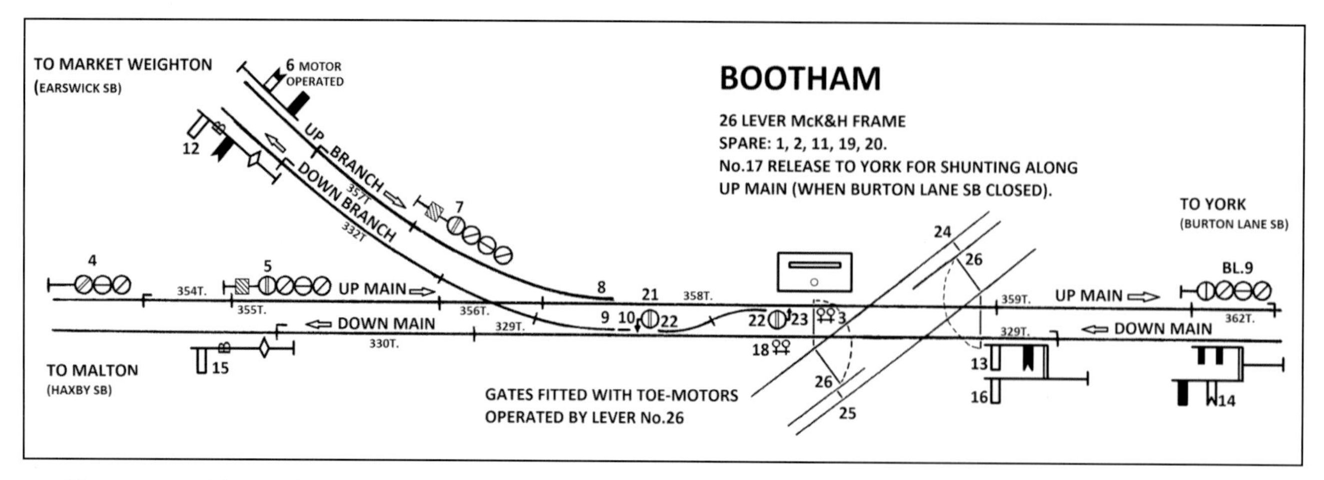

Illustration 136. Bootham: sketch diagram of the signalling based on the signal box diagram dated 1959. (Richard Pulleyn)

Most of the line was to have been singled, retaining double-line connections some 1,000 yards long approaching the two junctions, and passing loops about $^{3}/_{4}$ mile long at Pocklington and $1^{1}/_{2}$ miles long at Market Weighton. Seven of the 10 intermediate signal boxes would have been dispensed with, and auto-half-barriers would have taken the place of 19 of the manually-operated level crossing gates.

It was proposed that control would be from a new console in York Box, with an illuminated diagram, indications, and thumb switches for the operation of points and signals, control of the ground frames and manned level crossings.

The outdoor equipment was delivered to various locations along the line and S&T staff spent many weekends preparing the track and bonding track circuits in preparation for what would have been one of the biggest Centralised Traffic Control installations in the country. Without doubt, operating costs would have been significantly reduced but, before the work could be completed, the Beeching Report recommended closure of the line and this was carried out on 29 November 1965. The equipment was recovered months later so the economies that could have saved the line were never realised.(1)

Illustration 137. Copmanthorpe: the signal box and level crossing is seen on 12 October 1974 from Moor Lane which provided access to two farms; wheel-operated gates have been replaced by motor-operated barriers controlled from one of the former gate release levers. (Christopher J Woolstenholmes, CJW 137 3)

Copmanthorpe

The two sets of gates worked by separate wheels (for the Leeds and Normanton lines) were replaced by electrically operated barriers *circa* 1962. They were actually operated by lever No 22 which had previously been a gate lock.

York Yard South, 1962

When the 1903 signal box and its equipment became life-expired, it was replaced on 29 July 1962 by a new signal box opened just 23 yards north of the old signal box but on the opposite (Up) side of the line between 'B' Line and the Van Siding. The signalling contractor was Henry Williams Limited, agent for the Swiss company of 'Integra', although the external signalling works were carried out by BR (NER) staff.

The NX panel and the operating console were known at the time as the 'Domino' type, being made up from a mosaic of 40 mm x 80 mm steel 'tiles'. The NX panel was so named because, to set a route and clear the relevant signal, it required the signalman to press a button at the eNtrance to the route, then another at its eXit. To set up a route on the panel installed in York Yard South, both the entry and exit buttons had to be pressed simultaneously and held until the white route lights appeared (whereas most NX panels require the entrance then the exit button to be pressed). For a second train, under Permissive conditions, the main signal entry and exit buttons were pressed, then alternate red and white route lights appeared. Where there was an alternative route, this could be set up by pressing and holding the entry button at the same time as the alternative route (blue) button, then the exit button until the required route lights appeared.

Geographical circuitry techniques were utilised to control 188 routes by 42 electro-pneumatic point machines, nine x 3-aspect colour-light signals fitted with multi-lamp route indicators, one 2-aspect colour-light with subsidiary, 36 ground position-light signals, and 51 track circuits.

(1) *Railway Gazette*, 19 May 1961.

Illustration 138. *(Above) York Yard South: this view shows the relationship between the 1903 York Yard South and its modern replacment across the tracks, commssioned 29 July 1962. (John Midcalf Collection)*

Illustration 139. *(Left) York Yard South: the signal box as seen in 1986 from outside the Yard Master's Offices which were almost opposite; it will be seen that the footbridge across to the former Wagon Repair Works has been removed. (Richard Pulleyn)*

Illustration 140. *York Yard South: the so-called 'Domino' style of panel was installed here in 1962 by signalling contractor Henry Williams Limited, agents for the Swiss company 'Integra'. Sitting behind is Ken Appleby, eminent railway historian, one-time Area Manager at York, and author of 'Britain's Rail Super Centres - York'. (John M Boyes / Armstrong Railway Photographic Trust, JMB T228)*

By the 1960s, the method of working was still quite complex:

* To and from York Box (Track Circuit Block with Train Describers):

 Down Scarborough Goods (with connections to and from Branches Yard);

 Up Scarborough Goods (with connections – still referred to as South View – to the Permanent Way Yard, GN engine shed, MR engine shed and NE engine shed);

 Up and Down Doncaster Goods;

 Up and Down Leeds Goods;

 Down Goods (with connections to and from Holgate Cattle Dock Sidings).

* To and from York Yard North, on the Down side, it controlled (north to south):

 Hump Line into No 1 Down Yard (Sidings 1 to 13);

 Nos 1 and 2 Down Reception Lines (Telephone Block);

 Down Main Goods (Permissive Block).

* On the Up side it controlled (by Telephone Block except where shown):

 Down Mineral (leading to Down Through and Branches Yard);

 York Line;

 Frodingham Line;

 Main Exit from Up Yard;

 'B' Departure Line;

 No 1 Up Goods;

 Up Goods (Permissive Block);

 Up Main Goods (Permissive Block).

Holgate Platforms, 1964

Holgate Excursion Platforms were last used for York races in 1939, although an RCTS railtour also called there in 1957 to pick up passengers; clearly they were surplus to requirements and were demolished in 1964.

Accident at York Station 1965

On 15 June 1965 an accident took place at the north end of the station when empty stock was being propelled from Platform No 8S in the Down direction along the Up Main towards Clifton Carriage Sidings; the driver of the shunting loco passed a colour-light running signal and two ground subsidiary signals at danger and collided side-on with the leading coach of a Scarborough – Leeds DMU on Waterworks Crossing.

York Platform No 1, 1966

In 1966, Platform No 1 was converted into a Motorail loading Dock.

ECML South from York

Extension of York Box 'Outer South' panel commenced in 1967.

In Stage 1, Naburn and Escrick South signal boxes closed on 2 April 1967, so York Box fringed temporarily to Riccall North, working by TCB in both directions.

In Stage 2, Riccall North and South signal boxes closed on 11 June 1967, and the level crossings at Riccall York Road gate box, Riccall South signal box, and Turnhead gate box were all converted to Automatic Half-Barrier (AHB) operation supervised from Barlby North signal box, which became the new fringe to York Box. The only change in York Box was the addition of indications for the automatic signalling on the Down line from Barlby North.

York Station North End

In 1974, a significant remodelling of the layout at the north end of York station took place: Waterworks crossing was completely removed, severing connections between Platform Nos 14, 15 and 16 and the Scarborough lines, also severing the connection to the Goods lines to York Yard South.(1)

Accident at York Station 1975

At 02:48 on Saturday, 11 January 1975, having passed at danger a multiple-aspect colour-light signal on the Down Main, the 23:15 King's Cross - Aberdeen passenger train came into sidelong collision with the rear two vehicles of the 19:20 Aberdeen - King's Cross passenger train which was running into Platform No 9 under clear signals. A possible cause was that the driver of the Down train had been misled by the rear lights on a theatre-type route indicator on an adjacent signal, a policy which no longer applied at new installations.

Platform No 8, 1975

Apparently some passengers were confused by Platforms Nos 8S and 8N, thinking that '8S' meant that end for trains to the south and '8N' for trains to the north; in an effort to remove this confusion, the platforms were renumbered Nos 8A and 8B respectively on 5 May 1975.

Skelton, 1977

By January 1977, Skelton New Sidings had become surplus to requirements and were closed in preparation for resignalling in that area and, on 13 March 1977, signalling and permanent way alterations were commissioned:

(1) BR(ER) Supplementary Signalling Notice No.65, 17 - 29 April 1974.

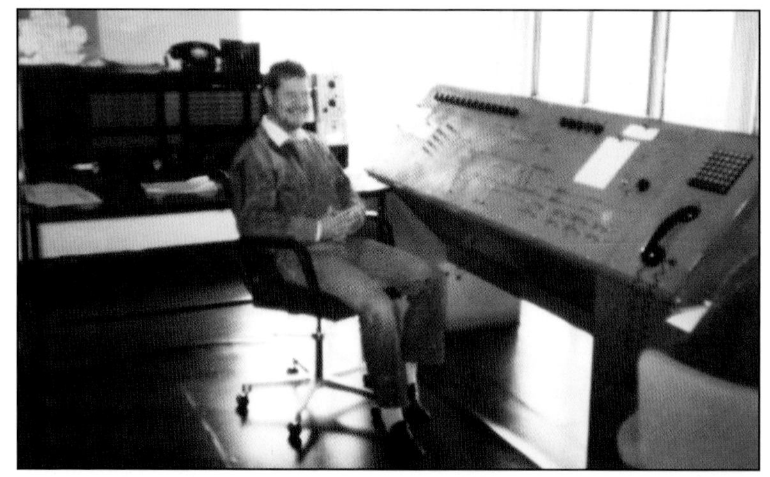

Illustration 141. *Skelton: following rationalisation of the layout, the lever frame and switch panel were replaced by a conventional NX panel located at the south end of the signal box where the windows provided a good view of passing trains. The train desciber to York Box is behind the seated signalman. The photograph was taken on 28 April 1986. (Richard Pulleyn)*

* A single lead 'Ladder' junction was installed to and from the Harrogate Branch.
* The junction into York Yards at Skelton was removed, so access to and from York Yards was at Skelton Bridge only.
* The Up and Down Independent lines from Skelton to Skelton Bridge became Slow Lines.

The new layout and signalling was controlled from a new NX panel installed at the York end of the signal box facing the window, so the frame and existing panel diagram was removed.

York Yard North

Landing Lane over-bridge immediately north of the signal box was replaced by a much wider road over-bridge in 1971 to connect with a new road and bridge over the river Ouse. Consequently, the pitched roof of the box was replaced by a flat roof giving the structure a rather abandoned appearance. Shortly before, on 9 February 1968, the 150-lever frame (which had 34 spare levers by 1966) was reduced to 60 levers (Nos 51 to 110, including eight spare). The large signal bridge spanning all of the lines outside the box was also replaced by a single colour-light with route indicator and a subsidiary aspect.

On 4 February 1984 the Up and Down Main Goods to and from York Yard South were converted from Permissive Block to Absolute Block; to and from Skelton they were converted to TCB (Bell).

Stageworks towards the major resignalling programme underway at York included:
* By 24 April 1988 a much simplified layout with many connections converted to be hand-worked and those few remaining controlled points converted to clamp-lock operation.
* By 21 August 1988 most remaining semaphores had been abandoned or converted to colour-light or ground position-light signals. The Up and Down Main Goods to and from York Yard South were converted from Absolute Block to Slow lines worked by TCB, so that henceforward they could be used by diverted passenger trains.

The signal box finally closed on 11 May 1989 when control transferred to York IECC.

Illustration 142. *Skelton: although Skelton Yard had closed when this photograph was taken on 28 April 1986, there was still sufficient telephone work, notably with York Control, to justify employment of a Train Register Lad on most shifts. (Richard Pulleyn)*

Illustration 143. *York Yard North: looking north in 1981, showing how a large part of the signal box was under the road bridge, which created a rather dark working environment on the operating floor. (Richard Pulleyn)*

Illustration 144. *York Yard North: levers have been removed from both ends of the 150-lever frame, reducing it to 60 levers (Nos. 51 to 110, including 8 spare). (Christopher J Woolstenholmes, CJW148 28)*

Illustration 145. *York Yard North: the view south from Landing Lane bridge towards York Yards. Class 56 No 56018 heads a heavy oil train towards Skelton; this locomotive was used by Dapol as the basis for an N Gauge model. (David R Vickers / 53A Models Collection, per Mick Nicholson)*

York Yard South, 1984

In February and March 1984, the layout was significantly simplified to reflect changing traffic requirements. The diagram reproduced as Illustration 146 shows the final layout.

Further rationalisation followed:

* July 1987, Up Doncaster Goods Line taken out of use.
* April 1988, Up and Down Scarborough Lines taken out of use; remaining Goods Lines worked by Absolute Block.
* May 1988, former Down Scarborough Goods Line reinstated as the ACE Siding with a temporary 'Triangle' level crossing (operated by train crew) to access to the IECC then under construction and the materials storage area.
* 21 August 1988, Goods Lines converted to Slow Lines worked by TCB Regulations.

The signal box closed on 11 May 1989 when control was transferred to York IECC.

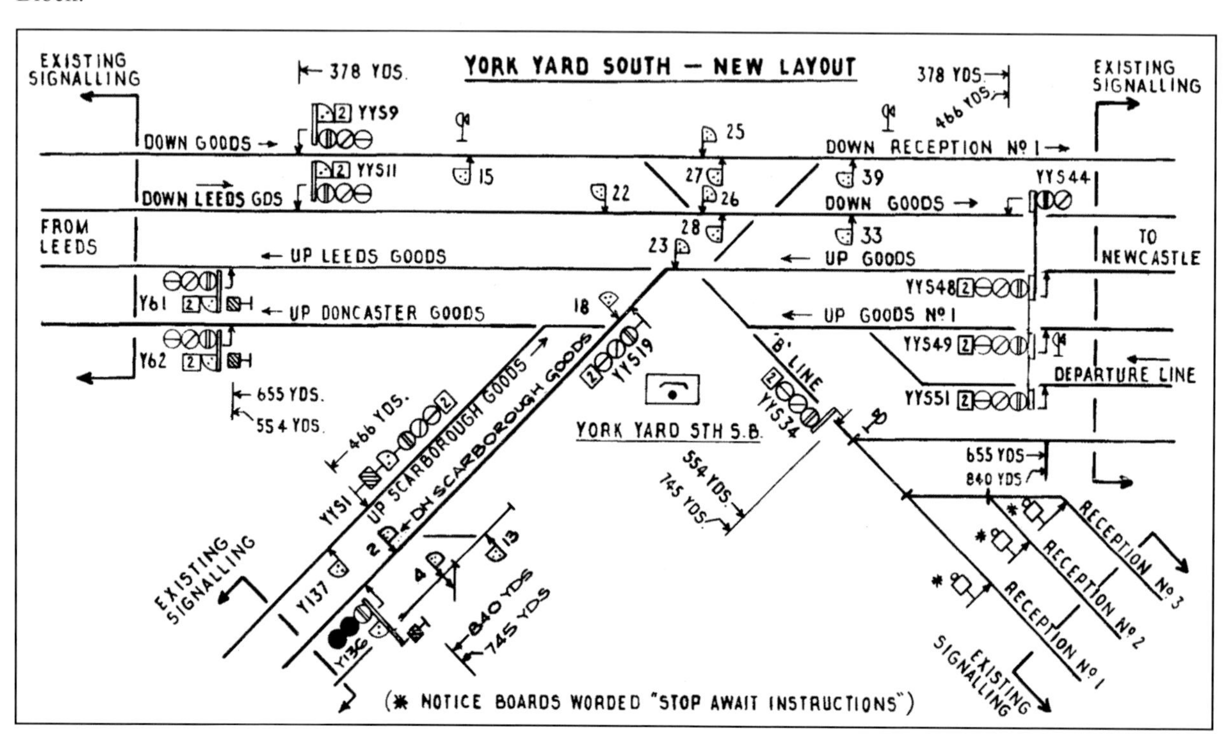

Illustration 146. *York Yard South: diagram of revised track and signalling arrangements. (BR Weekly Operating Notice NS10 dated Saturday, 3 March to Friday, 9 March 1984)*

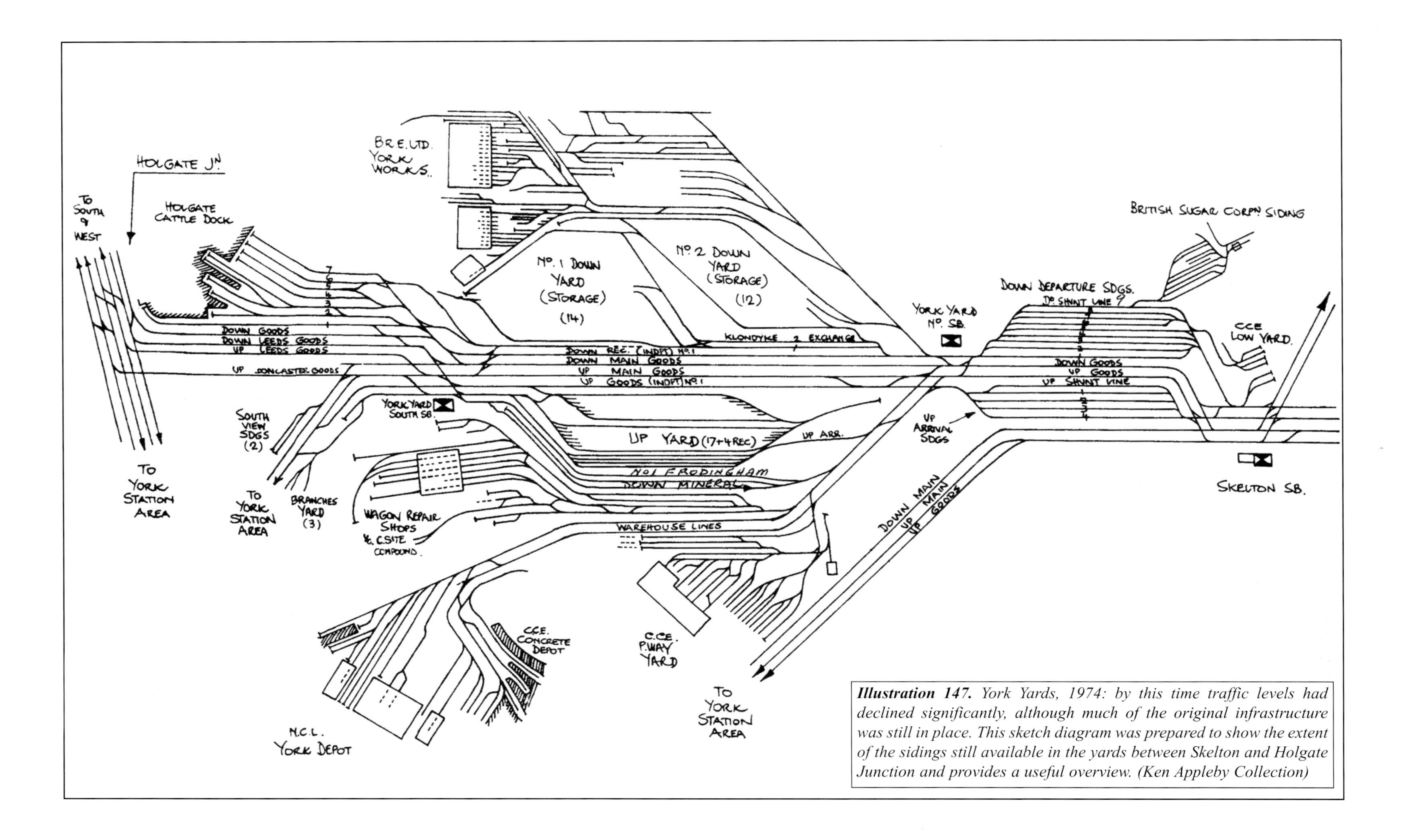

Illustration 147. *York Yards, 1974: by this time traffic levels had declined significantly, although much of the original infrastructure was still in place. This sketch diagram was prepared to show the extent of the sidings still available in the yards between Skelton and Holgate Junction and provides a useful overview. (Ken Appleby Collection)*

Chapter 17 : Operation 'Big Switch' – the New ECML

Clifton Carriage Sidings

At Clifton, major changes were made to the layout in connection with provision of new carriage maintenance and servicing facilities. A new control tower was also constructed to operate local points and signals away from the running lines; the tower was fitted with an Individual Function Switch (IFS) panel, brought into operation on 6 February 1983. However, as will be noted below, the considerable investment involved would soon be wasted as the requirement for these impressive facilities would soon diminish leading to closure.

New Main Line

During the 1970s a programme to develop a new Selby Coalfield was announced; it was recognised that removing coal from below the existing ECML would inevitably result in subsidence and significant speed restrictions, contrary to British Rail's programme for accelerating services. However, to leave sufficient coal under the line to provide support for the line would mean the loss of some 40 million tonnes of fuel, so it was agreed instead to divert the main line – a huge undertaking.

The new line was just over 14 miles long, stretching from a new junction at Temple Hirst (south of Selby) to Colton Junction between Copmanthorpe and Bolton Percy on the Leeds and Normanton lines. It would also be crossed by the Leeds - Selby - Hull line at Hambleton where curves were built from north to east (for the York - Hull service) and from south to west (as a useful diversionary route in case of problems on the former GNR route from Doncaster to Leeds). This would be achieved by a staged approach.

Copmanthorpe and Bolton Percy Signal Boxes

It was decided to control the new line from an additional Westinghouse M5 NX panel in York Box, working traffic south of Chaloners Whin through to just south of Temple Hirst where it fringed with Doncaster PSB; at Hambleton, the panel also fringed with Selby signal box in the east and Gascoigne Wood signal box in the west.

Accordingly, Copmanthorpe and Bolton Percy signal boxes closed on 13 March 1983 and the panel was first brought into use. At Copmanthorpe, Moor Lane had previously crossed the line adjacent to the signal box from which the barriers were operated; to avoid the need for this crossing the road was diverted to run through the former goods yard, thereby connecting with the overbridge just north of the site of the former station.

***Illustration 148**. Clifton Control Tower: brought into operation on 6 February 1983 to operate local points and signals from an Individual Function Switch (IFS) panel. However, withdrawal of coaching stock in 1987 led to the closure of Clifton Carriage Sidings so the control tower was taken out of use. The photograph was taken on 28 April 1986. (Richard Pulleyn)*

***Illustration 149**. Copmanthorpe: the signal box here closed on 13 March 1983 when a new panel was commissioned in York Box in preparation for opening of the Selby Diversion route from Temple Hirst to Colton. Moor Lane was diverted to run through the former goods yard, thereby connecting with the overbridge just north of the site of the former station, which enabled the level crossing to be dispensed with. (Christopher J Woolstenholmes, CJW30 5)*

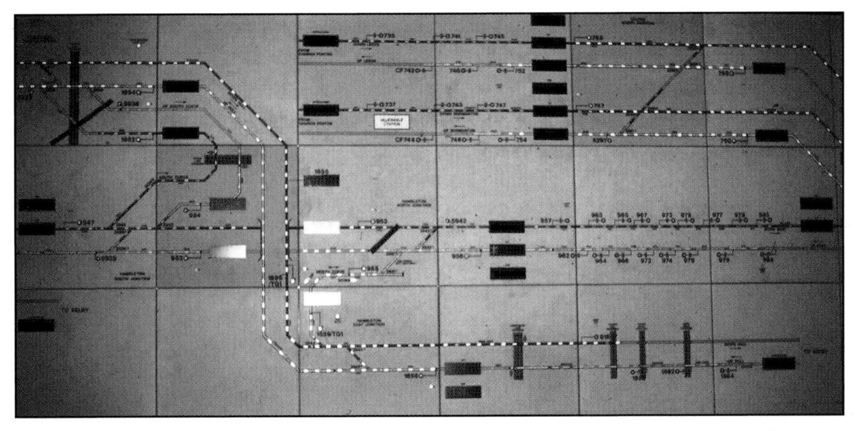

Illustrations 150 and 151*. York Box, Hambleton Panel and Desk: a new NX panel was commissioned on 13 March 1983 to control the Selby Diversion line from Temple Hirst to Colton; the desk was separate from the diagram which was mounted above. (Christopher J Woolstenholmes, CJW198 37 and 38)*

The new junction at Colton was commissioned on 9/10 April 1983, so from that date the ECML panel in York Box worked the northern portion of the line.

Chaloners Whin and Dringhouses Yard

On Sunday 25 September 1983, Chaloners Whin Junction points and all adjacent running connections were secured out of use pending removal. At 23:30 that evening the former East Coast Main Line between Barlby North Junction (Selby) and Chaloners Whin Junction was permanently closed to traffic in preparation for the opening of the new route from Doncaster via Temple Hirst Junction, Hambleton South and Hambleton North Junctions on Sunday 2 October 1983. In the interim period, all traffic between Doncaster and York was diverted via Askern and Knottingley.

The Down and Up Normanton lines between Colton Junction and Chaloners Whin Junction and their continuation (between Chaloners Whin Junction and York Holgate

Illustration 152*. Dringhouses Cold Store: the goverment cold store seen here on the left of the photograph was built during the Second World War and was rail connected at South Points. With Dringhouses Up Sidings to the right, Class 47 No 47006 heads an express towards Manchester on 18 August 1974. (53A Models Collection, per Mick Nicholson)*

Junction) into the Down and Up Doncaster Main Lines were renamed Down and Up Main throughout.

The mileposts applicable to all lines between Colton Junction and Chaloners Whin Junction were converted to bear Kings Cross - York mileages, and their location adjusted accordingly.

Dringhouses New Junction (between Chaloners Whin and Dringhouses Yard) centred at 188m 67c, and formed from a series of running (ladder) crossovers, was brought into use controlled from York Box.

Dringhouses Yard South end was remodelled and the sidings renamed or renumbered. A new Dringhouses South Shunters Ground Switch Panel was brought into use, housed in the TOPS Office, released from York Box, to control a number of local points and signals.

Finally, on Sunday 2 October 1983, the new ECML was opened throughout.

Further alterations to improve access at south end of Dringhouses yard were made in November 1984.(1)

(1) BR (ER) Supplementary Signalling Notice No.125, 25 September 1983.

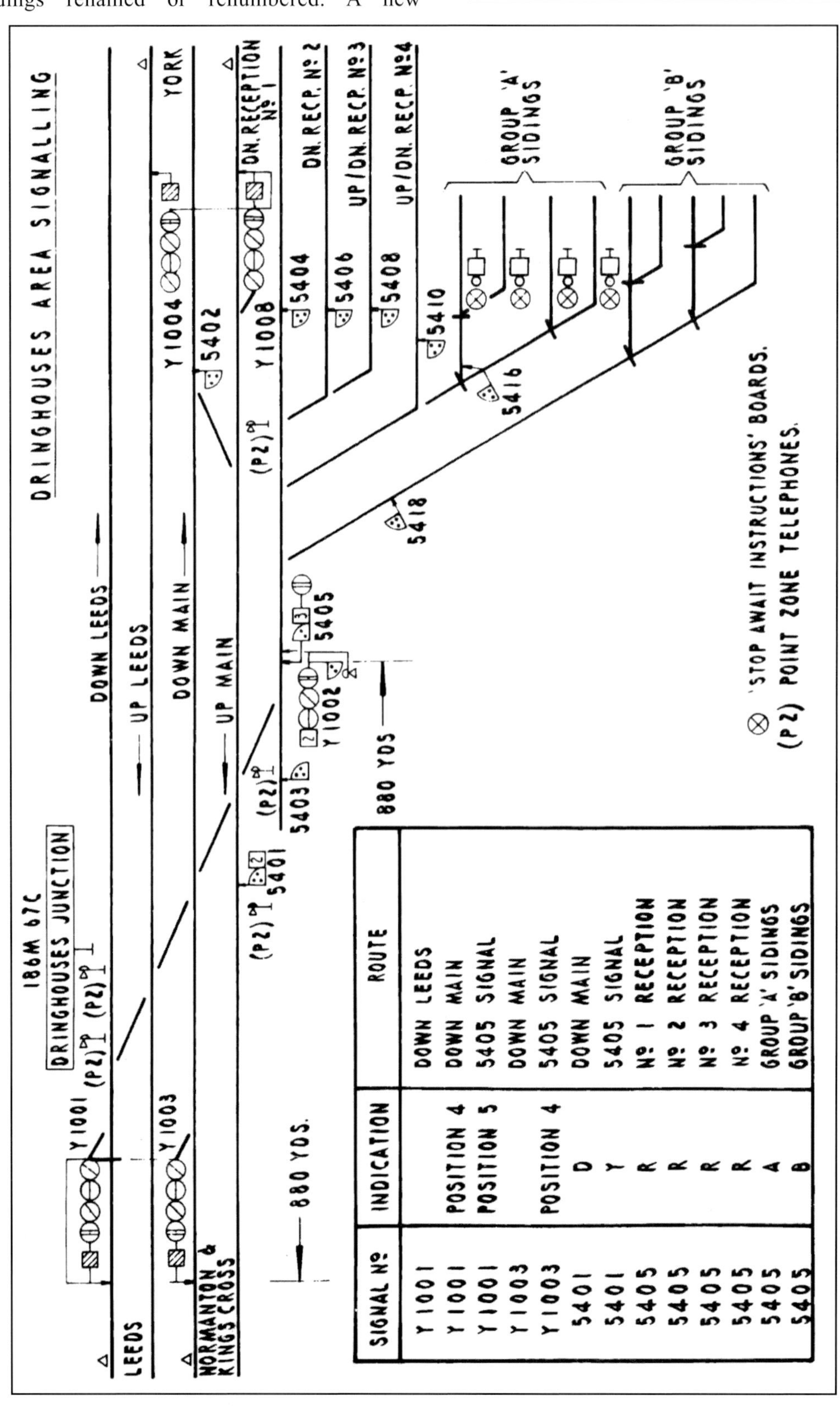

SIGNAL No	INDICATION	ROUTE
Y1001		DOWN LEEDS
Y1001	POSITION 4	DOWN MAIN
Y1001	POSITION 5	5405 SIGNAL
Y1003		DOWN MAIN
Y1003	POSITION 4	5405 SIGNAL
5401	D	DOWN MAIN
5401	Y	5405 SIGNAL
5405	R	No 1 RECEPTION
5405	R	No 2 RECEPTION
5405	R	No 3 RECEPTION
5405	R	No 4 RECEPTION
5405	A	GROUP 'A' SIDINGS
5405	B	GROUP 'B' SIDINGS

Illustration 153*. Dringhosues Yard, 1984: showing Dringhouses New Junction formed from a series of running (or ladder) crossovers, and the remodelled South end to the Yard. (BR (ER) Weekly Operating Notice NS47 dated 17 to 23 November 1984)*

Chapter 18 : 'All Change at York' – the 1980s

Prior to electrification of the ECML, a major scheme was developed to significantly simplify the complex layout at York, especially south of the station where arrangements still reflected the needs of a steam age railway with shunting, changes of train locomotives *etc*. Planning for the staged scheme began as far back as 1984.

Dringhouses and Clifton

Freight traffic patterns were changing significantly: by 1985 fast, air-braked freight services under the title 'Speedlink' were generally operating long distance only. Dringhouses Yard was nominated as a network yard, although there was no longer a requirement for a hump yard so, on 3 March that year, the control tower at the north end of Dringhouses Yard was taken out of use. Similarly, withdrawal of coaching stock in 1987 led to the closure of Clifton Carriage Sidings when the control tower was taken out of use; it had been demolished by 1988 when the site was used for storage of materials in connection with the York electrification and resignalling.

Foss Islands Branch

Foss Islands Depot itself had closed on 6 August 1984 so Staff & Ticket working was replaced by One Train Working on the branch for the occasional train using the connection to the DVLR.

During the early planning stages for remodelling the York area and commissioning of the Integrated Electronic Control Centre (IECC), it was anticipated that the remaining Dringhouses Yard would be closed and traffic concentrated in York Up Yard; however, Nestle had become the owners of the former Rowntree Mackintosh business, and they decided to concentrate on road transport with effect from April 1987. Since they were the principal customer in York for Railfreight, the future of the Foss Islands Branch was placed in real jeopardy: only the occasional transfer of oil traffic to the DVR Yard at Layerthorpe remained in use and, when the contract expired in October 1988 that sealed the fate of the line, so the planned transfer of control to York IECC never took place. The last passenger train from Rowntree Halt had left on 8 July 1988.

York Station Stagework

Implementation of the major remodelling at York was undertaken in stages. During Stages 1 and 2, between 10 September and 28 November 1988, the layout at the north end of York station was further simplified; the Up and Down Main lines through the station were removed on 8 November 1988 leaving just the through platform lines; Platform No 12 and all of the Scarborough Bays except one were taken out of use.

The Engineer then switched attention to simplification of Holgate Junction and the complex layout immediately south of York; the difficult five-stage operation at the south end of the station, commencing on 19 February 1989 and, as a result of meticulous planning, this was completed successfully and on schedule on 4 June 1989.

Scarborough Line Stagework

The major resignalling at York extended out as far as Strensall where preliminary stagework started on 28 February 1988 when a panel replaced the frame in Strensall signal box (6*m* 48*c* from York); Track Circuit Block working with colour-light signalling was brought into operation between Bootham signal box (1*m* 51*c*) and Strensall over both Up and Down lines. Control of Haxby station level crossing (4*m* 18*c*) by CCTV from Strensall was assumed on the same date: the gates had been removed and the gate box demolished on 14 February 1988. Haxby Road gate box (3*m* 27*c*) remained open, but became released from Strensall panel.

Next, on 14 January 1989, Haxby Road gate box was replaced by a temporary structure on the Up side of the line, north of the crossing; full barriers were installed under the control of Strensall panel, with local attendance pending demolition of the former gate box and implementation of full CCTV operation.

Strensall No 1 gate box (6*m* 00*c*) closed on 5 February 1989, when the gates were replaced by full lifting barriers worked from Strensall panel, again with temporary local attendance. On the same date, Strensall panel also assumed MCB (TV) control (Manual Controlled Barriers with TV overview) of the full lifting barriers at Strensall No 2 level crossing

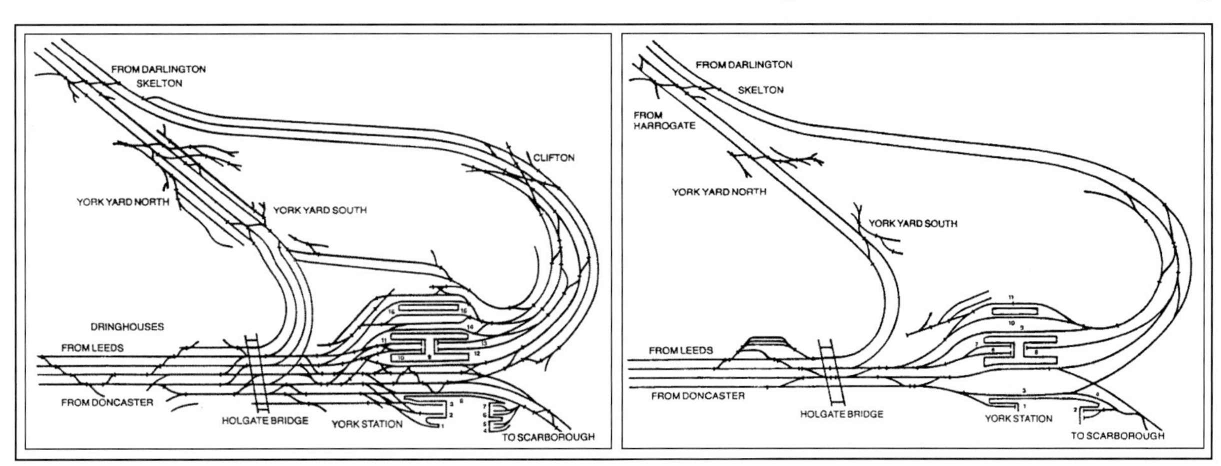

Illustration 154*. York Station Stagework: extracted from an information leaflet, these sketchmaps show the track layout at York both before track rationalsation in 1989 and afterwards. (BR / Richard Pulleyn Collection)*

(6*m* 11*c*); these barriers had been RC (Remote Control) operated from Strensall No 1 gate box since 31 May 1981 when Strensall No 2 gate box closed. These temporary arrangements at No 1 were replaced on 12 February 1989, also by MCB (TV) working but from Strensall panel.

At Burton Lane signal box (lm 09c) the facing points giving access to the Foss Islands Branch were replaced by plain line on 16 April 1989 and local instructions for working the branch were effectively deleted from the Sectional Appendix from the same date. Then on 30 April 1989, both Burton Lane and Bootham signal boxes closed.

The level crossing at Bootham was converted to an ABCL (Auto Half-Barriers Locally Monitored): red lights flashed continuously in both directions along the railway except upon the approach of a train, when road signals and barriers operated, correct operation being proved by a change to flashing white lights. From the same date Track Circuit Block (Bell) working was introduced between Strensall panel and York Box.

York IECC Commissioning

At 00:01 on Thursday, 11 May 1989, the four Westinghouse OCS panels in York Box were taken out of use, and the following signal boxes were closed: York Yard South, York Yard North, and Skelton.

Emergency hand-signalling, supervised from two workstations in the new Signalling Centre at York, was introduced in the area between signals at Copmanthorpe (south of York on the Doncaster and Leeds lines) and Beningbrough (on the ECML north). Commissioning of the 'York Integrated Electronic Control Centre' (IECC) with solid state interlocking (SSI) was signed in at 0708 on Sunday, 14 May 1989. At that stage, the fringe boxes were: Poppleton on the Harrogate branch, Tollerton on the ECML north, Strensall on the Scarborough line (as referred to above), and the Selby Diversion panel in York Box which was retained at this stage to continue to work the ECML south as well as the Leeds and Normanton lines as far as Colton North Junction, although all connections at Dringhouses Junction were secured permanently out of use pending removal.(1)

The IECC (also referred to as York Signalling Centre) was located west of Platform No 11 at York station, roughly on the site of the former Scarborough Goods lines. Externally, the purpose of the single storey building, clad in blue corrugated material, was not immediately apparent.

Five workstations (WS) were provided in the IECC: two for signalmen (north and south), and one each for communications, supervisor, and train announcer. Automatic Route Setting (ARS) applied for most train movements by interfacing the IECC with the National Computerised Timetable. For additional train movements and during out of course running, the signalmen could set up routes manually using either a conventional keyboard or a 'tracker-ball' system.

* York South Workstation controlled the line from south of Temple Hirst to just north of York station.
* York North Workstation controlled from just north of York station as far as Northallerton on the ECML, including the junctions for the Redmire and Harrogate branches, and York Yards.

The workstations were built to the 'BRR / Sema Group IECC Classic' design, and the centralised control system was supplied by CAP Industry Limited using three micro-computer interlocking modules which checked each other; if any of the modules was faulty it would automatically shut down. Control information was conveyed via simple duplicated cable routes to solid state lineside units which operated and monitored lineside equipment.

(1) BR (ER) Signalling Notice No.150, 11 to 14 May 1989 – Key Stage.

***Illustration 155**. York IECC: this April 2014 view of the nondescript building, located behind a security fence, also includes the York Rail Operating Centre in the distance. York ROC would take over control from the IECC on 27 December 2018; see Chapter 19. (Richard Pulleyn)*

There were eight interlockings within the York IECC area:

* Route Relay Interlockings at Temple Hirst, Hambleton and Colton.
* Solid State Interlockings at York South, York North 1, York North 2, Tollerton / Thirsk, and Northallerton.

As commissioned, the IECC controlled:

* 80 route miles.
* 246 track miles.
* 126 controlled main signals.
* 183 semi-automatic and automatic signals.
* 52 position-light shunting signals.
* 700 routes.
* 96 points.
* 1 ground frame.
* 22
* level crossings of various types.

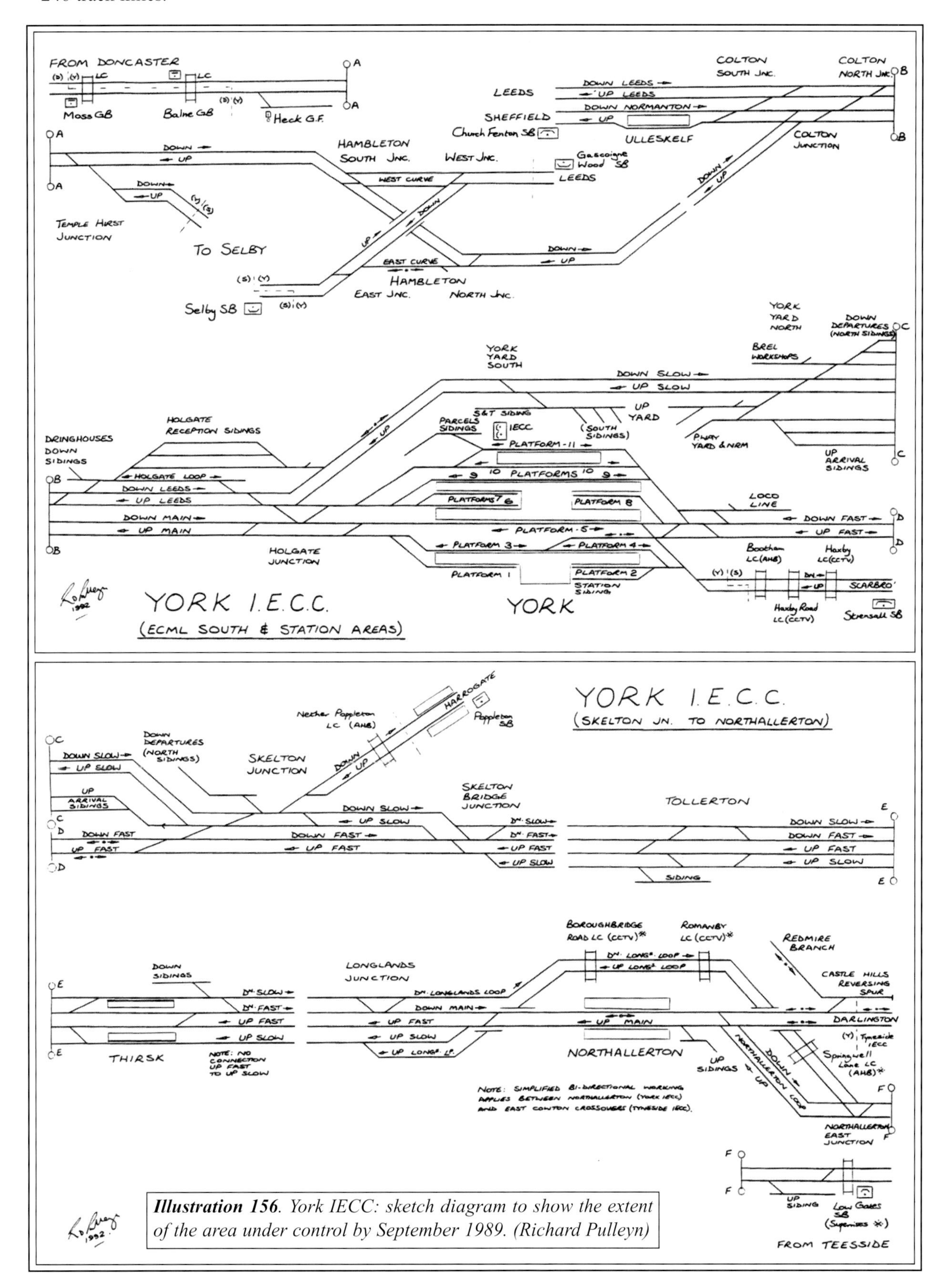

***Illustration 156**. York IECC: sketch diagram to show the extent of the area under control by September 1989. (Richard Pulleyn)*

***Illustration 157**. York IECC: in the foreground is the Shift Supervisor's Desk which does not incorporate any controls, with the original North Workstation beyond by the windows. (Richard Pulleyn Collection)*

***Illustration 158**. York IECC: a closer view of the North Workstation with the South Workstation beyond. The 'Trackerball' and keyboard are both located on the desk in front of the signalman, either of which can be used to initiate changes such as setting or cancelling routes. (Richard Pulleyn Collection)*

Concurrently with opening of the IECC on Sunday 14 May 1989, the platforms at York were renumbered, as follows: (Note: all platforms bi-directional.)

Former Number		New Number
3	Up side bay at south end	1
10	Up side (Scarborough) bay at north end	2
8S	South end of main Up platform	3
8N	North end of main Up platform	4
9	Down side main platform	5
10	Down side bay at south end	6
11	Down side bay at south end	7
13	Down side (Harrogate) bay at north end	8
14	Down side through	9
15	Down side through	10
16	Down side through	11

Re-Control of ECML Panel and Closure of York Box

At 00:33 on Sunday 10 September 1989, the York Box (Selby Diversion) panel was taken out of use and York Box finally closed. Control transferred to York IECC, which then had new fringe boxes at Doncaster PSB on the ECML south, Church Fenton on the Leeds and Normanton lines, Gascoigne Wood (at Hambleton), and Selby (at both Hambleton and Temple Hirst).

Meanwhile, the ECML electrification project from Kings Cross had been progressing rapidly and the first passenger carrying electric train service from Kings Cross arrived in York on Sunday 24 September 1989.

Extension of North Workstation

Further northwards extension of the area controlled by York IECC took place in four stages: on Sunday 10 December 1989 Tollerton signal box closed, and at 05:00 on Saturday 20 January 1990 Thirsk signal box closed (control passed to York IECC at around 22:40 later that day).

Next, at 01:30 on Sunday, 15 April 1990, Northallerton signal box closed so York IECC then fringed with Darlington PSB on the ECML north, and with Low Gates signal box on the former Leeds Northern towards Teesside. As part of this work, York IECC also controlled Northallerton East Junction, which had previously been worked by Low Gates box (following closure of Northallerton East signal box on 6 March 1960); however, on the Low Level route between Longlands Junction and Northallerton East Junction, Low Gates continued to monitor the CCTV level crossings at Boroughbridge Road and Romanby and to supervise Springwell Lane AHBs, even though the protecting signals were worked from York IECC; in effect, Low Gates 'slotted' the York signals by using the relevant 'Crossing Clear' buttons.

York IECC also controlled the Wensleydale branch connections at Castle Hills where there was a reversing line, although traffic rarely consisted of more than one daily limestone train between Teesside and Redmire. However, Bedale (which had been reduced to gate box status on 5 February 1985) was reinstated as a signal box on 8 April 1990 to facilitate weekday engineering work; from that date, instead of being worked as a single section, the branch was then worked by two One Train Working staff sections: Castle Hills - Bedale and Bedale - Redmire. Therefore, while the daily freight was occupying the upper end of the branch beyond Bedale, the engineers could have possession of the lower end. The One Train Working train staff for the Castle Hills – Bedale section was kept at Low Gates box when not in use.

It was originally intended that Low Gates signal box would be retained simply to supervise local level crossings. On the old Leeds Northern route from Northallerton to Teesside, York IECC would then work to Bowesfield (which controlled the layout at Eaglescliffe); however, following a reappraisal, it was decided that at this stage York IECC would work to Low Gates signal box which was retained and worked to Long Lane by Absolute Block. Nevertheless, on 29 November 1997 Long Lane and Picton signal boxes closed and the York IECC area of control extended close to MP 43¾, just north of Low Gates level crossing. Track Circuit Block working then applied from York IECC to Low Gates (which then worked to Bowesfield; unusually, therefore, Low Gates signal box, being adjacent to the level crossing, is not located within its area of signalling control).

Finally, on 11/12 May 1991 Darlington PSB closed as part of the Newcastle resignalling scheme, so York IECC then worked to Tyneside IECC, interfacing near Danby Wiske, a few miles north of Northallerton and on 8 July 1991 the ECML electrification project north from York was officially brought into use.

Impact of the 'Leeds 1st Project'

In 1967 Leeds PSB had been incorporated in offices above City station and further extension panels had been added over the years, but by the 1990s the original equipment was becoming unreliable and in some cases life expired. Consequently the initial 'Leeds 1st' station regeneration plan included provision of a new, purpose built Leeds Signalling Centre. However, Railtrack national signalling strategy was evolving so it was decided subsequently to locate control in an extended York IECC.

ADtranz was awarded the £30m contract for the design, installation, commissioning and transfer of the new signalling to York; this included installation of AWS (Automatic Warning System) and TPWS (Train Protection Warning System) throughout, together with 64 new signal posts, 117 new three- or four-aspect signals, 120 new point machines, 290 new track circuits, and 153 new lineside telephones.

Construction of a £10m building extension to York IECC commenced on 15 December 1999 to house the additional workstations, with commissioning anticipated in December 2001. The IECC was doubled in size, and completely refitted with the latest, ergonomically designed workstations. The SSI (Solid State Interlocking) included ARS (Automatic Route Setting), monitored by signallers at their VDU (Visual Display Unit) Workstations. As a consequence of the extension it also became possible to accommodate Railtrack Zone Control in the same building.

Phase 4 of the Leeds 1st Project, between 23 December 2000 and 7 January 2001, was probably the most important and complex phase of the project when decommissioning of the signalling at Leeds commenced and new signalling controlled from York was progressively introduced.

At 00:45 on 25 December 2000, Leeds West End, Leeds East End (Neville Hill / Marsh Lane) and Engine Shed panels were all signed out, although Leeds PSB retained control of the Leeds North West panel (Skipton / Ilkley/ Bradford Forster Square), and Leeds Ardsley Panel (Copley Hill West Junction exclusive to South Kirkby Junction inclusive).

From 00:01 on Wednesday 27 December 2000, control from Neville Hill West Junction to Manston level crossing was transferred to York (Leeds East Workstation) and brought back into use. Internal signalling at Neville Hill was not affected, but the depot consoles then obtained releases from York IECC. In recognition of the high number of moves taking place an additional Leeds East Assist Workstation was provided so that the area could be controlled by two signalmen, for example during early mornings when units were being released from Neville Hill depot to go into traffic.

At 05:15 on 2 January 2001, further new trackwork and signalling in the Leeds area was commissioned and controlled from York IECC. Consequently, at this stage York IECC (South) Workstation worked to Church Fenton which in turn worked to York (Leeds East) Workstation. York (Leeds West) Workstation worked to:

* Stourton PSB (with a boundary at Hunslet South Junction);
* Leeds PSB (Ardsley panel, with a boundary at Beeston);
* Leeds PSB (Leeds North West panel, with a boundary at Kirkstall);
* Horsforth signal box on the Harrogate line, with a boundary at Armley on the Down and Woodside on the Up;
* Batley signal box with a boundary at Cottingley station.

All signal ID plates on lines formerly controlled from Leeds PSB retained their 'L' prefix.

The Bradford lines were reinstated on 19 May 2001, so York IECC (Leeds West WS) then worked to Mill Lane (Bradford) signal box, and on 17 August 2001, the Leeds North West panel transferred to York IECC, which then fringed to Hellifield signal box. Ardsley panel became the only remaining panel in Leeds PSB.

At 08:52 on Sunday 21 April 2002 Church Fenton signal box closed and control from York IECC was fully commissioned at 18:40. Consequently, Leeds East Workstation then worked to York South Workstation, also to Milford and Gascoigne Wood (and, of course, to Leeds West Workstation). York South Workstation worked to Gascoigne Wood and Leeds East Workstation (and, of course, to York North Workstation, Selby, Doncaster and Strensall).

On 16 June 2002 at 08:00, Leeds PSB finally closed when the Ardsley panel transferred to York IECC (Leeds Ardsley Workstation).

Finally, signalling controlled from the panel in the Portacabin Stourton signal box transferred to York IECC on 28 July 2002, so the panel in the Portacabin at Castleford then became the fringe box to York on the former Midland lines south of Leeds.

Chapter 19 : York Rail Operating Centre (ROC)

York IECC did not represent the final page in the history of signalling in York because the city was chosen by Network Rail in 2012 to be the location for one of 12 planned Rail Operating Centres for England, Scotland and Wales. Furthermore, ultimately it will be the largest in the country and will control signalling and rail operations on the whole of the East Coast Main Line from London King's Cross to the Scottish borders together with associated lines.

The site chosen for York ROC was known as the 'Engineer's Triangle', a wedge of land at the junction between the main line and the lines through York Yard, originally occupied by engine sheds; ironically, therefore, the largest ROC has been built on the site of Locomotive Yard signal box which had the largest mechanical frame in the world.

The building was formally opened on Friday, 12 September 2014 by Phil Verster, (Network Rail, Route Managing Director) and Hugh Bailey (Member of Parliament for York). For photographs, see the front cover and Illustration 155.

In addition to the Signalling Workstations, the building includes Route Control and a Workforce Development Centre, both of which are described separately below.

North Lincolnshire Resignalling

The first workstations to become operative in York ROC were commissioned in connection with the North Lincolnshire Resignalling scheme on Wednesday, 30 December 2015. Eleven signal boxes (SB) and two gate boxes (GB) were abolished as detailed below:

Name	Type	Scope
Appleby	SB	Re-signal
Elsham	SB	Re-signal
Wrawby Junction	SB	Re-signal
Barnetby East	SB	Re-signal
New Barnetby	GB	Converted to CCTV on call
Brocklesby	SB	Re-control
Roxton Sidings	SB	Re-signal
Stallingborough	SB	Re-signal
Marsh Junction	SB	Re-signal
Pasture Street	SB	Re-control
Ulceby	SB	Re-signal
Barton Road	GB	Converted to ABCL
Immingham East	SB	Re-control*

* Became the 'Immingham Token Exchange Point' for operation over the Grimsby Light Railway.

Signalling control was transferred to new VDU based workstations located in the York ROC, known as the North Lincolnshire No 1 and No 2 Workstations. North Lincolnshire No 1 Workstation normally controls the area, with North Lincolnshire No 2 Workstation being used at busy times and during periods of perturbation.

Re-Control of Sheffield PSB

Following re-control of Sheffield PSB, the Sheffield and Rotherham Workstations were next commissioned at York ROC. Sheffield Workstation in York ROC was brought into operational use from 05:00 hrs on Monday, 2 May 2016, with the Rotherham Workstation following the next day from 0500 hours on Tuesday, 3 May 2016.

The existing Sheffield signal box (PSB) was closed although the signal boxes that fringed to Sheffield PSB remained unaltered so limits of control unchanged. Since this was a re-control exercise, no alterations to trackside signalling equipment, signage, permanent way or permissible line speeds were necessary.

Sheffield Workstation controls the areas between the following approximate fringe locations:

* 154*m* 46*c* on the Manchester lines fringing to Totley Tunnel East signal box.
* 149*m* 49*c* (Dronfield Inclusive) on the Main lines fringing to East Midlands Control Centre (EMCC) Chesterfield Workstation.
* 159*m* 16*c* on the Worksop lines fringing to Woodburn Junction signal box.
* 163*m* 22*c* on the Barnsley lines fringing to Barnsley signal box.
* 162*m* 48*c* on the Main lines fringing to York ROC Rotherham Workstation.

Rotherham Workstation controls the areas between the following approximate fringe locations:

* 147*m* 60*c* on the Barrow Hill lines fringing to East Midlands Control Centre (EMCC) Chesterfield Workstation.
* 47*m* 60*c* on the Beighton lines fringing to Beighton Station Junction signal box.
* 3*m* 57*c* on the Tinsley lines fringing to Woodburn Junction signal box.
* 162*m* 48*c* on the Meadowhall Main lines(exclusive) fringing to York ROC Sheffield Workstation.
* 16*m* 14*c* on the Pontefract lines fringing to York IECC Ardsley Workstation.
* 19*m* 47*c* on the Conisbrough lines (previously Doncaster lines) fringing to Doncaster signal box.

Re-Control of Huddersfield and Healey Mills PSBs

In connection with the re-control of Huddersfield and Healey Mills PSBs, which were then closed, Huddersfield Workstation was brought into operational in York ROC use from 05:00 hrs on 20 January 2018.

Calder Valley Resignalling and Re-Control of Bradford Mill Lane

Known as the Huddersfield to Bradford Re-signalling Project, this resulted in closure of the signal boxes at Hebden Bridge, Milner Royd Junction, Halifax, and Mill Lane Junction. The re-signalling was designed to incorporate journey time improvements including a 4 minute headway for non-stopping trains between Hebden Bridge and Bradford Interchange. The layout in the Bradford Interchange / Mill Lane Junction area was also enhanced with two additional crossovers.

Consequently, Halifax Workstation was commissioned in York ROC on 28 October 2018 to control the line from Hebden Bridge to Bradford Interchange and on towards Leeds as far as Wortley Junction, working by Track Circuit Block (TCB) with train detection by axle counters.

Ferriby to Gilberdyke and Saltmarshe Resignalling

From 05:15 hours on Monday, 26 November 2018 signalling equipment associated with the following locations was decommissioned: Gilberdyke Junction SB, Oxmardyke SB, Broomfleet SB, Cave Crossing SB, Crabley Creek SB, Brough East SB, Welton GB, Melton Lane SB, Green Oak Goit GB, and Saltmarshe SB. All of these locations were closed except Crabley Creek which was downgraded to become a gate box.

New signalling equipment was commissioned incorporating VDU Signalling Control Systems controlled from Brough Workstation at York ROC. Track Circuit Block (Axle Counters) Regulations applied throughout with a predominantly 4-aspect signalling system, but also some areas of 3-aspect signalling. All signals were of the LED type. Nine level crossings were upgraded to Manned Controlled Barriers-Obstacle Detection (MCB-OD), although Crabley Creek LC remained as Manned Controlled Gates (MCG).

King's Cross - Hertford Workstation

As the first step towards re-control of King's Cross PSB, the Hertford Workstation was transferred to the ECML South Section of the Rail Operating Centre in York with effect from 04:05 on Monday, 3 December 2018.

The WestCAD VSCS Workstation had been commissioned at King's Cross as part of the Digital Railway Programme with the second phase of the ERTMS testing in 2013. This saw the opening of an ETCS National Integration Facility based at Hitchin. When required for operational ETCS testing this can control 5 miles of the Down (northbound) line of the Hertford Loop – between crossovers installed at Molewood Tunnel (21*m* 22*c* from King's Cross) and Bragbury (at 26*m* 20*c* from King's Cross).

During peak hours, the Down Hertford Loop line operated normally, controlled from the workstation; however, when the Down line was needed for ECTS tests, control could be transferred to the test facility located at Hitchin, using a special switching facility.

When transfer of control was confirmed the Down Hertford line was then 'greyed out' on the Workstation screen, normal traffic then using the Up line in both directions. For this reason, bi-directional signalling was installed on both the Up and Down Hertford Loop lines.

York IECC

As mentioned above, York IECC did not represent the final page in the history of signalling in York because the city was chosen by Network Rail to be the location for a Rail Operating Centre. Consequently, with effect from 05:00 on Thursday, 27 December 2018, signalling in the areas controlled by York South, York North, Leeds West, Leeds East, Leeds Ardsley, and Leeds North West Workstations, previously located in York IECC, were moved to the York ROC. The respective areas controlled by each of these workstations remained unchanged. Shortly before this transfer all of the existing workstations in the ROC were transferred to a separate floor from Control which had expanded to include Electrification Control.

King's Cross

As work progressed on the ECML Upgrade Programme, and the associated ROC Migration Programme, the existing York ROC Hertford Workstation (which had transferred in December 2018) and control of King's Cross Signal Box Panels 5, 4 and part of Panel 3 was transferred to three new workstations in York ROC over the weekend of 14 / 15 September 2019.

The new workstations and their approximate areas of control (mileages from King's Coss) were:

* Wood Green Workstation, 5*m* 39*c* to 17*m* 65*c*.
* Langley Workstation, 18*m* 54*c* to 27*m* 54*c*.
* Hitchin Workstation, 28*m* 31*c* to 42*m* 0*c*.

Illustration 159. *York ROC: photographed in July 2018, before relocation to the separate signalling floor above, this is the Huddersfield Workstation which came into use on 20 January 2018. The screens provide a clear overview of the whole area under control although the signalman can zoom in on any one particular location as required. Despite the introduction of ARS (Automated Route Setting) this work still requires intense periods of concentration. (Richard Pulleyn)*

Chapter 20 : Traffic Control Offices in York

In the period leading up to and during the First World War, the volume of freight traffic being handled by the NER was so great that it was creating congestion and delay, particularly around centres of heavy industry such as Tyneside and Teesside. In an attempt to address this problem, the NER introduced a Freight Traffic Control at Newport (Middlesbrough) in 1910, followed by a Tyneside Local Traffic Control at Newcastle in 1917. These offices, improved efficiency by regulating freight and mineral traffic flows to avoid congestion, besides monitoring wagon supply and supervising train performance.

York Main Line Control, located in the Main Headquarters building, opened on 9 November 1922 to supervise the whole of the ECML between Shaftholme Junction (north of Doncaster) and Newcastle Central station – approximately 108 route miles. In particular, it regulated freight traffic to and from the marshalling yards at York, Darlington and around Tyneside. Located in the Main Line Control Office was a diagram board representing all lines being controlled; this board was fitted with a series of cords which moved relative to the average speed of various classes of train. Different coloured tickets were then hung on to a carrier to 'ride' on the cord moving nearest to the average speed for the class of train involved; when signalmen at various reporting locations telephoned in, the position of the carriers could be adjusted as necessary by three train controllers on each shift.

When a train was stationary, for example in a yard, the ticket was taken off the cord and placed on a peg. The traffic and locomotive controllers were seated behind the train controllers and, by looking at the diagram board, they could determine their next moves.

A second 'York District Control Office' was opened by the LNER in 1937, located at 37 Tanner Row (which once was the 'North Eastern Hotel' adjacent to the original passenger station), and from 1940 onwards this office controlled the ECML south of Skelton Bridge with the following controllers' positions:

* York Station and Freight Yards.
* York to Selby and Doncaster.
* York to Normanton.
* The Leeds Northern to Northallerton.
* York to Northallerton.
* York to Scarborough (Saturdays Only).

Taking the York to Northallerton section as an example, all trains were reported from the signal boxes at Skelton, Alne, Thirsk and Northallerton, although other boxes could also be contacted if necessary. The times reported were then plotted on specially-printed graph paper: the location of every signal box and colour-light signal section was shown on the vertical axis and the time was shown on the horizontal axis. Different coloured pencils were used to distinguish the type of train and whether the train was running on the Main / Fast or Relief / Slow line. Regulation of the traffic generally rested with the signalmen at key locations although control staff could intervene where they were aware of some over-riding circumstance. See Illustration 161.

In the following year, 1938, the main line as far as Northallerton was also transferred to York District Control; northwards, separate District Controls were also opened at Darlington, Sunderland and Newcastle.

Main Line Control subsequently became known as 'Central Control' until the merger of the BR Eastern and North Eastern Regions in 1967 when a further major reorganisation was initiated: so, with effect from 13 April 1969, Central Control became 'Regional Control' for the whole of the Eastern Region, located in Room W107 on the first floor of West Offices (this was the former Y&NM Board Room in York 'Old' station buildings).

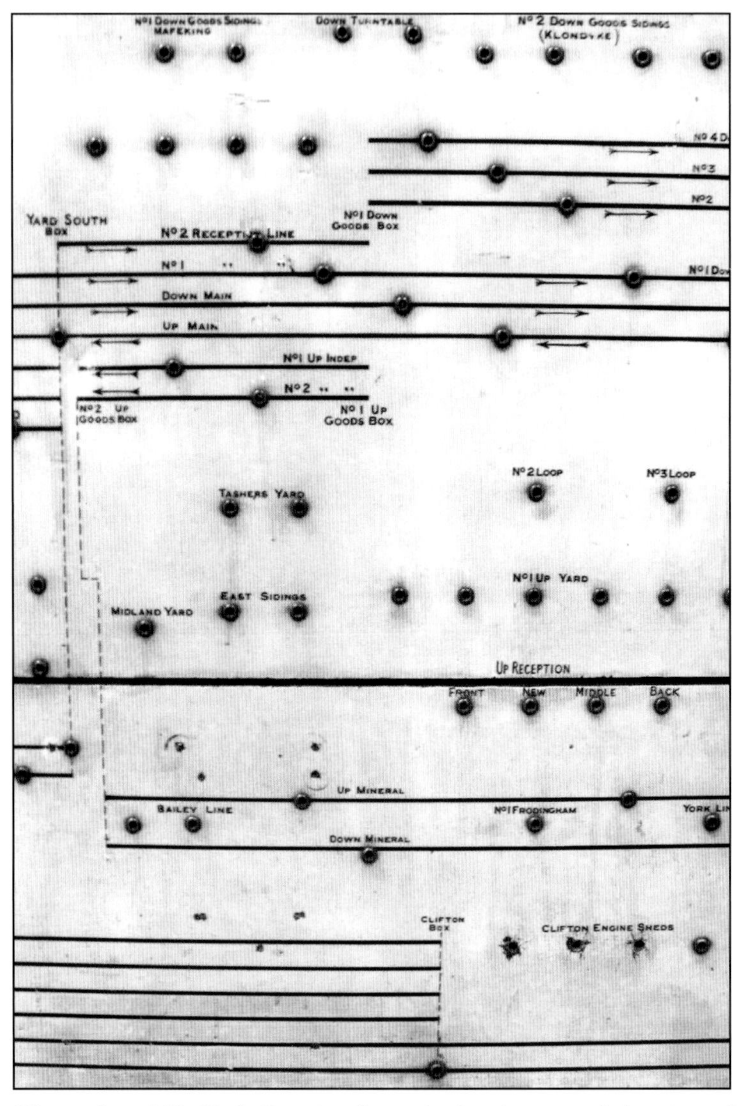

Illustration 160. *York District Control: this is part of the control panel for the York Yards Area showing where pegs could be inserted with details of trains at the various sidings and running lines. (Richard Pulleyn)*

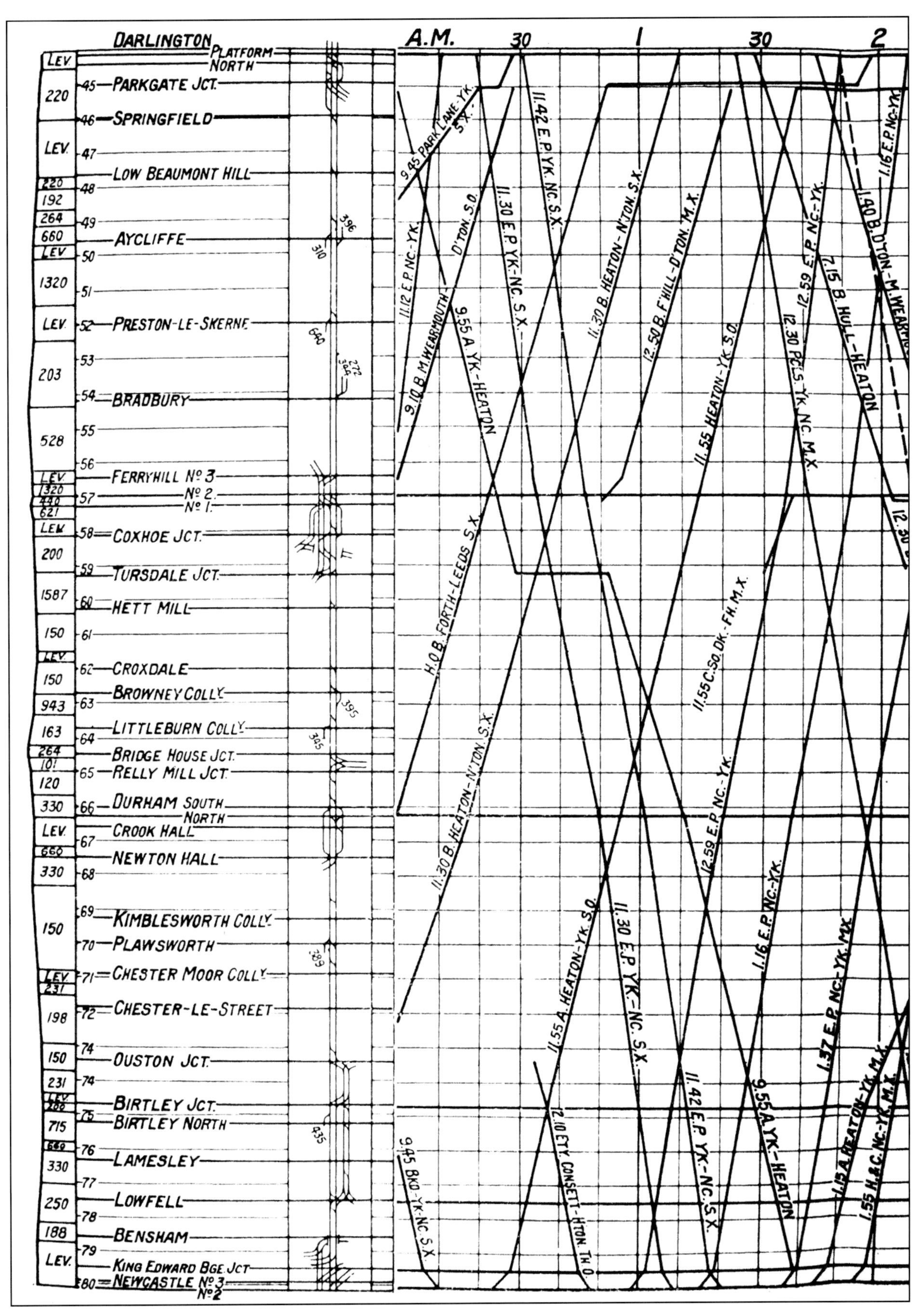

Illustration 161. *York District Control: an extract from one of the control graphs which was maintained by one of the controllers to keep an overview of traffic in the area. (BR / RM, September / October 1949, 24 Hours at York, OS Nock)*

York District Control was closed on 3 October 1982, when its functions were transferred to the Divisional Control at Leeds, then when the Regions were replaced by a new organisational structure, Regional Control became 'Route Control' from 6 April 1992 and by February 2000 (following privatisation) it had become Railtrack Control; 'Short Notice Scheduling', otherwise known as 'Very Short Term Planning' (VSTP) was in room W105. Great North Eastern Railway (GNER) and Northern were in the same building, but Jarvis were next door in Hudson House. In 2002, most of Railtrack's operations were transferred to the state-owned non-profit company Network Rail.

Route Control

Route Control, as it now was once again, moved over to the IECC in 2002, initially in the same room as the signallers and the Electrical Control Room (ECRO). This was in the south end of the building, which had been extended to accommodate the Leeds workstations, Control and ECRO moving in. The ECRO function moved in from Hornsey and Doncaster Ten Pound Walk.

The IECC was further extended northward and control staff moved into the new extension in 2004, co-located with GNER and Northern. TransPennine Express and Grand Central also had a presence for a short time in this office. The former Jarvis staff also moved in at this time, but worked as a separate function, merging the following year.

Route Control was the first occupier of the York ROC (Rail Operating Centre) when it opened on 16 September, 2014.

The changing nature of rail traffic, in particular the introduction of bulk trainloads, significantly affected the role of Route Control: an overview can now be obtained by the signalmen themselves by using computerised functions including CCF (Control Centre of the Future) and TRUST (Train Running System derived from TOPS), which latter in itself is an abbreviation for Total Operations Processing System. However, Route Control now takes a prominent role in what is referred to as 'incident management' – for example, train failures, mishaps *etc.* – irrespective of which Train Operating Company might be involved.

Illustration 162. *York District Train Control: the LNER Control Office at York which incorporated the ECML as far north as Northallerton. (LNER / NRM BR (NER) HQ photographs, 1994-7245)*

Illustration 163. *York Rail Operating Centre: the ROC was officially opened on 16 September, 2014 by which date Route Control had become established, although it was not until December 2015 that the first signalling workstations were commissioned to control North Lincolnshire. Sam MacDougall, NwR Route Control Manager, explained that most of the first floor of the ROC would be occupied by Controllers from Network Rail and the Train Operating Companies working alongside each other (Richard Pulleyn)*

Chapter 21 : S&T Offices and Workshops

In addition to signalling operations, York was also an important centre for the Signalling & Telecommunications Engineers, with offices and workshops constructed by the NER and perpetuated by its successors.

A more detailed history of the early development of these functions can be found in *A History of North Eastern Railway Signalling* (edited by Neil Mackay). In summary, in early years the Engineer's (Permanent Way) Department, with teams of fitters and blacksmiths, was responsible for the design, installation and maintenance of signalling, although gatemen, pointsmen and signalmen (also employed by the PW Department at that time) were responsible for ensuring that their apparatus was kept in proper working order, including regular testing and oiling.

Illustration 164. *Signal Engineers based at York, from 1899 to the privatisation of British Railways. The Railtrack ECML Zone went live on 1 April 1995, then combined with the NE Zone in 1996. Charles Weightman became the Signal Engineer for the combined LNE Zone in April 1997 and remained until September 2001. The role then became vacant in 2008 by which time a further reorganisation had been announced, which had the effect of converting the role of a Signal Engineer to that of an Signalling Asset Manager which it still is in 2020.*

However, the introduction of interlocking, followed by adoption of the block system, required new skills to be developed so the NER established a Telegraph Department responsible for maintenance of block instruments and bells, single-needle telegraphs, and later the telephone system. In 1870, to oversee this important work they recruited Adolphus Graves as Telegraph Superintendent reporting direct to the General Manager in York. Graves retired in 1902 to be replaced by Charles Ellison, again based in York where offices and stores had been established.

In 1894, Arthur Hurst of the Engineer's Department in York became more closely involved in signalling and in 1899 he was appointed to the new position of Signal Engineer for the Southern Division until his retirement in 1914, when he was replaced by Ernest Fleet whose responsibility covered the whole of the NER system. Finally, in 1928 the Telegraph Department merged with the Signal Engineer's Department under Arthur Tattersall.

Photographs of all the Signal Engineers from NER days until privatisation of the rawilays are included in Illustration 164.

York S&T Workshops

Together with Gateshead (Park Lane), York was one of the principal signal engineering workshops, based until the 1930s at Toft Green.

So called 'shop work' in connection with locking frame renewals and significant locking alterations, as well as construction of new lever frames for the North Eastern Area of the LNER, was concentrated at York. In addition to a locking shop, there was a separate blacksmiths' shop and a materials store. In the locking shop itself foundations were provided for the erection of frames, consisting of channels bolted on plates and running along both sides of the shop, set into shallow trenches some 2 feet wide. The materials store contained both new and recovered items which could be refurbished.

Preparatory work for relocking large frames could be undertaken in the workshop to minimise disruption on site. A wood template of the frame was prepared on which the centres of the plungers or tappets were marked; the locking fitters could then work to the template in conjunction with the locking plan or chart. The newly prepared tappets were then taken to site, marked off and stamped with the corresponding lever number before being returned to the shop so that the locks could be cut to match the markings.

Illustration 165. *York S&T Instrument Workshops in the LNER era; in the foreground we see Instrument Maker Lewins. In case of air raids, his steel helmet hangs within easy reach behind him. (LNER / NRM BR (NER) HQ photographs, 1994-7245)*

Chapter 22 : Signalling Staff Training and Development

LNER Signalling School

William Whitelaw, Chairman of the LNER, opened a new signalling school at York on 16 October 1930. The school had been instigated by John Miller, Engineer, and Arthur Tattersall, Signal & Telegraph Engineer. It was located in a number of wooden sheds alongside the Tanner Row side of the York Offices, with a twofold purpose:

* Technical – to provide a training facility for the new generation of signal fitters and others concerned with the installation and maintenance of modern electric or electro-mechanical signalling apparatus and appliances.
* Operating – to enable students attending lectures on Rules & Regulations to become conversant with the operating side of signalling (a 20-lecture course provided for not only signalmen but also for all other grades who desired to progress their careers).

The school was provided with a $1^{1}/_{4}$" gauge model railway, some 50 feet x 3 feet, incorporating typical features such as double junctions, single line junctions *etc*., controlled from five signal boxes. For example, all the 'outside connections' at signal box 'B' were worked from a 25-lever locking frame quarter full size, with electric locks and no less than 15 track circuits. Full size block instruments were fully linked to the signalling. Automatic colour-light signalling was also represented.

Full size equipment provided for the technical staff included a set of points with directing signals, point motors, mechanical and motor-operated semaphore signals, searchlight colour-light signals, 2- and 5-lever mechanical frames, a 3-lever all-electric power frame, relay cabinets *etc*.

Telegraph and telephone equipment was also represented, including a 10,000 line Strowger automatic telephone exchange, both Standard Telephones and Cables key and selector and General Electric Company dial system control phones, and two single-needle telegraph instruments with a repeater.

The school could accommodate up to 60 students at each session and the series of lectures or demonstrations proved extremely popular.(1)

It is known that the signalling school lasted until at least the 1960s, but no trace has been found subsequently of any of the equipment or models.

LNER Mobile Signal School

In addition to signalling schools based in York and Newcastle, the LNER Engineer's Department invested in a Mobile Signal School which could be taken round the Districts as required.

The mobile signal school included examples of many items of equipment which would have to be installed and maintained by S&T staff; this enabled them to have access for training purposes without disruption or risk to services.

(1) *Railway Gazette*, 31 October 1930 and *Supplement*, 2 January 1931.

Illustration 166. *At the LNER (North Eastern Area) Signalling School, York, on 16 April 1931, LNER Chairman William Whitelaw presents a prize to Lineman G Smith (Castle Eden).The full list of those present, from left to right, is: Relief Lineman A Hendry (Manors); Electric Fitter F Benneworth (York); Lineman G Smith; Electric Fitter R Ord (York); Lineman SL Short (Manors); Chairman William Whitelaw; Viscount Grey of Fallodon and Clarence D Smith (LNER directors); S&T Engineer AE Tattersall; Engineer John Miller. (LNER / W Fawcett Collection)*

Network Rail : Workforce Development Centre

Alongside the ROC and in the same building, a Workforce Development Centre was set up to provide a leading training facility with lecture theatres, classrooms and areas to simulate track and signalling repair and maintenance; this enables up to 200 delegates to be trained at any one time.

The Workforce Development Centre includes simulators for training signallers on mechanical signalling with Absolute Block, NX panels with Track Circuit Block, and the latest VDU-based workstations. See Illustration 168.

On the ground floor there are facilities for practical training of track and S&T Engineers.

National Railway Museum
L&Y Signalling School

It may seem strange to make reference to the L&Y Signalling School in a description of signalling at York, but this is relevant because the model railway from that school has been preserved at the National Railway Museum in York. See Illustration 167.

Illustration 167. *NRM L&Y Signalling School: in an extract from the NRM's website, the author is seen explaining the basics of Absolute Block signalling to a young visitor who was visiting with a school party.*

Illustration 168. *Network Rail Workforce Development Centre: the simulator lever frame, block instruments and illuminated track diagram, all connected to an instructor's control desk, for training signalling staff on Absolute Block. (Richard Pulleyn, 16 September 2014)*

The Gauge 1 electrified model railway was built in 1912 for the Lancashire & Yorkshire Railway by its apprentices at Horwich Works, and by the Bassett-Lowke Model Engineering Company. It was commissioned in January 1913 and situated in the offices above Manchester Victoria station. Although it was not the first such layout built, it was probably the first to use electric trains, and to have several signal boxes – just three to start with but later as many as five.

Like the LNER Signalling School described above, it was an interactive training aid used to demonstrate, in a safe environment, all situations that students could be faced with in reality, and to give them confidence in using the signalling equipment. It continued in use with many updates, as signal systems and rules changed, until 1995 when it was the last such layout in use by British Rail. Because of its historic importance it was donated to the Museum by its then owners Railtrack.

The layout was taken down and moved to York, and the task of rebuilding and restoration by a small group of volunteers commenced in 1999. It is now used for regular public demonstrations, and for training railway staff such as new recruits employed by signalling contractors but with no previous knowledge of the basic principles. It now has four signal boxes and an in-section ground frame which is electrically released. The locomotives are operated by remote control.

In 2013, the layout achieved its centenary and was awarded a certificate from the Guinness Book of Records as the oldest, complete model railway which is still fully operational and demonstrated on a regular basis to the visiting public by a team of volunteers.

National Railway Museum
Signalling Collection

It is recorded that, from as early as 1880, JB Harper of the NER had been collecting historical material, much of which was exhibited on the occasion of the Stockton & Darlington Railway Centenary in 1925; this formed the basis of York Railway Museum opened by LNER in 1928. The smaller exhibits were housed in the Old Station buildings and the rolling stock and other large exhibits in the former locomotive erecting and repair shops of the Y&NMR at Queen Street. See Illustration 169. Inevitably, the collection was dominated by items from the LNER although it certainly contained many items of signalling interest.

The York collection was combined with the Museum of British Transport in Clapham, London, in 1973 and in 1975, 150 years to the day that the first passenger train ran on the Stockton & Darlington Railway,

BR Chairman Richard Marsh handed over the keys to the National Railway Museum to the then Department of Education and Science.

There are plans for change at the National Railway Museum but, in addition to the L&Y Signalling School described above, visitors can also see NRM Central which is a simulator signal box again demonstrated by volunteers.

Alongside NRM Central is a set of 'slave screens' which show visitors trains being signalled at York in real time. These screens have been linked to York IECC and are to be updated to link with the screens at York ROC.

Signalling Principles & Practices, Rules & Regulations Classes

For many years it was a tradition among drivers to operate what were known as 'Mutual Improvement Classes' where experienced staff would share their knowledge with colleagues who wished to learn more. These classes were run on a purely voluntary basis and were held outside normal working hours. Signalling and operating staff were similarly provided for in so-called 'Block Classes' which ran alongside the MICs; as explained above (in the section outlining the LNER Signalling School) these were aimed at both signalmen and those who aspired to be station masters or inspectors.

Phil Graham, then an Operations Manager with BR, Railtrack and Network Rail started running classes at Middlesbrough in 1987, moving on to Leeds in 1989 and finally York in 1996, as his career progressed. When he first started these evening classes, there were still about six others elsewhere in the country, as well as correspondence courses based in each of the Regions; however, he has been the sole provider since about 2000. People attend his classes in York from as far away as London, Norwich, Liverpool and Newcastle. Vocational refresher training during working hours is now a key requirement for all operating grades and as signallers benefit from this it is inevitable that the demand from them has fallen. Although a few signallers do still attend there is no need for them to do so in order to get to and remain at the top of their competence tree; they are now outweighed by the number of drivers and staff from non-operating departments who wish to understand how the railway works; typically between 100 – 120 sign up each year.

The classes are entirely voluntary, held purely for information and interest and take place over winter months, spread over two years which are alternated: Year 1 provides an introduction and then covers Absolute Block Rules & Regulations, with Year 2 covering Track Circuit Block, Control of Single Lines, Accidents and Emergencies, and Level Crossings. Each year includes 12 Lessons which are repeated in alternate weeks to accommodate staff working shifts. At the end of each course there is a voluntary examination where trainees can test their knowledge; certificate awards are presented to those who succeed.

Illustration 169. *York Queen Street Museum: a view of just some of the signalling displays, including in the foreground the original route-setting switch panel installed at Thirsk. (BR / NRM Collection of BR (NER) HQ photographs, 1994-7245)*

Chapter 23 : the Future?

York Central

By 2020 York Yards, formerly a hive of activity, were being used for temporary storage of redundant rolling stock. However, a collaborative development partnership which includes York City Council, Network Rail, the National Railway Museum and Homes England envisaged big plans for this large brownfield site. The 'York Central' project recognises that this land provides a unique opportunity for housing and economic growth in the centre of York, even though it is contained by operational rail lines. The area already contains some private housing and businesses which will be retained alongside the National Railway Museum, but the rest of the site is largely underused so relocation of the remaining rail site will allow new development to take place.

The current proposals include:

* York City Council providing up to 2,500 homes together with offices, leisure and retail uses.

* The National Railway Museum is hopeful that Leeman Road, which divides the site, will be realigned so that the museum can be further developed to meet the changing needs of visitors.

* Network Rail is planning a new West Entrance to York station.

York ROC

Although it is not possible to forecast the future accurately, it is quite clear that the number of workstations in the ROC will continue to expand as further lines are transferred; plans are in hand for much of the signalling on Teesside and the Durham Coast to be included in the near future.

Ultimately it is planned that York will be the largest ROC in the country, and will control signalling and rail operations on the whole of the East Coast Main Line from London King's Cross to the Scottish Borders together with many of the associated lines. Provision has been made in the building for further developments in the 'digital railway' planned by Network Rail which may include commissioning of ERTMS (European Rail Traffic Management System), although it remains to be seen whether Britain's exit from the European Union will impact upon that policy.

It is fitting that, as a signalling centre, York developed such that it had the largest mechanical lever frame and will in future have the largest Rail Operations Centre in the UK.

Index of Signalling Locations

(Numbers in **bold** indicate a diagram or photograph)